METHODISM AND AMERICAN EMPIRE

METHODISM
and
AMERICAN
EMPIRE

Reflections on Decolonizing the Church

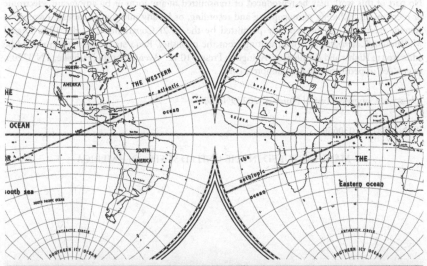

Edited by David W. Scott and Filipe Maia

Nashville

METHODISM *and* AMERICAN EMPIRE
Reflections on Decolonizing the Church

Copyright © 2023 by Abingdon Press

Library of Congress Control Number: 2023950280

ISBN: 9781791030650

MANUFACTURED IN THE UNITED STATES OF AMERICA

CONTENTS

PREFACE

Joerg Rieger

Why worry about empire, imperialism, and colonization? Are these topics not just distractions from the Methodist charges of making disciples, spreading scriptural holiness, and transforming the world?[1] And how is any of this related to basic Methodist identity?

The problem is that churches, even when they mean well and are committed to the transformation of the world, are often unaware of what goes into the formation not only of the world but also of the church. Formation includes things visible and invisible, from the official teachings laid down in commonly accepted doctrinal standards, to ecclesial education efforts, to relationships of power that shape us all the way to the core. Today, we are perhaps more informed than ever before about how relationships of power shape us: we know that family systems shape us profoundly, that our communities mold us in many ways, and that our cultures and nations impact us.

What is still mostly unaccounted for, however, is how imperial and colonial relations of power and money in politics and economics also shape us to the core, including our churches. This is why I started studying and writing about empire almost two decades ago as a theologian, realizing that large-scale relations of power shape our innermost convictions and beliefs as individuals and communities, often without any awareness of it. *Empire*, as I argued back then and referenced in several of the chapters here, can be defined as conglomerates of power that seek to shape every-

---

1. See the United Methodist *Book of Discipline*'s mission statement: "The mission of the Church is to make disciples of Jesus Christ for the transformation of the world" (*The Book of Discipline of The United Methodist Church, 2016* [Nashville: The United Methodist Publishing House, 2016], ¶120, p.93).

thing.[2] These dynamics are still with us, and this is what is at the core of colonial as well as neocolonial relations, both in the past and now.

It has taken a long time for theology and the church to understand how deeply we are shaped by the powers that be, both hard and soft, especially political and economic ones. But the good news is that we are becoming clearer about not only the problems but also the solutions. The chapters in this book provide various accounts of the problems, providing valuable details, many of which are still very little known. To be sure, this is not just a matter of keeping track of what is going on around us; this is also a matter of giving an account of what touches the heart of our Wesleyan traditions. In the traditions of the Holiness movements to which Methodism belongs, the point of faith is to become aware of our sinful state (through prevenient grace) in order to overcome it and to enter through the experience of justification into the long-term flows of sanctification.

In other words, without a thorough awareness of sin, as that which is to be overcome, the process of sanctification gets stuck. By the same token, without a deeper awareness of how we are affected by empire, imperialism, colonialism, and neocolonialism, the church gets stuck as well. No wonder we are at an impasse in Methodism today. The problem has to do not only with the imperial aspirations of conservative U.S. culture warriors who are waging all-out efforts to maintain control of politics, culture, and religion with fantastic amounts of funding, expert political strategies, and right-wing think tanks such as the Institute for Religion and Democracy.[3] The problem has also to do with the imperial naivete of well-meaning mainline Methodists who falsely assume that the problems of empire can be solved by including more people (be they sexual and racial minorities or global majorities) into what might be considered the mainstream.

Those looking for details of widespread Methodist collusions with imperialism and colonialism in recent decades will find a wealth of informa-

---

2. Referenced in the introduction to this book and the chapter by Darryl Stephens.

3. The broader framework is well documented. See, for instance, Kevin Kruse, *One Nation Under God: How Corporate America Invented Christian America* (New York: Basic Books, 2015); Steve Askin, "IRD 89 Percent Funded by the Right," *National Catholic Reporter* (1983), 19:15, 7.

tion in this book. Much of this material is not readily available elsewhere, and there is no doubt that much more will be discovered as time goes by. However, there is another side to these developments that shines through in these chapters in varying intensities as well: there exists a theological surplus (a term I coined years ago and picked up in several of the chapters) and an ecclesial and spiritual surplus that cannot ever be controlled completely by the schemes of empire builders and colonizers.

In the midst of the undeniable imperial aspirations for power and money described in this volume (the chapters about the efforts of conservative U.S. Methodism in Africa by Lloyd Nyarota and Taylor Denyer are particularly eye-opening), there is a Wesleyan theological surplus that keeps pushing against empire. Wesley's own critiques of the slave trade, certain expressions of British imperialism, and his support for those impoverished by early capitalism's drive for profit set the stage, remained alive in Methodist commitments to transform the world, limited as they may be, and to put an end to exploitation along the lines of gender, race, and class. While the current volume does not go into detail, this has been developed elsewhere.[4]

Unfortunately, much of the current Methodist tug-of-war is not only lacking more profound engagements of imperial and colonial tendencies in the church manifest on all sides; worse are widespread self-congratulatory attitudes about being somehow "countercultural." Conservative Methodists claim to be countercultural because they oppose cultural changes that affect gender and sexuality, seeking to uphold standards that reflect older cultural mores established during the industrial revolution promoting narrow definitions of male and female as well as the nuclear family, which they consider natural and eternal. By contrast, somewhat more open mainline Methodists, who sometimes are labeled "liberal" or "progressive," consider themselves countercultural because they seek to be inclusive of and hospitable to those who have too long been excluded by the dominant status quo.

---

4. See, for example, *Sanctification and Liberation: Liberation Theologies in Light of the Wesleyan Tradition*, edited by Theodore Runyon (Nashville: Abingdon, 1981); *Methodist Revolutions: Evangelical Engagements of Church and World*, edited by Upolu Luma Vaai and Joerg Rieger (Nashville: Wesley's Foundery Books, 2021).

To be sure, there is indeed a culture of empire—what some of us have called the "spirit of empire"—that needs to be challenged. Thus, efforts to be countercultural in the midst of the culture of empire are commendable, but it can be argued that neither of the above claims to be countercultural is going to make much difference. Neither the defense of fading cultural (but still surprisingly powerful) arrangements by the conservatives nor the inclusion of a few more people into an emerging cultural status quo by the liberals is addressing the culture of empire at its core because the real power differentials at work under the conditions of empire are not being addressed. The problem, as I have argued in my book *Christ and Empire*,[5] is not merely the relation of Christ and culture (as H. Richard Niebuhr would have it in his famous book *Christ and Culture*[6]), but the relation of Christ and culture and power.

So where do we find real alternatives to the culture of empire? Is there a Methodist theological surplus that makes a difference and that can still lead to the transformation of the world? Today, we are beginning to understand better how dominant power continues to distort the witness of the church, not only in the global situation but also at home. Many of our ancestors in Europe and the United States were caught up in these scenarios, even though they did not necessarily benefit from the dominant powers themselves. The missionaries of the past may serve as an example: while they often served the spirit of the respective European and American empires, they rarely benefited much themselves (living far away from their loved ones, often precariously). And, unlike others engaged in imperial and colonial enterprises at the top, they were not the ones to gain wealth and riches.[7]

A theological surplus emerged, however, whenever people began to pay attention and listen to the suffering and the struggles of their time. The American Methodist John R. Mott (1865–1955), drawn into imperial and colonial schemes in his own way, might serve as an example. Mott believed that Christianity was destined to become the dominant global

---

5. Joerg Rieger, *Christ and Empire: From Paul to Postcolonial Times* (Minneapolis: Fortress, 2007).

6. H. Richard Niebuhr, *Christ and Culture* (New York: Harper, 1951).

7. For examples, see George E. Tinker, *Missionary Conquest: The Gospel and Native American Cultural Genocide* (Minneapolis: Fortress, 1993).

religion in his generation, and he held that mission and the formation of global relationships was crucial, to be led by the benevolent efforts of European and American mission boards. Nevertheless, Mott also developed an awareness of the plight of workers at home, chairing a commission of inquiry into the 1919 steel strike in various U.S. states, documenting common abuses of workers, including twelve-hour workdays, low pay, seven-day weeks, long shifts, and lack of input from workers.[8] While almost forgotten today, this was a time when mainline churches would take the sides of workers and at times successfully challenged the capitalist economic system that still underwrites much of contemporary imperialism and (neo)colonialism. The anti-imperial and anti-colonial efforts of those days are still with us, despite ongoing efforts to turn back the clock. That these particular efforts are hardly reflected in the revised Social Principles of the UMC[9] shows the ongoing reach of empire even into circles that consider themselves progressive.

In the end, it comes as a surprise that decolonizing the church is a goal that is claimed across the Methodist divide. Representatives of the Global Methodist Church claim it (see the chapter by Filipe Maia) and so do representatives of the mainline of The United Methodist Church. Yet despite lofty claims, decolonization remains impossible without deeper understandings of colonialism, what drives it, and who benefits from it. Moreover, decolonialization remains impossible without siding with those who are most affected by continued colonial relationships. Finally, decolonization is impossible without a theology that promotes images of God that deconstruct imperial images of God that are deeply engrained in the hearts and minds of all, not only of the colonizers but also of the colonized. There is much to do for Methodists in the 2020s, but some of our histories can inspire us to remain hopeful for the future.

---

8. See Joerg Rieger, *Grace under Pressure: Negotiating the Heart of the Methodist Traditions* (Nashville: United Methodist General Board of Higher Education and Ministry, 2011), 65–68.

9. General Board of Church and Society, "2020 Social Principles of the UMC," https://www.umcjustice.org/documents/124.

Introduction

METHODISM AND THE
SPIRIT OF EMPIRE

David W. Scott and Filipe Maia

This book investigates historical trajectories and theological developments that connect American imperialism in the post-World War
II period on the one hand and Methodist and Wesleyan traditions on the
other. Methodist and Wesleyan traditions have been shaped by the imperial practices and mindsets of their American members, even when they
aspire to be global denominations united by a shared Methodist conviction in connectionalism as an ecclesial principle.[1] The United Methodist
Church, the largest denomination in the Wesleyan family, was founded in
1968 and strove to uphold the connectional principle in an ecclesial structure that was global in scope. United Methodists are unique in both the
fact that they represent a typical example of an originally Unites States-
based denomination and that they currently embody the distinct tensions
and fractures of a global church. The complex negotiations that take place
across different national, cultural, and political contexts have set up the
historical backdrop for the imminent schism of The United Methodist
Church. They might also be perceived as symptoms of lingering forms of
American imperialism that persist in global Methodism.

---

1.   *Connectionalism* is variously defined but signifies a conviction that the church extends beyond local fellowships and even (potentially) beyond state or national borders. Thus, a connectional ecclesiology
stands in contrast to the congregational ecclesiology that characterizes Baptists, for instance. For more on
the principle of connectionalism, see Russell E. Richey, *Methodist Connectionalism: Historical Perspectives*
(Nashville: United Methodist General Board of Higher Education and Ministry, 2009).

The guiding question that informs the reflections in this volume is: to what extent is Methodism's vision of global connection marred by American imperialism? To tackle this question, *Methodism and American Empire* offers a series of historical and theological analyses that focus on the entanglement of Methodism and empire in the second half of the twentieth century and the twenty-first century. This chronological focus recognizes the significance of the recent wave of globalization in shaping American empire, Empire writ large, and global Methodist denominations such as The United Methodist Church. It also seeks to capture the intersections between global and American tensions in church and society. With this volume, we seek to provide a historical perspective to understand the specific context of The United Methodist Church while also raising ecclesiological questions about the impact of imperialism on how United Methodists have understood the nature and mission of the church over the last century.

From the start of North American colonies of European powers, empire has characterized the American experience.[2] The role of empire in shaping the United States extends far beyond its origins as an imperial hinterland itself or its turn-of-the-twentieth-century heyday of possessing its own colonies. Empire as concentrated, top-down power that seeks to control others for the sake of its own agendas is a constant within U.S. history. Empire goes beyond particular political parties, presidential administrations, or theological groupings. The impulses and perspectives of empire have characterized and continue to characterize American politics, economics, culture, and religion in a thorough-going way. Imperialism has functioned and continues to function both within and beyond the territorial boundaries of the United States as a nation-state. Empire is a basic strategy by which those with power in the United States have sought to unite larger groups for the sake of asserting power over others, even

---

2. There is an extensive literature on the historical relationships between empire and the United States. See, for instance, Daniel Immerwahr, *How to Hide an Empire: A History of the Greater United States* (New York: Farrar, Straus and Giroux, 2019); Anthony G. Hopkins, *American Empire: A Global History* (Princeton, NJ: Princeton University Press, 2018); Julian Go, *Patterns of Empire: The British and American Empires, 1688 to the Present* (New York: Cambridge University Press, 2013); Richard H. Immerman, *Empire for Liberty: A History of American Imperialism from Benjamin Franklin to Paul Wolfowitz* (Princeton, NJ: Princeton University Press, 2012); Alfred W. McCoy and Francisco A. Scarano, eds., *Colonial Crucible: Empire in the Making of the Modern American State* (Madison: University of Wisconsin Press, 2009).

as those within these in-groups often act against their own interests by participating in such imperial projects. Thus, empire is a technique of exploitation of those within and beyond the empire, especially those on the margins.

At the turn of the twenty-first century, the category of Empire became an important concept in political philosophy with the publication of Michael Hardt and Antonio Negri's *Empire*.[3] The book traces changes in the political constitution of sovereignty over the last decades of the twentieth century to suggest that we no longer live in the age of *imperialism*. In contrast to it, the concept of Empire speaks to a political and social situation that lacks a clear center of power and where national imperialist interests give room to transnational corporations and political alliances. For Hardt and Negri, Empire represents a new dispensation of sovereign power "composed of a series of national and supranational organisms united under a single logic of rule."[4] Under the conditions of Empire, sovereign power no longer rests at the seat of the monarch or the head of government; it has been dispersed throughout transnational entities that, though still potentially connected to nation-states, transcend the agency of any one nation.[5] Empire is quite adept in accepting and incorporating regional and cultural differences while proliferating structures of power that remain more homogenous, more widespread, and more global. Empire is more insidious because it is more subtle, more incisive because it does not rely exclusively on imposition, and more ubiquitous because it shapes people's subjectivities on a deeper level.

The passage from imperialism to Empire is therefore a central aspect of Hardt and Negri's analysis of power in the latter portion of the twentieth century. For them, this also signifies that colonialism represents a regime of power that has lost steam in recent decades. According to postcolonial and decolonial critics, however, Hardt and Negri's account omits how the leg-

---

3. Michael Hardt and Antonio Negri, *Empire* (Cambridge, MA: Harvard University Press, 2000).

4. Hardt and Negri, xii.

5. Hardt and Negri stress how conquest and military intervention are not absent from Empire, but they serve different purposes. As opposed to creating a new colonial administrative apparatus connecting a territory to the national capital, military interventions in the age of Empire serve the purpose of opening new markets for transnational corporations.

acy of colonialism persists in the political and military structures of nation-states. For these critics, the concept of Empire tends to ignore how colonialism has shaped what power is and how it is constituted in the modern period. Coloniality, in the expression coined by decolonial theorist Aníbal Quijano, is more than the power of colonial nations.[6] Rather, it is the central matrix of power in the modern period, one that shapes culture writ large as well as fundamental forms of knowledge and worldviews. Its force is not weakened by the end of *de facto* colonialism. In this perspective, it is less important to trace the historical end of imperialism than it is to attend to how power in our epoch is still tainted by colonial forces whose shape-shifting presence is still operative in the postcolonial era.

Moreover, the rise and spread of new forms of nationalism in recent years complicates Hardt and Negri's narrative about the end of imperialism and the diminishing force of nation-states. As constructive theologian Catherine Keller poignantly claims, soon after the publication of *Empire* in 2000, "the world was subjected to a new U.S. manifestation of state sovereignty, aggressively *nationalistic*—and boundary-fixated."[7] While the immediate context for Keller's claim is George W. Bush's administration and the U.S. invasion of Afghanistan and Iraq, the more recent explosion of right-wing nationalism—of a peculiar Christian brand—only deepens her insight. If Empire today can operate beyond the central control of a nation-state, it remains true that concentrations of power continue to be clustered around the United States and its wealthy global partners. Whether as symptom of a passage to Empire or as the stubborn nature of sovereign power, the force of the nation-state remains steadfast and has been reclaimed by nationalistic movements as of late.

This book demonstrates that global Methodism is an example of the complex interplay between imperialism and Empire, between a U.S.-centric perspective on globalization and a transnational ecclesial body that

6.   See Aníbal Quijano, "Colonialidad y Modernidad / Racionalidad," *Perú Indígena* 13:29 (1992): 11–20; Aníbal Quijano, "Colonialidad Del Poder, Eurocentrismo y América Latina," in *La Colonialidad Del Saber: Eurocentrismo y Ciencias Sociales: Perspectivas Latinoamericanas*, ed. Edgardo Lander (Buenos Aires: Consejo Latinoamericano de Ciencias Sociales, 2000).

7.   Catherine Keller, "The Love of Postcolonialism: Theology in the Interstices of Empire," in *Postcolonial Theologies: Divinity and Empire*, ed. Catherine Keller, Michael Nausner, and Mayra Rivera (St. Louis, MO: Chalice, 2004), 228.

lacks an exclusive center of power but that nevertheless finds itself structurally caught up in a typically American mindset. By paying close attention to the impact that the United States has had in the shaping of global Methodism, specifically The United Methodist Church, this book will point out that ecclesial developments can be situated in this larger context of Empire. That is to say, when Methodists in multiple settings negotiated a common understanding of a "global denomination," they did so in a "globe" that was being created in the image and likeliness of Empire. We will show that these negotiations were always tied to the central role the United States played in global Methodism. At times, it is possible to observe Methodist traditions that have too quickly been subsumed by the logic of Empire. In other instances, we hope to demonstrate, Methodist voices might be perceived as resisting imperial forces and shaping what might be understood as a subversive view of the globe.

Methodism and Empire

Methodism has its own share in the history of Empire. The British Empire launched itself onto global dominance in the eighteenth-century as John and Charles Wesley set out to spread "scriptural holiness over the land." The Wesley brothers themselves were present in the founding days of the British colony in Georgia, and Charles served as Secretary for Indian Affairs, even if unwittingly and unsuccessfully.[8] John's own perception of his ministry in Georgia was connected to his commitments to "primitive Christianity," and he seemed to have assumed that the colony would provide a site for that.[9] His comments on Native Americans are often a mix of curiosity and the assumption that indigenous peoples were "primitive" and could therefore offer a glimpse of Christianity in its purest form.[10] This claim, albeit well-meaning, is not innocent and stands on a

---

8.   See Julie Anne Sweet, "Charles Wesley: Georgia's First Secretary for Indian Affairs," *Methodist History* 50:4 (2012): 212–26.

9.   Geordan Hammond, *John Wesley in America: Restoring Primitive Christianity* (Oxford: Oxford University Press, 2014).

10.   For a reflection on John Wesley's views of indigenous peoples, see Theodore W. Jennings, "John Wesley," in *Empire and the Christian Tradition: New Readings of Classical Theologians*, ed. Don H. Compier, Kwok Pui-lan, and Joerg Rieger (Minneapolis: Fortress, 2007), 257–69.

long line of European reflections about the "primitives."[11] On the other hand, Theodore W. Jennings, Jr. points out that Wesley opposed two of the "main pillars" of British imperialism: the transatlantic slave trade and the colonization of India via the East India Trading Company.[12] Wesley's opposition to these put him in direct confrontation with the center of gravity of the British Empire. For Jennings, he "keenly diagnoses the economic interests" behind imperialism and, though he lacks the analytic tools to offer a systemic critique of his social context, Wesley did indeed notice that imperial forces engender human suffering and run against the advancement of the reign of God.[13] Historian David Hempton has situated Methodism as a global tradition tied to imperial systems in the eighteenth and nineteenth centuries and argued that the success and failures of global Methodism ought to be understood in this imperial context.[14] Whether the Methodist revival enforced or resisted imperial forces, the fact remains that the world that Wesley envisioned as his parish was a world already shaped by British imperialism.

Britain would consolidate its global reach in the nineteenth century while the material conditions for the emergence of a new imperial force were being laid in one of its former colonies in the Americas. In December 1823, U.S. President James Monroe's message to Congress warned Europe that the western hemisphere was the United States' sphere of influence and that European interventions in the continent were not to be tolerated. The "Monroe Doctrine," as it became known, was repeatedly invoked to justify American interventions in Latin America and the Carib-

---

11. See M. Munro, "Wild Thing: Noble Savages, Exoticisms and Postcolonial Space in Jacques-Stephen Alexis's Les Arbres Musiciens," *French Studies* 57:1 (2003): 55–67, https://doi.org/10.1093/fs/57.1.55. For an example of the impact of the category of the "primitive" in supporting a nationalist project, see Helen Carr, *Inventing the American Primitive: Politics, Gender, and the Representation of Native American Literary Traditions, 1789–1936* (New York: New York University Press, 1996).

12. Jennings, "John Wesley," 258.

13. Jennings, 268.

14. David Hempton, *Methodism: Empire of the Spirit* (New Haven: Yale University Press, 2005).

bean throughout the nineteenth and early-twentieth centuries.[15] By 1845, it had merged with manifest destiny as a political and religious principle underlying expansionist policies that established the United States as a nation destined to expand its Christian and political values to other places.[16]

Historians have documented how this theological and political impetus drove the westward expansion of the United States. Jeffrey Williams, for example, argued that in this context Methodists started to accept violence against Native Americans as a necessary element of the Christianization of the nation. For him, during the antebellum period, Methodists "began to embrace the evolving civic theology of the nation as birthed by God and providentially chosen for spreading national moral, economic, and political values to the world."[17] As the political identity of the nation deepened its theological dimension, Methodists increasingly came to understand that defending the nation, especially against first nations in its territory, was both their civic and ecclesial duty. The well-documented Methodist role in the Sand Creek massacre of 1864 is just one example of this entanglement of a violent nationalism with an equally violent religious fervor.[18]

From a global perspective, Methodism has been widely recognized as a premier American experiment in international mission. The Methodist Episcopal Church was one of the most well-distributed organizations in the world in 1900, with 180,000 members and as much as five times as

---

15. See Jeffrey J. Malanson, "Manifest Destiny: The Monroe Doctrine and Westward Expansion, 1816–1861," in *The Routledge Handbook of American Military and Diplomatic History: The Colonial Period to 1877*, ed. Antonio S. Thompson and Christos G. Frentzos (New York: Routledge, 2015), 215, https://doi.org/10.4324/9781315817347-39; Jay Sexton, *The Monroe Doctrine: Empire and Nation in Nineteenth-Century America* (New York: Hill and Wang, 2011).

16. See Anders Stephanson, *Manifest Destiny: American Expansionism and the Empire of Right* (New York: Hill and Wang, 1995).

17. Jeffrey Williams, *Religion and Violence in Early American Methodism: Taking the Kingdom by Force* (Bloomington, IN: Indiana University Press, 2010), 95.

18. For more on the massacre, see Christopher M. Rein, "'Our First Duty Was to God and Our Next to Our Country': Religion, Violence, and the Sand Creek Massacre," *Great Plains Quarterly* 34:3 (2014): 217–38, https://doi.org/10.1353/gpq.2014.0055; Gary L. Roberts, *Massacre at Sand Creek: How Methodists Were Involved in an American Tragedy* (Nashville: Abingdon, 2016).

many adherents in twenty-eight countries on five continents.[19] Beyond the Methodist Episcopal Church, the prominence of mission holds true across the various Methodist bodies that have existed throughout American history. The Methodist Episcopal Church, South; African Methodist Episcopal Church; African Methodist Episcopal Church Zion; Wesleyan Methodist Church; Church of the Nazarene; Free Methodist Church; Evangelical Association; United Brethren in Christ; Methodist Protestant Church; and other smaller Methodist bodies have all been significantly engaged in international mission as well. Thus, Methodism as a tradition has been both emphatically American and enthusiastically expansionist.

Methodism's relationship with empire has been at times ambiguous, and there are ambiguities and ambivalences in how empire has played out historically. There have been differences among various groups of Methodists in terms of their views on and practices of empire. There have certainly been Methodists who have been vociferous supporters of both ecclesial and political forms of American empire. On the other hand, there have also been those who have pushed back against imperial instincts, and those on the margins of empire have appropriated the openings created by empire for their own purposes.[20] Moreover, the exploitation and injustice that are inherent to empire go against basic tenets of Christianity, especially in its Wesleyan expressions, which have tended to emphasize the equality of all believers before God, thus leading to theological tensions between Methodism and empire.

---

19. The 180,000 figure comes from *Annual Report of the Missionary Society of the Methodist Episcopal Church for the Year 1900* (New York: Missionary Society of the Methodist Episcopal Church, 1900), 7. For the five times as many adherents, see David Hempton, *Methodism*, 1–2. By 1900, the MEC had missions and members in North America (Mexico and Costa Rica), South America (Argentina, Uruguay, Paraguay, Brazil, Chile, Peru, and Ecuador), Africa (Liberia, Mozambique, and Angola), Europe (Germany, Switzerland, Austria-Hungary, Italy, Bulgaria, Sweden, Norway, Denmark, Finland, and Russia), and Asia (India, China, Korea, Japan, the Philippines, and Malaysia). See J. Tremayne Copplestone, *The History of Methodist Missions: Twentieth-Century Perspectives (The Methodist Episcopal Church, 1896–1939)* (New York: United Methodist Church Board of Global Ministries, 1973).

20. For instance, Kenneth Mackenzie has documented instances of all three of these positions in how American Methodists thought about the Philippines at the beginning of the twentieth century. See *The Robe and the Sword: The Methodist Church and the Rise of American Imperialism* (Washington: Public Affairs, 1961).

American Empire and American Denominations

Methodism has historically been a significant expression of Christianity in the United States. It was the largest denominational tradition in the United States during parts of the nineteenth century,[21] and it has remained the second largest denominational group within American Protestantism over the past half century.[22] The United Methodist Church is the second largest denomination in the United States.[23] Beyond numbers, historian Nathan Hatch has argued that Methodism is a better representation of the mainstream of American religious history than Puritanism and its descendants.[24]

The international denomination is a distinctively American model of being church. The United States, with its traditions of separation of church and state and vibrant voluntary associations pioneered denominationalism as a form of organizing church life.[25] Out of the 41,000 denominations in the world identified in the *Atlas of Global Christianity*, 6,200 are in the United States.[26] Yet there is something beyond sheer numbers of denominations at work here. Most of the prominent examples of centralized worldwide denominations are American in origin. The Roman Catholic Church is admittedly the most worldwide Christian body, though it does not see itself as a denomination. Beyond Roman Catholicism, most significant examples of Christian bodies with membership across multiple

---

21. Roger Finke and Rodney Stark, *The Churching of America, 1776–1990: Winners and Losers in Our Religious Economy* (New Brunswick, NJ: Rutgers University Press, 1992).

22. "Denominational Affiliation (Over Time)," The Association of Religion Data Archives, https://thearda.com/quickstats/qs_102_t.asp, accessed February 2, 2022.

23. "Religious Landscape Study," Pew Research Center, https://www.pewforum.org/religious-landscape-study/, accessed February 2, 2022.

24. Nathan O. Hatch, "The Puzzle of American Methodism," *Church History* 63:2 (June 1994): 175–89.

25. Russell E. Richey, ed., *Denominationalism* (Nashville: Abingdon, 1977).

26. Todd J. Johnson and Kenneth R. Ross, eds., *Atlas of Global Christianity 1910–2010* (Edinburgh: Edinburgh University Press, 2009), 60.

nations and centralized global decision-making are American in background, with a few recent additions from the global South.[27]

By contrast, worldwide traditions that emphasize national or congregational autonomy (even within a framework of transnational fellowship) are predominantly European in origin.[28] European Christian traditions mostly have roots in the Peace of Westphalia and the European experience of political colonization and decolonization, both of which have emphasized national religious identity.[29] The recent inclusion of denominations from the global South on the list of worldwide denominations, most of which have developed through global migratory diasporas and/or global media distribution, gives further credence to the notion that what is at the root of the desire to be a global denomination is the experience of globalization.[30] It is fair to say that many of these denominations, while emerging in the global South, replicate and readapt models that have been previously deployed by churches in the United States.

More important for the purposes of our analysis in this volume, many of the worldwide denominations with an American background are Methodist/Wesleyan, Holiness, and/or Pentecostal traditions.[31] (The Mormon Church and Jehovah's Witnesses are two notable exceptions.) Other expressions of Wesleyanism that have developed outside the United States, in contrast, have not aspired to worldwide organizational unity to the same extent that their American counterparts have, or in the case of

---

27. For a more thorough treatment, see David W. Scott, "Varieties of World-Wide Denominations," *UM & Global* (June 10, 2019), http://www.umglobal.org/2019/06/varieties-of-world-wide-denominations.html.

28. Anglicans, Lutherans, Reformed, Baptists, Moravians, and Mennonites all fall into this category.

29. Lutheran, Anglican, and many forms of Reformed/Presbyterian policy are predicated on national churches as a basic polity unit.

30. Examples of such denominations include the Universal Church of the Kingdom of God (Brazilian in origin), the Redeemed Christian Church of God (Nigeria), the Apostolic Church – Ghana (Ghana), and Jesus Is Lord Church Worldwide (the Philippines). Other scholars have made an explicit connection between the spread of such groups and globalization. See, for instance, Martijn Oosterbaan, ed., *Global Trajectories of Brazilian Religion: Lusospheres* (New York: Bloomsbury Academic, 2019).

31. For instance, the African Methodist Episcopal Church, the African Methodist Episcopal Church Zion, the Christian Methodist Episcopal Church, the Church of God (Cleveland, Tennessee), the Church of God in Christ, the Church of the Nazarene, the Free Methodist Church, the International Church of the Foursquare Gospel, The United Methodist Church, and The Wesleyan Church.

the British Methodist Church, have severed their organic connections to other countries in favor of national denominational autonomy.

There is a close connection between Americanism, Methodism, and denominational aspirations for global extension. Wesleyan theological convictions about connectionalism and the trans-local nature of the church reinforce drives toward global structure, but the American context is important as well. The desire to be a worldwide denomination, so common in the Methodist/Wesleyan family of churches, is grounded in peculiarly American experiences of and assumptions about the world and the church, assumptions shaped by American conceptions of and experiences of empire. A key explanatory factor for this dynamic lies in the American experience of globalization as a framework for worldwide expansion. While the debate on the nature, extent, and forms of American empire is voluminous, there is a consensus that the sorts of economic, cultural, and soft political power characteristic of globalization (as of Hardt and Negri's concept of Empire) has been the main way in which the United States has projected its power over other regions of the world, especially since the mid-twentieth century.[32] American empire is an empire of globalization more so than an empire of government.[33]

Because of the distinctive American experience of economic and cultural rather than political imperialism, it is possible that American denominations think of themselves as worldwide because of their positive experiences with globalization. The American-led creation of multinational corporations, worldwide organizations like the Red Cross, and global governance organizations like the World Bank and the United Nations have served as models, implicitly or explicitly, for how American denominations have thought about their relationships with their co-religionists around the world.[34]

---

32.   For a review of the historiography of American empire, see James G. Morgan, *Into New Territory: American Historians and the Concept of US Imperialism* (Madison: University of Wisconsin Press, 2014).

33.   Daniel Immerwahr argues that, since World War II, new techniques and technologies have allowed the United States to exert imperial power without control of territory. See Immerwahr, *How to Hide an Empire*.

34.   In some instances, Methodists, especially lay Methodists, were involved in the development of such organizations and in the promotion or sponsorship of international Methodist missions.

This globalized approach has been supercharged by American cultural and intellectual traditions. Notions of exceptionalism and the American national mission have provided further ideological sources for the desire for American denominations to become worldwide denominations.[35] Yet the surest conclusion is that the American desire to create global denominations is rooted in historical experiences of globalization more so than in an expression of some primordial aspect of American character. Thus, the drive to create global denominations, denominations that reflect American preeminence in other spheres, is historically situated.

Like most other historical processes, the drive to enshrine globalized American imperial dominance into the structures and practices of international Christian communities has been contested. Various groups of Christians, both from outside the United States and from within American Christianity, have repeatedly pushed back on the notion that the United States should be at the center of church power, arguing instead for a more egalitarian approach to Christian fellowship. These contestations have been historically situated as well. Thus, both the drive to inscribe American dominance in church structures and the drive for greater international equality among fellow Christians have played out in historically influential ways.

Empire and the Church's Self-Understanding

This volume insists that imperial forces do not exist apart from religious imaginaries. By tracking down the ecclesiological debate in global Methodism, we call attention to the forms in which visions about the church are marked by imperial forces. This is not new in the history of the Christian tradition, a faith tradition that emerged in the context of the Roman Empire. Neither is it new to Methodism, a tradition that emerged in the context of the British Empire in the eighteenth century and grew exponentially alongside the increasing role played by the United States in the global stage

---

35. The notion of America as a country with a self-identified and religiously-driven mission to the world has been explored in books such as William Hutchison, *Errand to the World: American Protestant Thought and Foreign Missions* (Chicago: University of Chicago Press, 1987) and Ian Tyrrell, *Reforming the World: The Creation of America's Moral Empire* (Princeton, NJ: Princeton University Press, 2010).

from the nineteenth century onward. Methodist and Wesleyan theologies have always been generated in tense relation to imperialism. How has this intimate connection between Methodism and imperialism shaped the vision of a global denomination in the twentieth and twenty-first century? Is the vision condemned to be just another example of the impact imperialism has on the Christian faith? Or might there be forms of imagining the Methodist theological tradition as offering an alternative to imperial theologies?

In several theological disciplines, the introduction of Empire as a central category of analysis has been extremely generative. Empire has served historical studies in support of research that observes the development of Christian traditions alongside the progress of imperial forces. Elisabeth Schüssler Fiorenza narrates how the study of empire reshaped biblical studies and the understanding of the formation of the Christian canon as well as its study in the present.[36] Similarly, Richard Horsley has amplified the study of early Christianity with a keen attention to how the context of the Roman Empire impacted the shape of a budding Christian identity, which often contradicted and resisted imperial forces.[37] A focus on empire has allowed theologians to scrutinize how theological categories have been shaped in political and social circumstances impacted by imperialism. As the authors included in the volume *Empire and the Christian Tradition* demonstrate, revisiting themes and figures in historical theology with the lens of Empire is a salient task that produces new perspectives in Christian thought.[38]

Theologians Néstor Míguez, Joerg Rieger, and Jung Mo Sung tease out the "spirit of Empire" to address the ethos engendered by imperialism. Its global reach "generates a 'collective spirit'. . . that allows and approves of certain behaviours, reactions, feelings, and attitudes."[39] Hardt and Negri's

36. Elisabeth Schüssler Fiorenza, *The Power of the Word: Scripture and the Rhetoric of Empire* (Minneapolis: Fortress, 2007). For a perspective on the impact of postcolonial studies in biblical research and hermeneutics, see Tat-siong Benny Liew and Fernando F. Segovia, *Colonialism and the Bible: Contemporary Reflections from the Global South* (Lanham, MD: Lexington, 2018).

37. Richard A. Horsley, *Jesus and Empire: The Kingdom of God and the New World Disorder* (Minneapolis: Fortress, 2003); Richard A. Horsley, *Jesus and the Politics of Roman Palestine* (Columbia, SC: University of South Carolina Press, 2014).

38. Compier, Kwok, and Rieger, eds., *Empire and the Christian Tradition*.

39. Néstor Míguez, Joerg Rieger, and Jung Mo Sung, *Beyond the Spirit of Empire: Theology and Politics in a New Key* (London: SCM, 2009), 2.

claims about the subject-forming force of Empire invited theological reflections on how theological imaginaries often remain caught up in an imperial paradigm. In their view, "Empire presents its order as permanent, eternal, and necessary."[40] The spirit of empire substantially shapes our visions of God and our ecclesial structures. From a theological perspective, that which is received in faith as a perennial truth ought to be investigated carefully so as not to be confused with imperial images being projected as coeternal. In terms of ecclesial structures, attention to Empire invites vigilance to scrutinize how power flows in the context of a global denomination. Empire seeks to be pervasive and all-controlling. No theology can claim immunity against these forces; no church can claim to be outside of the spirit of empire.

In Joerg Rieger's concise definition, empire refers to "massive concentrations of power which permeate all aspects of life and which cannot be controlled by any one actor alone."[41] Empire's reach is therefore insidious but not all-consuming. While imperial forces amass significant power and aspects of life, their claims for omnipotence tend to fall short. For theologians engaged in empire studies and anticolonial theologies, this prompts the thought of new images of God that emerge in the cracks of imperial power. Rieger states, "One of the key purposes of the study of Christian theology in the context of empire has to do with a search for that which cannot be co-opted by empire, and which thus inspires alternatives to empire."[42] Rieger refers to this as a theological *surplus*. The term speaks to the residues that empire seeks to suppress and that nevertheless show up, contrary to the policing efforts of imperial forces.[43]

But in its expansion and its global reach, in its impetus to shape all according to its image and likeness, it also fosters that which it cannot contain. A justice-seeking theology must continuously assess its premises, discern the spirits, and seek out the movements of God's Spirit beyond the

40. Hardt and Negri, *Empire*, 10–11.

41. Joerg Rieger, "Christian Theology and Empires," in *Empire and the Christian Tradition*, ed. Compier, Pui-lan, and Rieger, 3.

42. Rieger, 1.

43. See Joerg Rieger, *Christ and Empire: From Paul to Postcolonial Times* (Minneapolis: Fortress, 2007), 9–11.

spirit of empire. For Keller, the imperial condition of Christianity might find its antidote in the *interstitial*, the sites where the inescapable reach of imperial forces nevertheless produces alternatives to Empire.[44] It creates the conditions for its own questioning, for its own potential dissolution. In its global aspirations, empire fails to completely create a world that replicates its models of power and its structure of authority. In its drive to globality, empire meets local stories that present a counter-story to the imperial vision of the "globe."[45]

It is the both the opinion and the commitment of the authors in the book that the Methodist traditions have not been subsumed by imperialism. While not uncritical to the impact of imperialism on Methodism, the testimony offered by the chapters gathered in this volume is that there is a theological surplus that remains active in Methodist communities and their theologies. While imperial forces seek to control everything, God's work exceeds the grasp of empire. The force and vitality of Methodism relies on its ability to encounter God's grace in the interstices of empire.

The flow of power under imperialism is an everlasting vertical force that moves from the centers of power to its peripheries. Contributors to this volume detect several instances whereby Methodism obeyed this logic. Paying close attention to these imperial forces has a double significance. On the one hand, it trains Methodist leaders and theologians to acknowledge that the church is not immune to the forces of empire, even when it seeks to preserve itself from the involvement in geo-political matters. All ecclesial debates are political and, we must insist, the task of forming a global denomination ought to be situated in the context of American national and corporate expansionism in the twentieth century. On the other hand, paying close attention to imperial forces might create the necessary space to discern counter-hegemonic ways of being the church. This is the constructive task that we seek to embrace in this volume. We hope that readers will be able to recognize how Methodism also found ways of negotiating forms

44. Keller, "The Love of Postcolonialism," 224.

45. See Walter D. Mignolo, *Local Histories/Global Designs: Coloniality, Subaltern Knowledges, and Border Thinking*, Princeton Studies in Culture/Power/History (Princeton, NJ: Princeton University Press, 2000).

of power that are cultivated on the underside of empire and whose flow is horizontal, integrative, and democratic.

A global ecclesial body need not obey the logic of empire. The central ecclesiological commitment to connectionalism that orients Methodist traditions can be perceived through the lens of a counter-hegemonic form of transnational and transcultural solidarity. In Wesleyan ecclesiology, connectionalism marks the commitment to a vision of the church that imagines itself as a network of communities gathered by the Spirit of God. The connectionalism of empire operates in the logic of annexation and homogenization. Its connectionalism is a vast network for the imposition of a singular perspective and of an exclusive and exclusionary mode of assembling. It is a gathering that gains shape through fundamental acts of exploitation and exclusion. Resisting this imperial ecclesiology would entail the formation of ecclesial networks where divine grace is received and perceived in the coming together of the planetary assembly. The connection puts the members of the church body in relation to a life that emerges in the spaces of grave tensions and amidst the struggle for just relations.[46]

The authors in this volume share historical and theological perspectives that indicate the negotiations that Methodists performed in their attempt to form a global ecclesial body. We shall see that imperialism is stamped in many of these negotiations. But we hope that readers will notice that this is not the whole story. In ecclesial connections so marred by imperialism, we share here glimpses of possible modes of transnational and transcultural connections. They testify to the possibility of a Methodist connectionalism that insisted on spreading its roots across the borders and boundaries set by empire.

Plan of the Book

As the above historical and theological overview indicates, this volume provides a critical perspective on the efforts of The United Methodist Church and other Methodist bodies in constructing a global denomina-

46. See Joerg Rieger, *Grace under Pressure: Negotiating the Heart of the Methodist Traditions* (Nashville: United Methodist General Board of Higher Education and Ministry, 2011).

tion. Through archival research, historical analyses, and theological reflections, this volume chronicles the formation of a global ecclesial ethos
amongst United Methodists since the mid-twentieth century. These accounts demonstrate how the denomination has struggled to find a balance
between centralized ecclesial authority and local and national autonomy.
The authors in this volume suggest that this ecclesial tension ought to be
understood in the context of imperialism.

Methodism and Empire is divided in two parts. The first part offers
perspectives on the historical roots of United Methodism and U.S. imperialism in the twentieth century. It begins with analyses of the history of
the Commission on the Structure of Methodism Overseas (COSMOS),
a committee first convened by The Methodist Church in 1948, incorporated into the structure of The United Methodist Church at its founding
1968, and dissolved in 1972. In chapter 1, Joon-Sik Park chronicles this
history to show that the challenges in implementing a global denomination accompany United Methodism since its inception and that concerns
about U.S. imperialism are anything but new. Park further shows that
United Methodists outside the United States expressed a desire to be part
of a global body but have repeatedly expressed concerns about paternalistic and colonial patterns that persist in the UMC. These patterns, Park
maintains, suppress the Wesleyan ecclesial principle of connectionalism
and hinder the mission of the church. Philip Wingeier-Rayo demonstrates
in chapter 2 that resistance to U.S. imperialism, combined with the social
and political contexts of the 1960s and 1970s, are to be treated as the
backdrop to understand the pursuit of autonomy by Methodists in Latin
America and the Caribbean. Wingeier-Rayo suggests that the Cuban Revolution and its impact in Latin America accentuated the perception that
Methodism was an American denomination and that Methodists in the
continent would be better off in autonomous churches.

In chapter 3, David Scott provides an "exercise in comparative polity" that contrasts the organization of The Wesleyan Church, the Church
of the Nazarene, the African Methodist Episcopal (AME) Church, and
the UMC. Scott shows how a combination of broader historical circumstances common across denominations and internal historical trajectories

and organizational decisions within each denomination have influenced the ways in which American dominance has both been expressed and mitigated in various U.S.-based Methodist denominations. This comparative approach allows for new perspectives on the relationship between Methodism and American empire. Of all these denominations, the UMC has made fewer changes to its structure to adapt to its global membership, although Scott concludes by saying that a window of opportunity is now presenting itself for United Methodism to address this issue.

Section 2 of *Methodism and Empire*, "Contemporary Perspectives," begins with Jørgen Thaarup's probing of General Conference as a "parallel structure" to the U.S. system of government. In particular, Thaarup points out the similarities between the three branches of government in the United States and United Methodist polity. In General Conference, this creates an unfavorable scenario for non-American delegates who find themselves in a foreign system of governance.

Chapter 5, written by Darryl Stephens, accounts for the Social Principles of the UMC and interrogates whether it can provide a truly global ethic for the denomination. Stephens addresses two major points of contention that currently divide United Methodists: competing perspectives on human sexuality and the implied white U.S.-centric character of the denomination. For him, the 2020 draft of the new Social Principles, while embedded in these tensions, has the potential to offer a global ethic that meets this divided church.

In chapter 6, Taylor Denyer reflects about how conflict in United Methodism in the United States exacerbates local tensions in annual conferences in Africa. Denyer documents how several groups with the UMC tried to intervene in her own North Katanga Annual Conference and other annual conferences in Africa to gain institutional power within the denomination. She perceives this as an attempt to construct an "ecclesiastic empire." Lloyd Nyarota, in chapter 7, situates United Methodism in Africa within the long history of colonialism and imperialism in the continent while arguing that current disputes arising from the U.S. context continue to have an impact on African United Methodists. Nyarota points out that certain groups in the United States saw African delegates to General Conference as "raw material" they could control to achieve their goals for the denomination. For Nyarota, some United Methodists in Africa have fallen for these imperial tactics. But his chapter affirms the Christmas Covenant as offering a genuine pathway that could allow for both a worldwide connection and regional contextualization.

A similar sentiment is shared by Cristine Carnate-Atrero and Izzy Alvaran, who endorse the Christmas Covenant in chapter 8. They argue for the importance of regionalization as the best alternative to confront the imperialist legacy still present in the ecclesial structures of United Methodism. Building on the voices from central conferences, Carnate-Atrero and Alvaran endorse the document "Out of Chaos, Creation: Imagining a Way to Be a Better United Methodist," claiming that it represents a model of a truly connectional, global, and diverse denomination. Filipe Maia's chapter concludes the volume offering a critical account of the recently established Global Methodist Church, which carries in its name the project and the desire of a worldwide church body. Maia suggests nevertheless that the guiding documents of the new church replicate distinctly American concerns and patterns, which might ultimately hinder the denomination's global aspirations.

Methodism as a denominational tradition has historically resisted U.S. imperialism even as it has often also succumbed to it. That process of struggle and contestation is ongoing, as references to an ongoing split in The United Methodist Church indicate. We hope this volume will give encouragement to those engaged in that struggle.

Section 1:
HISTORICAL ROOTS

1

THE WORLDWIDE NATURE OF THE UNITED METHODIST CHURCH

A Historical and Missiological Reflection[1]

Joon-Sik Park

I had the privilege of serving on the Study Committee on the Worldwide Nature of The United Methodist Church (UMC) from 2009 to 2012. What I soon realized was that the task of the committee was nothing new; in fact, it was commissioned to address a century-old debate. According to Bishop Patrick Streiff, "Few Methodists are aware of how old the debate is and how many times in its history The United Methodist Church and its predecessors have oscillated between these two options"—whether they "should become more global or whether all parts outside the U.S. should become autonomous."[2] Exploring and examining the worldwide nature of the UMC, I came to be convinced that to know and be mindful of the history of the debate, or to place it within a broader historical context, would be crucial for the denomination to make right decisions regarding future directions for its global connection.

1. Research for this article was supported in part by the Florence Bell Scholar Award in 2018 from the Department of Special Collections and University Archives of the Drew University Library. I thank Robert J. Harman for helpful comments on an earlier version.

2. Patrick Ph. Streiff, "The Global Nature of The United Methodist Church: What Future for the Branch Outside the United States?" *Quarterly Review* 24:2 (Summer 2004): 182.

A Historical Reflection

The UMC and its predecessors have long grappled with their worldwide nature and structure. As early as in 1928, the Board of Foreign Missions of the Methodist Episcopal Church recommended to its General Conference that some constitutional changes be made in order to allow the Central Conferences "the standing necessary to become autonomous units" and that a Central Conference be established also in the United States. It envisioned the Central Conferences to be "organically united into a real ecumenical Conference" with its major role "to discuss and legislate on the increasingly vital world issues" that were often eclipsed by "a jam of local interests."[3]

However, it was not until the 1960s that The Methodist Church came to consider seriously making changes to its global structure. The most focused and sustained study on its global connection was undertaken by the Commission on the Structure of Methodism Overseas—also known as COSMOS—from 1964 to 1972.[4] It is worth revisiting and probing the COSMOS reports and responses, as they can still shed critical light on the proper understanding of the relationship between the U.S. Methodist Church and the Methodist Churches in other parts of the world.

COSMOS was first established in 1948 by the General Conference of The Methodist Church. In 1964, its membership consisted of "four bishops administering in Jurisdictional Conferences, four bishops administering in Central Conferences, one minister and one [layperson] from each Jurisdictional Conference, and one person from each Central Con-

---

3. "The Board of Foreign Missions," *Journal of the 30th Delegated General Conference of the Methodist Episcopal Church* (New York: Methodist Book Concern, 1928), 1257. Currently, in each of the seven geographic areas outside the United States—located in Africa, Europe, and the Philippines—annual conferences are organized together in a central conference. Among its major responsibilities are to connect annual conferences for common mission and to elect bishops and fix their tenure.

4. The Commission's minutes, reports, study documents, and correspondence are in the collection of the United Methodist Archives and History Center (UM Archives) of the General Commission on Archives and History in Madison, New Jersey.

ference." They were all "nominated by the Council of Bishops and approved by the General Conference."[5]

The work of COSMOS was guided by five core and foundational principles. New structures should:

1. contribute to "the development of responsible, indigenous churches of integrity" which are not "under the control of a foreign body."
2. be shaped by the centrality of mission.
3. foster "interdependence in mission, that is, provision of ties of partnership and fellowship in common tasks between Christians across national and regional lines."
4. be considered provisional and "interim" in nature and thus be "flexible."
5. "provide for equality of relationship and accompanied by a mutual search for renewal."[6]

The COSMOS report to the 1968 General Conference stated that The Methodist Church then was "in reality not a world church in structure but an American church with overseas outposts," and that "to drift or make minor shifts in present structure is to decide against a world church by default."[7] In a presentation to COSMOS titled "The Need for Structural Flexibility," Bishop Prince Taylor, who served as Chairperson of COSMOS from 1968 to 1972, contended that the then-current structure did not "provide for a world church of equals" but was "still a paternalistic one." He argued for the creation of a world church "out of world partners" without delay, since "later may be too late."[8]

COSMOS identified four possible alternatives for the global structure. The first was "modification of the present structure" allowing greater

5. *Doctrines and Discipline of The Methodist Church 1964* (Nashville: The Methodist Publishing House, 1964), ¶1812. A central conference with a membership of 200,000 and above was allocated two representatives. Further, four persons, two women and two men, were added to the Commission by the Board of Missions.

6. "Study Guide for a Consultation on Methodist Church Overseas Structure" (1966), 1336-1-3-7, UM Archives (Madison, NJ), 13–14. For slightly different wordings of these principles, see also "The Methodist Church [USA]—A Change in Structure Required" (ca. 1965), 1335-1-4-52, UM Archives (Madison, NJ), 14, which stresses the importance of the new structure supporting the "unity with other Christians."

7. *Journal of the 1968 General Conference of The United Methodist Church*, vol. 2 (Nashville: The United Methodist Publishing House, 1968), 1784–85.

8. Prince A. Taylor, Jr., "The Need for Structural Flexibility" (1964), 1335-1-5-3, UM Archives (Madison, NJ), 3.

freedom and responsibilities for the Central Conferences. The second alternative was to encourage Methodist churches outside the United States to become autonomous or to form united churches. One major concern about this proposal was the possibility of autonomous churches becoming intensely nationalistic.

The third was to create "a truly decentralized, international Methodist Church," consisting of regional conferences including one in the United States. It envisioned a World General Conference that would only legislate on matters of global and connectional concerns. Much of the current authority of the General Conference would be transferred to the Regional Conferences. The last alternative, proposed by D. T. Niles, was to form "a World Methodist Conference of Churches" that serves not as "a legislative body but a consultative body" for autonomous regional churches. The focus was to be on fellowship and common mission among churches from various Methodist traditions.[9]

It was known that COSMOS favored the third model of an "International" or "World Church," which would share "a common basis of faith, ministry, membership and general episcopacy." The Regional Conference would "write its own Discipline and provide administration and organization suited to the region." Such a structure was thought to be able to allow both "local autonomy and inter-dependence."[10]

However, COSMOS stopped short of recommending a specific proposal for the global structure to the 1968 General Conference, where the union of The Methodist Church and the Evangelical United Brethren Church took precedence over all other matters. Instead, the Commission requested and was granted the authority to hold jurisdictional consultations and a World Methodist Structure Congress in the coming quadrennium with the purpose of presenting a definitive proposal to the next General Conference.

By the time the 1972 General Conference was gathered, however, COSMOS had abandoned the "World Church" alternative in which the U.S. Church would become a regional or central conference. It was no lon-

---

9. Lawrence Turnipseed, "New Structures for Methodism Overseas" (1966), 1335-1-5-6, UM Archives (Madison, NJ), 3–6.

10. "The Beginning of a New Era" (1968), 1335-1-2-51, UM Archives (Madison, NJ), 3.

ger considered a viable option as it would be "costly in time and money" and "take years to implement." COSMOS instead recommended the reorganization of the World Methodist Council "for worldwide fellowship and cooperation of all churches of the Methodist traditions."[11] The UMC in reality settled for the status quo with little structural changes, and "left churches choosing autonomy without a promised link to each other in their regions and beyond."[12]

As Lawrence Turnipseed perceptively noted, the 1972 General Conference signaled a major negative turning point in the history of The United Methodist Church's efforts to become a genuinely global church. Most significantly, "the understanding of 'global connection' was gradually narrowed to focus only on the Central Conference relationships," resulting in weakening of ties with the autonomous churches.[13] Ever since 1972, new attempts and efforts to shed light on the worldwide nature of the UMC have ensued. However, the proposals from the subsequent studies, including the one by the Study Committee on the Worldwide Nature of the UMC in 2012, neither significantly differed from nor meaningfully enhanced those of COSMOS.

Since almost the beginning of the last century, the UMC and its predecessors have sought to address their global connection through multiple study commissions and consultations, as well as General Conference deliberations. Yet, thus far, there have only been slow, reluctant, and modest modifications but no integral changes in the worldwide structure. It is very hard not to raise the question why such has been the case.

---

11. R. Lawrence Turnipseed, "A Brief History of the Discussion of The United Methodist Church as a 'World Church,'" in *The Ecumenical Implications of the Discussions of "The Global Nature of The United Methodist Church"* (New York: General Commission on Christian Unity and Interreligious Concerns, 1999), 25. According to Robert J. Harman, "when the subject of responsibility for funding [the] global vision of Methodism arose, the project [of a world church] seems to have been dropped" (*From Missions to Mission: The History of Mission of The United Methodist Church, 1968–2000*, United Methodist Church History of Mission Series, vol. 5 [New York: United Methodist General Board of Global Ministries, 2005], 454).

12. Robert J. Harman, "Worldwide Nature of the Church: How We Got Here!" (Paper delivered at the Meeting of the Study Committee on the Worldwide Nature of the UMC, Atlanta, GA, August 24, 2009), 14.

13. Turnipseed, "A Brief History of the Discussion," 25.

One probable reason could be the U.S. Methodist Church's preoccupation with its own local concerns and interests, including the two mergers in 1939 and 1968. Whenever the issue of the worldwide structure was brought up to the General Conference, other pressing U.S. issues or interests led to opting for the status quo over substantial changes. However, more fundamentally, it could have been due to the desire of the U.S. Methodist Church to be in and retain the dominant position, which could be traced back to the Western colonial ethos. The following observations were shared at the COSMOS jurisdictional consultations held in 1969:

> The present structure of the United Methodist Church is basically a result of the experiences and worldview of the 19th century—the century of Western expansion. There have been adaptations and accommodations to needs overseas but the basic ideas and patterns were developed for and by the U.S.A. The church here and overseas cannot afford that image of imperialism and colonialism.[14]

It is noteworthy that the UMC and its predecessors have not attempted to provide a biblically or theologically based reasoning for their desire or intent to be and remain a global church. For instance, the report of the Commission on Central Conferences of the Methodist Episcopal Church to the 1932 General Conference described two contrasting approaches to mission churches—centralizing and decentralizing. Unlike U.S. Methodists,

> Practically all other Protestant denominations, both in America and in Europe, have had the policy of setting up independent, self-governing churches from the beginning in their missionary activity. . . .
> Indeed, most of these denominations have maintained a fixed purpose of creating self-supporting, self-governing and self-propagating churches from the beginning and have been eager to have the younger churches set up in their own households as quickly as possible. For all these churches it is just as natural for them to think of having . . . the development of independent church units in the various countries of the world as it has been for the Methodists to think of a centralized control of their far-flung church line.[15]

---

14.   J. Robert Martin, "A Report on the COSMOS Jurisdictional Meetings" (1969), 1336-1-4-1, UM Archives (Madison, NJ), 5.

15.   "The Commission on Central Conferences," in *Journal of the 31st Delegated General Conference of the Methodist Episcopal Church* (New York: Methodist Book Concern, 1932), 1442–43.

Yet, the report neither offered a value judgment on either approach nor provided a critical self-reflection on why U.S. Methodists had settled on the centralized control policy.[16]

For the integrity of the life and mission of the UMC, however, it is crucial that the motivation behind its desire to be a global church be probed. Writing on the historical connection between colonialism and mission, Joerg Rieger poignantly argues that "even though direct patronizing structures at the political level have been discontinued with the end of colonialism, . . . even in a postcolonial age, colonial mentalities have not disappeared." Most dangerously, those with colonial or neo-colonial mentalities desire "to form the other in [their] own mirror image" and tend to consider the other merely as objects of benevolence rather than as equal partners.[17]

It is a disturbing truth that "failure to consider our colonial heritage may result in failure to understand who we are today."[18] It is thus imperative that the United Methodists in the United States take a hard look at themselves and see whether colonial paternalism might still linger with and keep them from confronting squarely the basis of their deep-seated desire to keep the current worldwide structure. If it is the aspiration "to maintain [its] image as big, powerful, worldwide, growing, and successful," says Dennis Campbell, then "it can be a dangerous new kind of United Methodist triumphalism."[19]

Yearning for Integral Autonomy

According to the study guide prepared for a COSMOS consultation held in Green Lake, Wisconsin, in 1966, there were several factors that were forcing The Methodist Church to examine its global structure: "the

16. Bruce W. Robbins, *A World Parish?: Hopes and Challenges of The United Methodist Church in a Global Setting* (Nashville: Abingdon, 2004), 51–52.

17. Joerg Rieger, "Theology and Mission Between Neocolonialism and Postcolonialism," *Mission Studies* 21:2 (2004): 207, 222.

18. Rieger, "Theology and Mission," 202.

19. Dennis M. Campbell, "Does Methodism Have a Future in American Culture?" in *Questions for the Twenty-First Century Church,* United Methodism and American Culture, vol. 4, ed. Russell E. Richey, William B. Lawrence, and Dennis M. Campbell (Nashville: Abingdon, 1999), 20.

growth and maturity of the Church overseas"; "the emergence of the new nations and a new awareness of self-identity"; "the growing urgency of mission" by the indigenous churches, resulting in or calling for "new relationships" between the church in the United States and the churches overseas; and "the emergence of the ecumenical movement," in particular "the rise and growth of regional Christian Councils."[20] There was a clear recognition that the churches in Africa, Asia, and Latin America "had 'come of age' and that, therefore, national leadership should be given increasing authority and responsibility."[21]

The diversity of the historical and geopolitical contexts of the central conferences and annual conferences overseas obviously affected the degree of their desire to seek autonomy. Some preferred stability to greater freedom and responsibility. However, there was an undeniable yearning for greater autonomy on the part of the younger churches, in particular those in Asia and Latin America, and autonomy was viewed as the goal toward which the church should move forward. Although the proposal for autonomy for the churches overseas was only one of the four alternatives, it was "ardently supported by an increasing number of Methodists."[22]

A working definition of autonomy for COSMOS was presented in three points: to be "responsible to no other church for the conduct of its own life"; to have "full legislative powers and full administrative responsibilities for managing its own life"; and "in its own right [to be able to] enter into relations with other churches through confessional and ecumenical bodies."[23] There was strong agreement that each church's selfhood and integrity should be protected and that each church should be responsible for its own life and mission.

---

20. "Study Guide for Consultation on Methodist Church Overseas Structure," 1336-1-3-7, 10.

21. Richard C. Raines, "Ecumenism and the Structure of Methodism Overseas" (1965), 1335-1-4-4, UM Archives (Madison, NJ), 3.

22. Richard C. Raines, "Autonomy" (1966), 1335-1-2-35, UM Archives (Madison, NJ), 5. Harman perceptively notes, "The force and lasting influence of this trend toward self-determination could not be underestimated. When asked in a survey by the Council of Bishops at the outset of their contemplation of a global church structure in the 1989–1992 quadrennium, few autonomous church leaders expressed any interest in returning to the fold of the central conferences in their regions" (*From Missions to Mission*, 446).

23. "[Memo] To: The Consultation on Overseas Structure" (1966), 1335-1-1-31, UM Archives (Madison, NJ), 1.

The statement issued by a consultation convened by the East Asia Christian Conference (EACC) in Kandy, Ceylon, in 1965 well reflected the then sentiment of the churches in Asia regarding autonomy. The central question raised was "whether a Church in a specific situation or region is free to make its own decisions in obedience to God and in the fullness of the life of grace." Gaining integral autonomy was viewed as "the end of one phase of the missionary enterprise and the beginning of another," signalizing "the transition from dependence to partnership."[24]

Commenting on autonomy following the Kandy Consultation, Ivy Chou lamented that the churches in Asia did "(1) continue to be legally and psychologically dependent on the 'parent' churches, (2) lack the sense of selfhood, and the sense of mission as the 'people of God' in their own land, and (3) fail to move beyond the 'family' life of their particular confession, into multi-lateral relationships with other churches in the same region as well as with other churches at large."[25]

Autonomy was not meant to sever all ties but to usher in relationships of equals. What the Methodists in Asia wanted was to gain true selfhood and freedom to pursue ecclesial structures that could possibly enable the integral life and witness of the church. What was desired of the Methodist churches in the United States was to "see autonomy as the fulfilment of their overseas missions, rejoice over its coming, and take conscious steps toward its realization."[26] In a memorandum to COSMOS in 1965, D. T. Niles even stated that a structure of true equality and partnership could not "be achieved by side-stepping the autonomy issue," and that "autonomy for a church is not a choice . . . [but] belongs to its very nature."[27]

The Methodist churches in Latin America also desired autonomy in order not to be regarded as "a foreign religious expression" but to be "fully identified with the realities, the aspirations, the tragedies, and the glories

---

24. EACC, "Statements Issued by a Consultation on Confessional Families and the Churches in Asia," *International Review of Mission* 55:218 (1966): 195–96.

25. Ivy Chou, "Comments on Autonomy—Following the Kandy Consultation" (1965), 1335-1-2-36, UM Archives (Madison, NJ), 1.

26. Chou, "Comments on Autonomy," 2.

27. D. T. Niles, "World Methodism: A Memorandum" (1965), 1335-1-6-16, UM Archives (Madison, NJ), 4, 8.

of [their] people."[28] They believed in both the universality and contextuality of mission: The scope of the mission of the church is worldwide and not bound by any boundaries, yet the church in each place is to determine how mission is to be fulfilled. Their aspiration toward autonomy was for the sake of critically discerning and faithfully carrying out their particular mission. For Latin American Methodism, autonomy was understood as freedom and "a space gained for the kind of thought, prayer, experimentation needed if Methodism will continue to serve in Latin America."[29]

José Míguez Bonino stressed that the identity and calling of the church in Latin America was to be construed more "by reference to the Gospel and to the Latin American location" than to a confessional tradition. Methodists in Latin America, if faithful to their calling, "shall not come out of [their] crisis . . . primarily as Methodists, or perhaps even as Protestants" but as Christians striving for the transformation of Latin America.[30] Autonomy would grant them the freedom and authority to determine the institutional structure and the nature of mission appropriate to their particular contexts.

One of the common concerns among the Methodist churches overseas regarding the central conference system was that it would still mirror "vestiges of colonialism or ecclesiastical empire-building of a world church."[31] They were "sometimes stigmatized as being a part of a foreign, rather than an indigenous, organization," which hurt the integrity and effectiveness of their witness.[32] One notable stigma of being a central conference was that it could not hold its own membership in regional or world councils.

When Bishop Raines requested personal responses to the proposal for an International Methodist Church, one respondent wrote:

---

28. "Summary Statement Adopted by Methodist Latin American Consultation on 'Life and Mission of the Church'" (1962), 1335-1-8-7, UM Archives (Madison, NJ), 3.

29. José Míguez Bonino, "Methodism in Latin America" (1970), 1336-1-4-7, UM Archives (Madison, NJ), 5.

30. Bonino, "Methodism in Latin America," 6–7.

31. L. Elbert Wethington, "The Central Conference of the Methodist Church: A Study-Paper for the General Conference COSMOS, 1960–64" (1962), 1335-1-2-56, UM Archives (Madison, NJ), 29.

32. Richard C. Raines, "A World Structure for a World Church or a World Structure for a World Mission?" (n.d.), 1335-1-5-24, UM Archives (Madison, NJ), 5.

I must say that as much as I appreciate your intention, I doubt that it takes sufficient of the aspirations and dilemmas of many of the overseas churches today. The proposal does very much sound like "possessive parents" choosing and prescribing for their "adolescent children" their own friends (and marriage partners!) and their development of their adult family relationship! If you can look at the picture less from the States' point of view, but more from the crucial situations and needs with which our churches are confronted, you will see that the next step has to be genuine support and positive guidance toward autonomy.[33]

A world structure without each church becoming autonomous was viewed as prone to perpetuating a relationship of dependence and inequality, a colonial pattern, and keeping the younger churches from gaining full maturity. Almost all central conferences expressed their strong desire to be a part of a world church, but at the same time were wary of the possibility of a continuing U.S.-dominated relationship.

Reflecting on the work of COSMOS, Bishop Taylor stated that "little or no consideration [had been given] to what might be done in the USA to make it *a partner in a world church, instead of it being the world church, extended overseas*, with the overseas structure designed to accommodate itself to the USA blueprint."[34] It was doubtful, considering its numerical and financial strength, whether the U.S. church was willing to surrender its dominance and control over Methodism for the sake of forming a truly international church. American Methodism was probably not ready to heed a warning issued by the Kandy statement: "To what extent can a Church in one region be a governing authority over a Church in another region without distorting its own life? Governing raises as many problems as being governed."[35]

In response to the yearning for autonomy on the part of some central conferences, one major concern was that it could lead to excessive nationalism or provincialism, isolating the churches from one another over national or regional boundaries. Yet, Bishop Yap Kim Hao argued:

---

33. "Personal Reactions to the Proposal for an International Methodist Church Expressed in Letters Written at the Request of Bishop Raines" (1965), 1335-1-5-14, UM Archives (Madison, NJ), 1.

34. Taylor, "Need for Structural Flexibility," 1335-1-5-3, 3, italics mine.

35. EACC, "Statements Issued by a Consultation on Confessional Families and Churches in Asia," 196.

Autonomy of the church has often been misinterpreted as the development of a national church. . . . Within Asia, no autonomous church can ever expect to become . . . a national church or a state church. . . . Autonomous churches in Asia are churches *for* the nation, *in* the nation and most certainly not *of* the nation. . . . We must remind ourselves that Asian nations are either secular or religious states which are Islamic or Buddhist but certainly never Christian.[36]

The thirst for autonomy originated from their desire to be involved in "all aspects of national life" and to be part of "the longing and hopes of a people, as well as [of] their frustrations and despair" so that they could be the church in their own locations.[37] For them, the presence of national churches was prerequisite to the forming of an international church. Thus, Ivy Chou contended that "the danger of 'isolation' and 'nationalism' [had] been overemphasized by those . . . opposed to autonomy," and that "the risk should not be used as an argument against autonomy."[38]

In the midst of the emergence of postcolonial nations in Asia, Niles urged the church to be actively involved in nation-building: "That a nation attains self-hood is part of the requirement for a church's full discharge of its mission in and to that nation."[39] He was conscious of and cautioned against the danger of falling into nationalism—"to slip from a concern to build a church for the nation into a desire to build a church of the nation."[40] However, he was also aware that, when such caution came from the churches of the West, it could have been motivated by their concern about losing influence over the younger churches.

36. Yap Kim Hao, "Methodism in Asia" (1970), 1336-1-4-7, UM Archives (Madison, NJ), 7, italics in original.

37. Ruth Anstey, "Autonomy" (1965), 1335-1-2-42, UM Archives (Madison, NJ), 4.

38. Chou, "Comments on Autonomy," 1335-1-2-36, 3. It is noteworthy that the early growth of Korean Christianity at the beginning of the twentieth century was inseparably intertwined with anti-Japanese Korean nationalism wholeheartedly embraced by Korean Protestants. See Joon-Sik Park, "Korean Protestant Christianity: A Missiological Reflection," *International Bulletin of Missionary Research* 36:2 (2012): 59–61.

39. D. T. Niles, *Upon the Earth: The Mission of God and the Missionary Enterprise of the Church* (New York: McGraw-Hill, 1962), 143.

40. Niles, *Upon the Earth*, 256.

It needs to be pointed out that "the movement toward autonomy was not uniform nor did it receive unanimous endorsement."[41] For instance, the Methodist churches in Europe did not seek autonomy, as they had not been "a Church founded by missionaries in a colonial situation" and had "always felt on an equal footing" with the churches in the United States. Historically, from the very beginning, their stance was not in conformity with state or national churches. Being minority churches, they were extremely conscious not "to live in a national ghetto" and not "to become or stay provincial."[42]

Another thorny issue in relation to autonomy was that of dependence of the Methodist churches overseas on the financial support of the Methodist Church in the United States. It took courage for the central conferences to choose autonomy over remaining part of the current structure, since it certainly had financial implications. Although the Board of Missions had promised that "a move to autonomy would in no way lessen its willingness to continue support in prayer, concern, funds and personnel,"[43] autonomous and united churches eventually came to lose the financial assistance that once they were privileged to receive.

The Methodist churches in both the United States and overseas failed to address squarely these questions: "What are the reasons Central Conferences desire to maintain . . . the relationship with the 'mother church'? . . . How much weight should be given to financial support?"[44] It probably cannot be denied that the financial advantage granted to the central conferences kept some of them from being motivated to pursue autonomy or explore an alternative global structure.

The overwhelming majority of the participants in the COSMOS consultations in the 1960s supported a certain structural change of The

---

41.   Harman, *From Missions to Mission*, 450.

42.   "Future Structures of the European United Methodist Church" (1970), 1336-1-4-7, UM Archives (Madison, NJ), 2–3. Streiff notes: "European Methodists had indigenous leadership and financial self-support. They viewed their relation to the U.S. part of the church as a partnership. World War II had shown them the danger of any church established along national borders" ("Global Nature of The United Methodist Church," 184).

43.   "Statement on Autonomy at Annual Meeting of the Board of Missions of the Methodist Church" (1964), 1335-1-2-43, UM Archives (Madison, NJ), 1.

44.   Elbert Wethington, "Central Conference of the Methodist Church," 1335-1-2-56, 26–27.

Methodist Church that would provide for greater freedom and local authority. They were, however, also concerned that the desire to pursue such a change might appear "ungrateful" to the U.S. Methodist Church and negatively affect its financial assistance.[45] There were undeniable "psychological pressures . . . from the system itself to maintain the status quo." The aspiration and striving toward autonomy was "looked upon as an abortive, negative, almost unfriendly gesture" rather than "encouraged as a logical development."[46] Whether intended or not, the paternalistic relations between the churches in the United States and overseas were perpetuated for both psychological and economic reasons.

Unlike The Methodist Church in the United States, the Methodist Church in the British tradition in general supported the establishment of autonomous churches (as in Nigeria, Ceylon [now Sri Lanka], and Ghana) or united churches (as in South India, Burma [now Myanmar], and Sierra Leone) overseas. British Methodists believed that it was right and desirable "for Founder-Parent Churches to exercise initiative in encouraging Churches to request autonomy" so that they could "become completely self-governing" and "come to terms with their role and mission within the life of the nation."[47] What the British Methodist Church envisioned was for the younger churches to become free of the taint of colonialism and rooted in their own cultural and national soil.

The Evangelical United Brethren (EUB) Church also considered it as its policy to encourage the development of indigenous autonomous or united churches outside the United States. When the EUB Church was formed in 1946, all of its overseas churches (except in Sierra Leone, Germany, and Switzerland) had become part of united churches in their own countries. According to John Schaefer, they were "free to choose their own structure, their own forms of worship, and determine their own doctrinal statements." Even when the EUB Church merged with The Methodist

45. Raines, "Autonomy," 1335-1-2-35, 3.

46. "A Preliminary Proposal for Legislative Revision of the *Discipline* in Light of the COSMOS Study Paper" (n.d.), 1335-1-5-23, UM Archives (Madison, NJ), 2.

47. Donald B. Childe, "Autonomy: The Need to Set the Churches Free" (1964), 1335-1-2-49, UM Archives (Madison, NJ), 1.

Church in 1968, one of its concerns was "that the united churches may find a significant place in the structure of United Methodism."[48]

Whereas the Methodist Church in Britain and the EUB Church were intentionally committed to helping overseas churches become indigenous and autonomous, "permissiveness" might well define the policy of the U.S. Methodist Church toward autonomy throughout its history.[49] It was reluctant to see autonomy as necessary and inevitable for the church to grow and mature with integrity in its own indigenous context. It certainly failed to provide positive guidance toward autonomy. Yet, as Yap strongly argued, "we cannot at one breath say that you can be autonomous if you want it and you can remain in the Central Conference pattern if you choose to do so."[50]

The yearning for integral autonomy and interdependence through relationships of equals, expressed at various COSMOS consultations, was not fully heard. Profound wisdom and insights that could have helped The Methodist Church find a way forward regarding its global structure were not fully integrated into the decisions adopted at General Conferences. Unfortunately, the work of COSMOS represented wasted opportunities and unfruitful toil.

Regrettably, the imaginations of the UMC and its predecessors regarding the worldwide structure were and have continued to be severely limited and stifled by their imperial tendencies and characteristics. For instance, the UMC is now working on a "global" *Book of Discipline* to allow for greater freedom for the central conferences to adapt the parts considered regional or local to their unique contexts and needs. Yet, as Hendrik Pieterse keenly points out, even "adaptation language" reflects the "center-periphery" mindset and "the continued privileging of U.S. designs in de-

---

48.   John F. Schaefer, "The Relationship of the Evangelical United Brethren Church with Churches Overseas," *The Seminary Review* 52 (January 1966): 19, 21.

49.   Richard Raines, "A History and Evaluation of Autonomy in Methodism" (1968), 1335-1-2-46, UM Archives (Madison, NJ), 4.

50.   Yap Kim Hao, "Encourage Autonomy" (n.d.), 1335-1-2-48, UM Archives (Madison, NJ), 14.

nominational deliberations and General Conference decisions." What is
sorely missing is "the recognition that we are all equally 'adapters.'"[51]
Míguez Bonino's apprehension still merits careful hearing:

> I must confess my concern that Methodism is particularly in danger of be-
> ing swallowed up by the structural model . . . which—however much it may
> claim to be participatory—functions as a center of power with subsidiaries
> throughout the world. . . . This is not a question of imperialist intention. It
> is the unavoidable effect when a church structure that grew out of a specific
> context (such as the UMC in the U.S.) attempts to form in its own im-
> age—either through law or through influence—corresponding structure in
> totally different contexts.[52]

Here a question to raise is, even with a global *Book of Discipline* and
other modifications, whether the current structure would allow United
Methodist churches outside the United States to attain the kind of integrity needed for authentic life and mission, countervailing American
dominance. For the sake of the denomination's equitable connection and
missional integrity, autonomy should be seriously considered for all parts
of the UMC outside the United States. As equal, autonomous partners,
Methodist churches in each region then could together decide on their
future worldwide structure.

A Way Forward

Serving on the Study Committee on the Worldwide Nature of the
UMC from 2009 to 2012 was an enlightening and transformative experience. Engaging with United Methodists in intense listening sessions in
the Philippines, Liberia, Cote d'Ivoire, and Spain as well as in the United
States, I came to a deeper appreciation of connectionalism. No matter

51. Hendrik R. Pieterse, "A Worldwide United Methodist Church? Sounding toward a Connectional Theological Imagination," *Methodist Review* 5 (2013): 12.

52. José Míguez Bonino, "A Latin American Perspective on Challenges of Mission in the Post Cold War Era," in *Mission and Transformation in a Changing World: A Dialogue with Global Mission Colleagues* (New York: United Methodist General Board of Global Ministrie, 1998), 41. As a reason for Latin American churches' adoption of autonomy in the 1960s, he cited their frustration with having to apply "a 400-page *Discipline* written for a 10,000,000-member church with a complex structure and vast monetary resources" to the context of a 10,000-member church (ibid.).

how fragile and imperfect the current global structure might be, the great majority of United Methodist churches desired to stay together in common mission and fellowship across cultural and geographical boundaries. Yet, I also came to learn how complex and challenging it would be to live fully and justly into the worldwide nature of the UMC. The study committee grappled with how the UMC could integrate and hold in creative tension those seemingly opposing values like unity and local autonomy, equity, and mutual accountability.

The study committee found it extremely difficult to bring about integral changes, not just minor modifications, to the global structure. United Methodist churches both in the United States and overseas had vested interests in the current structure and were still not willing to journey beyond the status quo into the future with all its promise and uncertainty. Furthermore, the concern about and interest in the worldwide connection were promptly eclipsed by other, often U.S.-centric, concerns and interests—with denominational restructuring becoming the most dominant issue at the 2012 General Conference. The study committee proposed a global model for the purpose of continued conversation and study by annual conferences during the 2012–2016 quadrennium. It seemed, however, to fail to generate denomination-wide ecclesiological and missional reflections on the future shape of the worldwide structure.

Connectionalism is foundational and central to the distinct identity and structure of Methodism. It has been an unmistakably Wesleyan ecclesial vision. *The Book of Discipline* of the UMC describes it as "a vital web of interactive relationships," in which the people called Methodists are connected by sharing a common doctrine, polity, and mission, inter alia.[53] As the UMC seeks to address its worldwide nature, a focused ecclesiological self-reflection on its connectionalism would be prerequisite to any changes in its organizational forms. Hasty responses to emerging needs and challenges would most likely result in shallow adaptations than genuinely transformative reforms.

---

53. *The Book of Discipline of The United Methodist Church, 2016* (Nashville: The United Methodist Publishing House, 2016), ¶132.

Aptly delineating the multifaceted nature of connectionalism as "a practical divinity," Russell Richey brings to the fore its rich meanings for Methodism, including "an ecclesial vision, a missional principle, [and] a covenantal commitment."[54] One aspect of connectionalism that I call attention to is its missional nature. The Methodist connection was originally missional or mission-shaped. It was intrinsically designed to provide a coherent framework for mission. As *Grace Upon Grace*, The United Methodist Church's mission statement, stresses, "connectionalism is a means of discovering mission and of supporting mission."[55]

It is crucial then that the missional nature of the connection be reclaimed, and that connectionalism as the missional principle guide and shape the UMC's structural and organizational deliberations. Mission is to determine both the local and global structures, and all efforts at reordering the current connectional structure should serve the church's missional life and practice. As Robert Harman well puts it, "[The UMC's] mission should . . . define its future shape. Its mission calling should take the discourse [of a global church] far beyond organizational boundaries and privileges of membership."[56]

Commenting on the request for autonomy by the Latin American Central Conference at the 1968 General Conference, Bishop Sante Barbieri said, "You will ask what the reasons are. . . . In the first place, we have come to the conclusion that laws, regulations, and structures have to be created as close as possible to the place where the decisions have to be made. . . . We do not seek autonomy for autonomy sake; it is an autonomy for a better discharging of the mission in each place."[57] It must be noted that historically greater local autonomy has usually led to greater missional consciousness and commitment.

---

54. Russell E. Richey, "Introduction," in *Connectionalism: Ecclesiology, Mission, and Identity*, United Methodism and American Culture, vol. 1, ed. Russell E. Richey, Dennis M. Campbell, and William B. Lawrence (Nashville: Abingdon, 1997), 3.

55. *Grace Upon Grace: The Mission Statement of The United Methodist Church* (Nashville: Graded Press, 1990), ¶50.

56. Harman, *From Missions to Mission*, 455.

57. *Journal of the 1968 General Conference of The United Methodist Church*, vol. 1 (Nashville: The United Methodist Publishing House, 1968), 437.

In order to become a faithful and effective instrument of mission, each church needs to discern and to participate in God's mission in ways responsible to its specific cultural and social context. And it requires sufficient local authority and freedom. The goal of any structural change is to help United Methodist churches in all regions "become responsible churches—standing on their own feet, conducting their own life . . . discharging their own mission," and making necessary changes "in structure and administration for the fulfillment of their mission in the light of their local situations and needs."[58]

Authentic missional commitment and faithfulness would cultivate and enhance the sense of mutual interdependence, a deep awareness that the churches worldwide need one another for mutual affirmation, correction, and transformation in the journey of mission. As responsible partners in the gospel, they would want to journey together and live into an interconnected web, constructing "missional relationships in which Christians across contexts . . . accompany one another into the work and understanding of the missio Dei."[59]

Partnership in mission "is based on the fundamental belief that God's love for the world is greater than any one church can possibly comprehend or realize." The commitment to mutuality in mission "broadens our awareness of how interconnected God's mission is at the local, national and global levels."[60] As Mark Wethington astutely states, "in covenantal relationship [in mission] we are able to discern and do together what we are unable to perceive and carry out alone."[61] Such awareness and mutual experience of the interconnectedness in mission is to be integral to the global connection of the UMC. Furthermore, the forming of missional partnership across national and regional boundaries would keep churches in each region from falling into isolating provincialism.

---

58. Ivy Chou, "Letter to Charles Parlin" (1965), 1335-1-4-40, UM Archives (Madison, NJ), 1.

59. Mark W. Wethington, "God's Mission and United Methodism," in *Connectionalism: Ecclesiology, Mission, and Identity,* vol. 1, ed. Russell E. Richey, Dennis M. Campbell, and William B. Lawrence (Nashville: Abingdon, 1997), 225.

60. Sherron Kay George, *Called as Partners in Christ's Service: The Practice of God's Mission* (Louisville, KY: Geneva, 2004), 122.

61. Mark Wethington, "God's Mission and United Methodism," 226.

Pursuing mutual interdependence in mission, the UMC is, first, to strive toward living out and expressing its worldwide connection at the level of local congregations. Since "it is primarily at the level [of the local church] that the church encounters the world," and since it is the local church that is "to participate in the worldwide mission of the church,"[62] the covenanting relationship of mutuality in the global connection is to be recognized, valued, and experienced in the very life and mission of the local church. Mutuality in mission needs grassroots interaction, and not just institutional or organizational structure. In order for connectionalism "to become a living practice,"[63] local congregations should be encouraged and supported to engage each other concretely and hospitably across cultural and geographical boundaries.

Second, the UMC is to discover ways to share financial resources while protecting and furthering the integrity of both the churches that receive and the churches that give. It can no longer avoid confronting the issue of an excessive and unhealthy dependency that the current structure has created and continues to perpetuate. It is regrettable that money from the U.S. churches has "unquestionably shaped mission into being more paternalistic than mutual" and "frequently displaced the Spirit's power."[64] Considering the enormous regional economic disparities existing among United Methodist churches, the resources of the churches in the United States should continue to be willingly and joyfully shared for the sake of the *missio Dei*. Yet, it is crucial that they be shared much more responsibly than in the past so as to discourage and prevent economic dependency and to increase mutuality in all areas of the life and mission of the church.

When money becomes "the primary focus" or basis of the relationship, it is extremely difficult "to establish a relationship of mutuality-in-mission" and not to cultivate a culture of dependency.[65] Since autonomy "involves integrity" and "responsibility for one's own life," it is vital that

---

62. *Book of Discipline, 2016,* ¶202.

63. *Book of Discipline, 2016,* ¶125.

64. Mark Wethington, "God's Mission and United Methodism," 234.

65. Wethington, "God's Mission and United Methodism," 236–37. Wethington shares a story of Methodist missions in Peru as a telling illustration of how challenging it is to cultivate a mutual covenant relationship, in which the wealth of the North American church does not become the primary focus.

"the question of self-support and of meaningful stewardship" be seriously grappled with.[66] At the same time, "with conditions in a global economy producing more poor communities," a future worldwide structure, if pursued, is "to offer a model of economic justice through an effective plan for the sharing of resources and authority in its policymaking domains."[67]

Throughout the history of the church, "the unforgivable sin is the fear . . . that God may lead us where we do not want to go."[68] United Methodist churches are called to live out together their missional calling as equal partners, overcoming the fear of the unknown and forming a new kind of unity in witness and life-together beyond national and regional boundaries. As Pieterse well expresses it, "resisting the deep-running transformation beckoning at this crucial juncture in our existence, whether through the exclusionary dynamics of center-periphery thinking, fear of change, benign neglect, or the comfort of the familiar betrays our most authentic connectional impulses."[69] United Methodist churches should neither relive the past nor perpetuate the present but live into the future, embracing even ambiguity and uncertainty. And it requires prayerful imagination, courage, and mutual respect and trust.

---

66. Robert L. Turnipseed, "Interpretation and Implications of the Green Lake Consultation on Methodist Church Overseas Structure" (1966), 1335-1-4-21, UM Archives (Madison, NJ), 5. Raines also underlined that integrity would require "greater seriousness of effort toward becoming self-sustaining" and responsible for mission ("Ecumenism and Structure of Methodism Overseas," 1335-1-4-4, 10).

67. Harman, *From Missions to Mission*, 453.

68. Elbert Wethington, "Central Conference of the Methodist Church," 1335-1-2-56, 33.

69. Pieterse, "A Worldwide United Methodist Church?" 22.

2

THE AUTONOMOUS PROCESS OF LATIN AMERICAN METHODISM

A Critical Review

Philip Wingeier-Rayo

John Wesley gave the Methodist movement great vision and direction when he wrote in the "Large" Minutes": "What may we reasonably believe to be God's design in raising up the Preachers called Methodists? To reform the nation and, in particular, the Church; to spread scriptural holiness over the land."[1] Since its inception, Methodism had an evangelistic zeal in its effort to share the good news, spread to different regions, and teach holiness to new believers. Methodism spread through the trade routes of the British Empire, often carried by immigrants who aimed to start Methodist societies in their new colonies. Converted by the preaching of John Wesley himself, Nathaniel Gilbert, a speaker of the House of Assembly of Antigua, returned to the Caribbean along with three enslaved women, Sophia Campbell, Mary Allen, and Bessie, to begin Methodist work in 1759.[2] Methodism spread to the American colonies through immigrants such as Barbara Heck, Philip Embury, and

---

1. John Wesley, *Works*, Jackson Edition, vol. 8 (Grand Rapids, MI: Baker, 1978), 299.

2. John C. Neal, "The Methodist Episcopal Church and Early Wesleyan Missions to the Caribbean," *Methodist History* 50:1 (Oct. 2011).

Robert Strawbridge, who started Methodist societies in New York and Baltimore, respectively.

Wesley did not initially envision the church polity necessary for such spread, as he considered Methodism to be a renewal movement within the Church of England, and thus he rejected early calls for schism. Once the United States gained its independence from England, Wesley conceded to allow American Methodists the freedom to organize their own church after the Revolutionary War, when the relations between the two countries were so contentious that a unified ecclesial body was an impossibility. Wesley saw that the die was cast and granted the new church a license for freedom:

> As our American brethren are now totally disentangled both from the State and the English hierarchy, we dare not entangle them again either with the one or the other. They are now at full liberty simply to follow the Scriptures and the Primitive Church. And we judge it best that they should stand fast in that liberty wherewith God has so strangely made them free.[3]

This innovative freedom to experiment in practical theology was an early trait of John Wesley's leadership and has been at the heart of Methodism from the beginning. This innovation within a new context, rather than top-down authoritarian control, allows for ministries to develop freely as context changes. After their autonomy from Wesley, Methodists in the newly formed United States of America, in turn, evangelized and planted new mission churches around the world with the vision for them to eventually become autonomous. This independence, however, was slow in developing, and often after many years of ongoing mission work, there was still a deep financial and organizational dependence upon the so-called "mother church."

This chapter will explore the process of autonomy in the 1960s and 1970s of some mission churches started by American Methodists, specifically in Latin America and the Caribbean. To set the context, this chapter will revisit the ecumenical conversations around missions in the post–World War II era and the resulting decolonization and self-deter-

---

3. This letter was sent with Thomas Coke and distributed to American Methodists in 1784 along with the Sunday Service and an edited version of the Articles of Religion. *Letters of John Wesley.*

mination movements. The chapter will review the influence of the Chinese and Cuban revolutions and anti-communist fears among Protestant mission leaders—especially in the United States. This chapter will recap the work of the Commission on the Structure of Methodism Overseas (COSMOS), which began in 1948, initially in The Methodist Church and ultimately in The United Methodist Church after unification in 1968, and which was disbanded in 1972. Most important, the chapter will scrutinize the decisions made by national church leaders to opt for autonomy and explore whether this was their free choice or was made under the urging of COSMOS.

The Ecumenical Movement in World Missions

Before delving into the work of the Commission on the Structure of Methodism Overseas (COSMOS) and the autonomy of Methodist churches in Latin America, it is important to establish the context of world missions. The 1910 World Missionary Conference in Edinburgh was entitled "The World Missionary Conference to consider missionary problems in relation to the non-Christian world." Out of approximately 1,200 delegates, the overwhelming majority were from the mission-sending churches in Europe and North America, and only seventeen were from the so-called mission churches in the global South. The emphasis of the conference was on the evangelization of non-Christian countries and peoples. This theme undervalued the contributions and participation of younger churches. Shortly after the conference, World War I broke out among northern European countries, precisely the countries that hoped to share Christianity around the world. These countries were also colonial powers with territories in Africa, Asia, and the Pacific Islands. Then, twenty years later, World War II ensued with many of the same countries. In the aftermath of the two world wars, between the years 1945 and 1960, three dozen countries in Africa and Asia gained their independence from their European colonial powers.[4]

---

4. "Decolonization of Asia and Africa, 1945–1960," Office of the Historian, U.S. Department of State, https://history.state.gov/milestones/1945-1952/asia-and-africa.

The second World War left the European colonial powers economically depleted and with little political will or manpower to put down multiple costly independence wars across the world. The colonized countries were seizing the moment and fighting for independence from their European colonizers. Vietnam, for example, waged a war of independence against France (1945–1954).

World missions followed a similar pattern, and the younger churches in the global South began to request autonomy. At the 1947 meeting of the International Missionary Conference (IMC, a successor body to the World Missionary Conference in Edinburgh) in Whitby, Canada, the participants approved a statement emphasizing cooperation between the former mission-sending countries and the younger churches:

> The task of world evangelism starts today from the vantage ground of a Church which, as never before, is really world wide. . . . It is working itself out today in a real partnership between the older and younger churches. The sense both of a common faith in Christ, and of a common responsibility for an immense and unfinished task, have brought us out of the mists of tension and re-adjustment to a higher level, from which we have been able to see our world task in a new perspective.[5]

The theme of the meeting in Whitby was "Partnership in Obedience." The delegates at this meeting also abandoned the use of the terms *Christian* and *non-Christian* countries, eliminating a false dichotomy. Soon the historically Western Christian nations would begin a decline in church membership, and the younger churches would begin to grow, thus eliminating this distinction. The emphasis on partnership highlighted that all Christians can participate in God's mission, and the younger churches would be equal members of the IMC with the churches in the global North. The trend toward partnership would reach its maximum expression in 1961, when the delegates of the IMC voted to merge with the World Council of Churches, thus putting younger and Western churches on equal footing as members of the WCC.

5. Quoted in T. V. Philip, *Edinburgh to Salvador: Twentieth Century Ecumenical Missiology, A Historical Study of the Ecumenical Discussions on Mission* (Delhi: CSS and ISPCK, 1999), 44.

Creation of the Commission on the Structure of Methodism Overseas

In concert with these ecumenical conversations and against the backdrop of the self-determination movements, the General Conference of The Methodist Church authorized the formation of the Commission on the Structure of Methodism Overseas with the purpose "to keep the church alert to change its world parish responsibilities."[6] In the words of Bishop William B. Oden, "COSMOS was authorized by the 1948 General Conference as a liaison between American Methodism and overseas churches that had come into existence through American missionary outreach."[7] COSMOS had the following task: "Recognizing the different conditions that exist in various fields of the world, and the changes taking place in those fields, this commission shall continue to study the structure and supervision of The Methodist Church in its work outside the United States and its territories and its relationships to other bodies and shall prepare such recommendations as it considers necessary for presentation to the General Conference."[8] The fundamental question framing the commission's work was how to be Christ's body given the political, social, and geographic climate where the church is located.[9] In spite of these missional goals, Bishop William Oden clearly named the rise of anticolonialism as one of the reasons that COSMOS' mandate became especially urgent.

The Context of Latin America and the Caribbean

The political movements for decolonization and independence from their colonizers influenced the church and theology. Specifically, within Roman Catholicism, Pope John XXIII convened the Second Vatican Council (1962–1965) to reconcile the church's beliefs with this period

6. *Journal of the 1968 General Conference of The United Methodist Church*, 242.

7. William B. Oden and Robert J. Williams, *The Council of Bishops in Historical Perspective: Celebrating 75 Years* (Nashville: Abingdon, 2014), 92–93.

8. *Journal of the 1968 General Conference of The United Methodist Church*, 242.

9. *Journal of the 1968 General Conference of The United Methodist Church*, 242.

of radical change and the challenges of modernity to church dogma. The Roman Catholic Church, as well as other churches, had benefitted and participated in colonialism, and Vatican II was part of the process of decentralization. In addition to greater acceptance of the sciences, the Catholic Church allowed greater participation by the laity, more openness to ecumenical relations, and the translation of the Bible into the vernacular. While these changes were worldwide, it wasn't until the Catholic bishops in Latin America met in Medellín, Colombia in 1968 that they could together interpret what these changes meant for their continent. The Council of Latin American Bishops (Consejo Episcopal Latinoamericano, or CELAM) had met only one time prior, in Brazil in 1958, but its second meeting, referred to as CELAM II, was monumental. The translation of the Bible into Spanish and Portuguese was significant because Catholics could read the Bible in their own language and interpret its meaning for their context.

At Medellín, the bishops named the obvious reality that they served a majority poor continent. CELAM II saw the poor as victims of injustice and called the church to address structural inequalities. This also had the effect of questioning the assumption that God had providentially created the existing order; on the contrary, the bishops proclaimed that this unjust social order was the result of society's collective sin and systematic injustice. For example, in the CELAM II document on "Poverty of the Church," the assembly affirmed: "In this context a poor church: denounces the unjust lack of this world's goods and the sin that begets it."[10] Moreover, the document on "Justice" declared that "since our continent is fundamentally peasants, Medellín directs special attention to this majority sector of the population."[11] This document also called on the bishops to be in solidarity with the poor, known more commonly as a "preferential option for the poor."[12]

---

10.   Conference of Latin American Bishops, "Poverty of the Church," Medellín, Colombia, September 6, 1968, par. 5.

11.   Conference of Latin American Bishops, "Justice," Medellín, Colombia, September 6, 1968, par. 14.

12.   "Poverty of the Church," par. 10.

This declaration went hand in hand with the emergence of Latin American liberation theology. Prior to Medellín, the Marxist ideology that prevailed during the Cuban Revolution did not conceive that a person could participate in a revolution out of religious convictions. However, the theological method affirmed by CELAM II created a space for people to use the inductive method of Bible study, incarnational theology, and read the "signs of the times" in light of scripture in a way that encouraged Christian participation for social change. This openness toward Christian participation in a Latin American revolution was influenced by Medellín. Liberation theology was not only influential within the Roman Catholic Church but also had many subscribers in Protestant circles and was translated into an anti-American and decolonization sentiment and subsequently into a desire for self-determination.

Self-Determination, Communism, and Anti-American Sentiment

Within Cuba, the self-determination movement proceeded liberation theology. A grassroots revolutionary movement led by Fidel Castro successfully ousted dictator Fulgencio Batista on December 31, 1958, thus opening the door for Castro to descend out of the mountains triumphantly to assume power in the island nation on January 1, 1959. It was not at all clear at that time that the revolution would become socialist and what attitude it would have toward religion. In fact, Cuba had historically been a religious country, and many participants in the revolution had religious beliefs. Fidel Castro himself attended a Catholic parochial school and many of the leading revolutionary figures espoused their beliefs. Yet the revolution occurred within the larger context of the Cold War and viewed the United States as the "Yankee" oppressor. The revolutionary government nationalized U.S. property, and this antagonized the United States. So, when a group of Cuban exiles in Florida attempted to invade the island on April 17, 1961, Fidel Castro declared the revolution to be "socialist" in character, thus strengthening its alliance with the Soviet Union. The United States broke diplomatic ties, and immediately church leaders began to fear the worst. This sudden turn of events sent shock waves throughout the world. Cuba continued to strengthen its economic, political, and military ties to the Soviet Union and adopt a Marxist-Leninist philosophy toward religion. In June of that same year, the government nationalized all church-related schools, universities, and hospitals, stoking fears that churches would be closed.[13]

Since their founding, the Protestant churches in Cuba had developed a loyalty and pro-American bias, which was a natural affinity. However, this alliance became problematic after the revolution and the rise of nationalism.[14] Many Cuban leaders were influenced ideologically by the North American context and anti-socialist sentiments.[15] The United States, on the other hand, was in a very different place ideologically. The United States and the Soviet Union were locked in an intense geopolitical battle, and the Cuban Revolution was interpreted in this context. McCarthyism had created a "blacklist" for anyone remotely tied to the Communist Party or communist ideology—real or not.

The impact and fear of the Cuban Revolution on American Methodist mission work in Latin America and the Caribbean cannot be overstated. The nationalization of church property, such as schools, universities, and clinics, created the fear that this could happen in other countries in the region. China had also experienced a Communist revolution where church property was confiscated, Western missionaries imprisoned, and Christians repressed.[16] Christianity was perceived as a Western religion, and Chinese Christians were persecuted for having any association with Westerners. The Cultural Revolution in China began in 1966, and all Western influence was severely restricted.

The events in China and Cuba were extreme examples of a larger decolonization and self-determination movement that was happening

13. Raoul Gomez Treto, *La Iglesia Católica durante la Construcción del Socialismo en Cuba* (San José: CEHILA, 1994), 44.

14. Carlos Camps Cruell, "La Herencia Misionera en Cuba: Implicacioónes en los Social," in *La Herencia Misionera en Cuba*, ed. Rafael Cepeda (San José: DEI, 1996), 123–30. My translation.

15. Israel Batista, "El Protestantismo Cubano en un Proyecto Histoórico," in *La Herencia Misionera en Cuba*, ed. Rafael Cepeda (San José: DEI, 1996), 65.

16. Olin Stockwell, *Meditations from a Prison Cell* (Nashville: Upper Room, 1954).

worldwide. The Soviet Union also emerged from World War II as a global power, and newly independent nations found the Marxist ideology appealing to their nationalistic movements. The United States had difficulty separating the self-determination movements from the Soviet influence, and this led to U.S. intervention in proxy wars such as Vietnam. Cuba was a similar battleground, and the United States narrowly escaped a direct confrontation with the Soviet Union during the Cuban missile crisis in October 1962.

In the midst of the strained diplomatic relationship with the United States, the Methodist mission church in Cuba tried to continue its missionary work. Prior to the revolution, the Methodist Church had 9,209 members in 150 preaching outposts; however, it was highly dependent upon support from the U.S. mission board. In fact, U.S. missionaries outnumbered Cuban pastors 54 to 51. The Cuban church also had 22 schools, six clinics, and several rural missions that were subsidized with support from the United States. When the U.S. government broke off diplomatic ties with Cuba in January of 1961, the Mission Board called back the missionaries out of a concern for their safety. Cubans actually encouraged the missionaries to return to the United States, not only out of concern for their safety, but also for the well-being of the Methodist work.[17] In a report prepared for the 1966 COSMOS consultation in Green Lake, WI, Robert Lonnie Turnipseed alluded to this concern of mission churches being perceived as a U.S. outpost when he wrote that "it is easy to see how persons opposed to the Christian faith can use them to brand the church as a foreign rather than an indigenous church."[18] The tensions between the enemy nations made church work more difficult, as Protestant churches, not to say all churches, were seen as pro-American, and anyone associated with them was suspected of being counter-revolutionary.

Former bishop of The Methodist Church of Cuba, Rev. Armando Rodriguez, recalled that the diplomatic tensions between the United States and Cuba triggered a period of crisis for the church. In 1963, the bishop of the Florida Episcopal Area, Bishop Roy Short, could not attend the an-

---

17. Telephone conversation with Larry Rankin, April 17, 1998.

18. Robert Lonnie Turnipseed, "New Structures for Methodism Overseas," paper prepared for the COSMOS, Green Lake, WI, February 10, 1966, p. 1.

nual conference in Cuba. So, Cuban leader Rev. Angel Fuster spearheaded a movement to request autonomy, and this request was sent to the 1964 General Conference in Pittsburgh. Prior to its approval, the Methodist Church in Cuba had to present its proposed *Book of Discipline* and Articles of Faith to be approved by the General Conference. Once accepted, the Methodist Church in Cuba was able to hold elections for bishop. The leading candidate was Rev. Angel Fuster; however, he died suddenly in an automobile accident in 1967 during a lay-over after attending a World Council of Churches meeting in Geneva. Nevertheless, the Cuban church elected him as their first bishop posthumously and then elected Rev. Armando Rodriguez, who was consecrated as bishop on February 11, 1968, by Mexican bishop Alejandro Ruiz.[19]

The Impact of the Self-Determination Movement on Methodist Polity

The anti-American sentiment and fear of the spread of communism in the region gave the 1964 General Conference greater motivation to expedite autonomy for the Methodist mission churches outside the United States. The loss of property and potential erasure of years of missionary work in China and Cuba were a blinking red light for what could be the tip of an iceberg. Recognizing the urgency of the situation, in addition to approving autonomy for the Cuban Methodist Church, General Conference expanded the mandate of COSMOS: "study the structure and supervision of The Methodist Church in its work outside the United States and its territories and its relationships to other Church bodies."[20] Taking up this mantle, the commission held study committees in every central and annual conference outside the United States, as well as consultations with British Methodists and the World Methodist Council. The General Conference left COSMOS with two principles to guide their work: 1) the

19. Telephone interview with Armando Rodriguez, February 1, 2018.

20. "Commission on the Structure of Methodism Overseas, Report No. 1," *1968 Advance Daily Christian Advocate*, 1778.

principle of freedom, and 2) the principle of fellowship or connectionalism.

Therefore, the 1964 General Conference authorized a study committee within COSMOS with a budget to organize a consultation with leaders from the central conference churches around the world. Prior to this gathering, the General Secretary for the Methodist Mission Board, Tracy Jones, reflected on the motivation for the gathering and the context: "During the past five years in Asia, Africa, Latin America, Europe, and in the United States, there has been a growing conviction that the time has come to more carefully examine these three patterns."[21] Jones continued, "But I think on reflection we will all agree that we cannot remain where we are. The pressure of the gospel and the changes in the world are leading into new relationships."[22]

Bishop William Oden acknowledged the three realities that forced the hand of The Methodist Church to consider autonomy for their mission churches: "1) a rapidly growing church in mission outposts, 2) the rise of anticolonialism, and 3) increasing nationalism with a number of churches seeking autonomy at the General Conference of 1964."[23] Bishop Roy Short wrote that "in effect, what eventually happened was the beginning of a process of dismantling what had been a world church."[24]

Tracy Jones laid out five main options for the future structure of world Methodism: continue as we are, centralized world church, limited world church, autonomous Methodist churches, and united churches. Jones appeared to be non-partisan and neutral, as one would expect a mission executive to be. In fact, the paper included some examples from around the world where these models have been used and their advantages or disadvantages. However, in his concluding remarks, Jones made the case for autonomous churches. Jones wrote:

21. Tracy Jones, "What Patterns for Methodist Churches Around the World?" *World Outlook* New Series 24:8 (March 1964), 7.

22. Jones, "What Patterns," 8.

23. Oden and Williams, *The Council of Bishops in Historical Perspective*, 93.

24. Roy H. Short, *History of the Council of Bishops of The United Methodist Church, 1973–1979* (Nashville: Abingdon, 1980), 165.

> From the days of John Wesley, we have assumed that the mission of the Church determines the structure of the Church. . . . In practical terms, this meant that the organizational structures of the church had to be related in some way to the situation in which people lived. . . . If it is true that the mission determines the structure, then in a day of change there should be no hesitation among Methodists in finding new structures, if the mission demands it.[25]

Jones then went on to give the example of autonomy of American Methodism following the War of Independence. Jones stated that "following the War of Independence the Methodists made a major decision about their future. They severed their ties with John Wesley and the Church of England. This made possible the emergence of an autonomous church. The creative organizational genius of Francis Asbury came to the fore."[26] Jones referred to the autonomy and successful mission outreach of American Methodism as a case for autonomy of the younger churches around the world.

Further complexifying the relationship between the mission churches around the world, The Methodist Church in the United States had begun conversations of unity with The Evangelical United Brethren (EUB) Church. In anticipation of the 1968 merger with The Methodist Church, the EUB Mission Board granted autonomy to all of its mission churches around the world—largely in the spirit of Christian unity.[27] In addition, the Methodist churches in Brazil, Mexico, and Korea had already become autonomous in 1930 due to other unique factors, such as the aftermath of World War I, the Mexican Revolution (1911–1919), the 1929 stock market crash, and the desire to merge the Methodist Episcopal Church with the Methodist Episcopal Church, South. The autonomy of the Methodist churches in Korea and Mexico and the EUB mission churches outside the United States created a precedent and a roadmap for COSMOS to follow.

COSMOS met on May 3, 1965, and planned for a major consultation with representatives from the mission churches in 1966. In a pa-

---

25. Jones, "What Patterns," 50.

26. Jones, "What Patterns," 50.

27. David W. Scott, "Autonomy, international division mark United Methodist tradition," *UM & Global*, June 1, 2022, http://www.umglobal.org/2022/06/autonomy-international-division-mark.html.

per prepared for the planning meeting, Mission Board executive Lonnie Turnipseed described the inadequacies of the current structure and the rationale for change. He described the centralization of the power in the U.S.-dominated General Conference. Basically, there were only a handful of international delegates to General Conference who would attend only to deliberate and vote on primarily U.S. domestic matters, and the number of delegates was too few to influence decisions of the larger church. Turnipseed wrote that the "[t]otal overseas representation [is] so small that [it] cannot influence legislation."[28] Moreover, the General Conference was always held in the United States, and the central conference delegates had to travel and assemble in an unfamiliar context and engage in the proceedings in English, which they may or may not have understood.

The central conference churches were also subject to the Methodist *Book of Discipline* that addressed the reality of the U.S. church. Even when it was translated into the language of the church abroad, the content was still intended for the U.S. reality. Furthermore, the composition of COSMOS had only one representative per central conference, for a total of 9 members in 1960, while the United States had 23 members. Even the word *Overseas* in the name of the commission emphasizes the otherness or secondary nature of the mission churches. Another impediment to the full inclusion of the central conference churches was that the Judicial Council was composed of all U.S. members. So basically, the whole structure and power base of The Methodist Church was centered in the United States.

1966 COSMOS Consultation in Green Lake, Wisconsin

The COSMOS consultation was held on October 29–November 5, 1966, in Green Lake, Wisconsin, where 250 participants came from all over the world and the United States, bringing their distinctive perspectives and interests with them. The commission did not have the authority to make structural changes in the denomination—merely to make recom-

---

28. Robert Lonnie Turnipseed, "Reasons Why Change in Methodist Overseas Structure Is Necessary," unpublished paper, May 3, 1965, 1.

mendations to the General Conference. Given the distinct contexts of each of the delegates, this could not be a "one size fits all" recommendation. This consultation considered four major options for the churches in the central conferences outside the United States:

1. Keep the present basic Methodist structure.
2. Encourage Methodist units outside the United States to become autonomous churches.
3. Create a truly international Methodist church that would have several regional conferences (the United States being one of several) and one General Conference with balanced representation between the United States and central conferences abroad.
4. Organize a world fellowship of autonomous Methodist Churches.

One representative from Singapore, Yap Kim Hao, speaking from his perspective from South East Asia, advocated for autonomy:

> Autonomy is not so much a question of self-government or independence as that of the principle of freedom. We are primarily interested and vitally concerned with the Church making her own witness in the social and political environment which is clearly delimited in our world today. We are attentive to the freedom of our people to make an unfettered response to God and His word which is spoken to us in our living situation.[29]

Yap Kim Hao, who would go on to become Malaysia and Singapore's first Asian bishop, argued that Methodist churches outside the United States could not afford to be seen as a Western institution imposed upon local people, and he advocated that they become affiliated autonomous Methodist churches with equal partnerships while still maintaining fraternal relationships with The Methodist Church in the United States.[30]

At the conclusion of the consultation, the delegates recommended that COSMOS take to the 1968 General Conference a proposal to grant autonomy to the Methodist churches in Malaysia, Argentina, Bolivia, Costa Rica, Chile, Panama, Peru, and Uruguay.[31] Cuba had already been recommended for autonomy at the 1964 General Conference due to the reasons previously stated.

---

29. Yap Kim Hao, *A Bishop Remembers* (Singapore: Gospel Works, 2006), 66.

30. Yap Kim Hao, *A Bishop Remembers*, 67.

31. "Commission on the Structure of Methodism Overseas, Report No. 1," 1782.

Based on its findings from the consultation, COSMOS reported to the 1968 General Conference that structural change of world Methodism was "desirable and necessary" and gave the following reasons:

1. There has been growth both in membership and in the strength of leadership in Methodist groups outside the United States. These groups want greater freedom to make decisions.
2. The spread of nationalism, finding expression in new nations, and a greater desire for independence and self-determination has created a new climate in which the church must carry out its mission.
3. Methodist churches outside the United States are now both receiving and sending missionaries. Present structures, created and controlled by a General Conference, 90 percent of whose delegates are from the United States and 90 percent of whose time is devoted to concerns of the American church, cannot give proper consideration to the different conditions of 45 countries involved.
4. The emergence of the World Council of Churches and regional conferences such as the East Asian Christian Conference raise questions as to how Methodist groups should be related in these areas and be fully participating members of these bodies and at the same time under the jurisdiction of the General Conference. Similar problems exist in Africa, Latin America, and India.
5. A deepening conviction that to drift or make minor shifts in present structures is to decide against a world church by default. [32]

Was Autonomy Encouraged or Sought by the Latin American Churches?

This leads to a debated question among Methodist missiologists and church historians on whether autonomy was a choice or encouraged by COSMOS. This question is especially complex while dealing with all the former mission outposts associated with American Methodism. There is not one clean and easy answer to this debate because there are multiple actors, and each country in the region has a slightly different context. As mentioned above, some global representatives attending the meeting in Green Lake held clear positions in favor of autonomy; however, this was not the uniform experience. Since this chapter deals only with Latin

---

32. "Commission on the Structure of Methodism Overseas, Report No. 1," 1784.

America and the Caribbean, I will briefly entertain here two possible interpretations.

One theory is that the Methodist mission churches in Latin America and the Caribbean freely sought autonomy out of a sense of mission and desired the freedom to be self-governing, self-sufficient, and self-propagating. This interpretation subscribes to the belief that the leadership of the various Methodist churches in Latin America and the Caribbean felt ready to assume the economic responsibility and leadership to contextualize the beliefs, structure, and mission of the church to their immediate reality. This position believes that the Latin American leaders felt ready to assume these responsibilities and were advocating for autonomy.

The other theory is that the sentiments in the Methodist mission board, COSMOS, and the broader ecumenical push toward autonomy coerced the mission churches in Latin America and the Caribbean to accept autonomy. Former Mission Board executive Robert Harman reacted to the suggestion that former mission churches were "encouraged" to become autonomous. Harman stated:

> At a consultation held in Green Lake Wisconsin in 1966, leaders from all churches in the world wide Methodist connection plus representatives of the EUB Mission board offered their thoughts about the future of the denominational structure and mission. The revolutionary changes occurring in the post colonial period impacting governments and social institutions in affected countries were strongly impacting the churches. Most presentations offered by church representatives themselves vigorously concluded that historical linkages suggesting any continuation of colonial patterns of dependency had to be jettisoned. The Commission on the Status on Methodism Overseas (COSMOS), the consultation host, only then agreed to engage in a follow up process that permitted regional conversations resulting in proposals for autonomy to be submitted to the 1968 General Conference.[33]

Harman comes from the EUB tradition that did not have the same predicament as The Methodist Church because all the former mission churches became autonomous prior to or at the merger that created The

---

33.   Robert Harman, "Historical Context for Affiliated Autonomous Methodist Churches and Their Standing in a Global United Methodist Church," *UM & Global*, June 9, 2016, www.umglobal.org/2016/06/robert-harman-historical-context-for.html.

United Methodist Church. However, within Methodist polity, the situation is more complicated.

One of the suggested structural changes that the 1964 General Conference had received was "to urge Methodist groups outside the United States to become autonomous and form united churches."[34] One of the main reasons for mission churches to separate from the mother church in the United States, as stated by Lonnie Turnipseed in his address to the consultation at Green Lake, was to avoid the anti-American sentiment in their various contexts.[35] This anticipated fear of leftwing movements and the reputation of Methodist work as pro-American led the commission to encourage the Methodist churches in Latin America to become autonomous. At the very minimum, the status quo was not an option. Therefore, a second interpretation of the movement toward autonomous churches is that it was encouraged by COSMOS.

The situation of the Methodist Church in Cuba was probably the most clear-cut, because the revolution and rupture of diplomatic ties with the United States made the practical matters of sending money, communication, and travel nearly impossible. The Cuban Methodist Church also launched a financial independence campaign in the early 1960s, sending pledge cards to 1,500–1,600 members, soliciting financial pledges for the economic solvency of the church.[36] Moreover, as previously stated, the close association between the Cuban church and the United States became an obstacle for the success of the Methodist work in Cuba.

The threat of more left-wing revolutions and the nationalistic spirit of Latin Americans led Methodists elsewhere in Latin America to ultimately choose autonomy—however, with mixed feelings. The Methodist Church in Peru published a doctrinal statement in 1965 called *Manifiesto a la Nación*, which led to an organizing conference in Lima on January 19, 1970, that launched The Methodist Church in Peru as an affiliated autonomous entity. Former Peruvian bishop and church historian Rev. Jorge Bravo believes that the Cuban revolution created a fear throughout Latin

---

34. "Commission on the Structure of Methodism Overseas, Report No. 1," 1785.

35. Turnipseed, "New Structures for Methodism Overseas," 1.

36. Interview with Armando Rodriguez, February 1, 2018.

America that other countries would become left wing and communist, and so COSMOS tried to "persuade" Methodist Churches to become autonomous to avoid similar conflicts or tensions—especially around properties. Many churches were not prepared to assume the administrative responsibilities, but still it happened.[37] Bravo laments, "some members were not in agreement with the autonomy of the church and long for the 'missionary era.' This situation produced the withdrawal of the majority of missionaries and a membership loss of 50% of pastors and lay members."[38] Bravo went on to claim that autonomy was not a true expression of the will of the national leaders, but rather an imposition of the will of the "Mother Church."[39]

Remembering the context and the urgency of the Methodist educational institutions in Latin America to become autonomous in the late 1960s and early 1970s, Hugo Ortega wrote, "On the one hand [the Methodist Church in the United States] tried to have less responsibility in the financing of the Latin American mission, and on the other, it wanted to respond positively to the desire for autonomy of Methodism in the region."[40] Ortega continued by suggesting that the work of COSMOS "worked to strengthen the process of autonomy (1969 to 1973)"[41] and described the context and rationale for autonomy as the backdrop of radical national movements in China and other countries that have nationalized Western schools and clinics, expelled and imprisoned missionaries as a main reason behind autonomy of national churches and institutions.

In the years 2018, 2019, and 2020, a group of mission executives and leaders from the autonomous Methodist churches in Latin America and the Caribbean held a series of dialogues to reflect upon the mission of the church. The group reflected on the origins of Methodism in the region and the process leading to autonomy. In the summary report, orga-

---

37.   Bravo, "Inicios del Metodismo en Perú," https://www.angelfire.com/pe/jorgebravo/iniciosmetodismo.html, accessed January 18, 2023.

38.   Bravo, "Inicios del Metodismo en Perú," my translation.

39.   Bravo, "Inicios del Metodismo en Perú."

40.   Hugo Ortega, "La Trayectoria de la organización Latinoamericana de las instituciones educativas," *Revista de investigación académica* 2 (November 1998), 65.

41.   Ortega, "La Trayectoria," 66.

nizer Humberto Martin Shikiya wrote, "The autonomy of the Methodist churches in Latin America and the Caribbean has implied that all of their members would assume, in an organized and systemic way, responsibility in the decision making process about life and mission."[42]

Argentine Methodist historian Daniel Bruno offers a more balanced perspective on autonomy. On the occasion of the fiftieth anniversary of the autonomy of *La Iglesia Evangélica Metodista Argentina* from The United Methodist Church in 1969, Bruno wrote that "the mission [churches] in Latin America needed to separate from the mother church."[43] He recalled that COSMOS sent the recommendation to General Conference to allow it to receive petitions from the churches in Chile, Peru, Argentina, and Uruguay to request its autonomy.[44] Bruno also recalls that as part of the process of autonomy, the Latin American churches would organize a new regional body to facilitate connectionalism. And so, the Council of Evangelical Methodist Churches in Latin America (and the Caribbean), known as CIEMAL for its initials in Spanish, was born in February of 1969.[45]

Elaine Robinson also reflected on autonomy for the Methodist Church in Argentina and likened it to "exile" from American Methodism. She states that, although the church continues to receive support from the General Board of Global Ministries, this financial support is much less than those churches who remain in The United Methodist Church as part of the Central Conference.[46] Robinson writes, "Despite its wish to remain in 'fellowship' with The United Methodist Church and its emphasis that it did not seek separation or isolation, the UMC, in many ways, has moved away from Argentina."[47] Robinson goes on to assert that "the

---

42. Humberto Martin Shikiya, "Mission Roundtables: A Paradigm of Sharing" (CREAS, 2020), 266.

43. Daniel Bruno, "50 años de autonomía de la Iglesia Evangélica Metodista en Argentina: Enfoque Histórico," *El Estandarte Evangélico* (October 13, 2019).

44. Bruno, "50 años de autonomía."

45. Bruno, "50 años de autonomía."

46. Elaine Robinson, "El Exilio del Metodismo Argentino," *Cuadernos de Teología* 26 (2007). Reprinted in *Revista de Historia Evangélica*, VII (2012). See also English version, "Recovering Los Desaparecidos," in *A Living Tradition: Critical Recovery and Reconstruction of Wesleyan Heritage*, ed. Mary Elizabeth Moore (Nashville: Kingswood Books, 2013).

47. Robinson, "Recovering Los Desaparecidos," 189.

UMC continues to marginalize and render invisible the affiliated autonomous churches in Latin America."[48]

Conclusion

Methodism was created as a renewal movement within the Church of England with the initial goal "to spread scriptural holiness throughout the land." While Wesley did not originally intend for Methodism to become its own denomination or split from the Church of England, this missionary zeal embedded itself in the British Empire and allowed Methodism to expand throughout the world. After the War of Independence, Wesley gave his blessing to the formation of the Methodist Episcopal Church, and this same missionary zeal was transplanted as American missionaries continued to plant Methodist churches around the world. The initial desire was that these mission churches would adapt and contextualize in the various countries and regions around the world, eventually becoming autonomous yet connected.

Autonomy for mission churches became an urgent matter following World War II and the decolonizing and independence movements of colonized nations. In particular, the revolutions in China (1949) and Cuba (1959) that fomented nationalistic and anti-American sentiments instilled a fear among American Methodists that the communist revolutions would have a domino effect and nationalize Methodist institutions. The self-determination and decolonization movements were gaining momentum. In countries with strong leftwing movements, The Methodist Church was branded as being a colonial outpost too closely associated with the United States, thus impeding its ministry effectiveness as a national church. China and Cuba were extreme examples of this phenomenon with the revolutionary governments imprisoning missionaries and confiscating valuable church property. The 1964 General Conference gave the Commission on the Structure of Methodism Overseas (COSMOS) a more urgent mandate to consider alternative relationships for the "younger" mission churches— especially the consideration of autonomy. The Methodist Mission Board

---

48. Robinson, "Recovering Los Desaparecidos," 190.

and COSMOS wanted to avoid this scenario in other countries. COSMOS reacted to these world conditions and engaged Latin American churches in the process toward autonomy. The status quo was not an option. The two main options presented to the national churches were to pursue autonomy on their own or as a union church in their country. One must realize that the dynamics in which national church leaders made this decision were fraught with a tremendous imbalance of power and money. The national churches in the region were heavily subsidized by the Methodist mission board and did not have the financial means to be self-sufficient.

Nevertheless, the recommendation from COSMOS to the 1968 General Conference was that several national churches in Latin America be granted permission to pursue autonomy, namely Chile, Argentina, Uruguay, and Peru. While those churches chose and were granted autonomy, they did so with the understanding that they would still enjoy a connection and the ongoing financial support of the newly formed United Methodist Church. Unfortunately, however, this affiliated autonomous status has resulted in much less financial support, status, and connectionalism with The United Methodist Church.

3

AMERICAN POWER IN THE GLOBAL CHURCH IN ECUMENICAL METHODIST PERSPECTIVE

David W. Scott

This chapter looks ecumenically to compare various ways of organizing a Methodist denomination that is at the same time based in the
United States and to some extent "global," "worldwide," or "international."[1]
By comparing the histories and practices of The Wesleyan Church, the
Church of the Nazarene, and the African Methodist Episcopal (AME)
Church with The United Methodist Church (UMC), it shows how a combination of historical circumstances common across denominations and
internal historical trajectories and organizational decisions within each denomination have influenced the ways in which U.S. dominance has been
expressed and mitigated in U.S.-based Methodist denominations. Each
denomination has sought to address the desire of members from outside
the United States for a say in denominational matters—in varying ways,
to varying degrees, and with varying success—while patterns of American
imperial domination persist, most notably within The United Method-

---

1. I do not distinguish between the three terms in this piece.

ist Church, which has made fewer structural changes to accommodate its non-U.S. members than its sister denominations. A comparative approach to these issues allows for new perspectives on the relationship between Methodism and American empire and suggests possible paths still open for the UMC to use to move toward more international equity.

The Historical Roots of Global Methodist Polities

There have been three eras in which questions of how to be a global denomination have been particularly pressing for American Methodist bodies. Each era involved questions about polity and practice that structured relationships between U.S. Americans and their co-religionists from other countries. While U.S. American dominance has recurred throughout these eras, these eras have also functioned as windows of opportunities for denominations to make changes to structurally reflect the international nature of their membership more fully, as the case studies in this chapter show.

The first era was the era of early missionary expansion. This era in the late nineteenth and early twentieth centuries saw the widespread extension of Christian missions from the West to the rest of world amid a wave of secular globalization. The British Empire and other European imperial systems were important players in both processes. American commercial expansion into international markets was its own additional force for globalization, and American companies helped pioneer modern forms of multinational corporations. Americans and Europeans joined together in forging a variety of international organizations. The extension of American Methodist missions around the world occurred within this context of empire and globalization and was deeply connected to it.[2]

For all four denominations, international mission first introduced questions of international polity. Especially for the Church of the Nazarene, mission was integral to the beginning of the denomination, and

---

2. See, for instance, David W. Scott, *Mission as Globalization: Methodists in Southeast Asia at the Turn of the Twentieth Century* (Lanham, MD: Lexington, 2016).

questions of global polity were already being worked out in the late nineteenth and early twentieth centuries. The Methodist Episcopal Church (MEC), forerunner of the UMC, also experimented with its global polity at the same time, creating central conferences and missionary bishops, but the MEC stepped back from fully thinking through the implications of these new structures to focus on the upcoming merger with the Methodist Episcopal Church, South (MECS), and Methodist Protestant Church.

The second era was the era of decolonialization, starting in the early 1960s and running through the early 1970s. The movement for political decolonization in Africa, Asia, and Latin America reconfigured secular international relations, and it also raised significant questions for the practices of mission that had been established in the colonial era. Cries of "Missionary, go home!" and a push for church autonomy accompanied the push for political autonomy. For denominations that sought to remain international bodies, this context raised serious questions about the nature of those international connections.

For the Wesleyans and Nazarenes, this period was an important time for beginning to shift structures to reflect a more international membership. The AME Church began to wrestle with the question of indigenous episcopal leadership. The Methodist Church had conversations about its international nature, especially through the Committee on the Status of Methodism Overseas (COSMOS),[3] but real changes were sidelined because the major focus of the time was on working out a merger with the Evangelical United Brethren (EUB) Church.

The third era is an era of contemporary globalization and world Christianity starting in the 1980s. Contemporary globalization and the rise of world Christianity have been separate but coinciding forces. Government policies, new technologies, and economic conditions in the latter decades of the twentieth century led to a vast expansion of international trade, communication, and travel. By the 1990s, this new expression of globalization came in for significant critique along several lines, including on issues of international equity.[4] At the same time, the number of Christians

---

3. See chapters in this volume by Joon-Sik Park and Philip Wingeier-Rayo.

4. For a review of such critiques, see David Held and Anthony G. McGrew, *Globalization/Anti-Globalization: Beyond the Great Divide* (Cambridge: Polity, 2002).

in the global South began to grow significantly, receiving increasing scholarly and popular attention through the end of the century and into the twenty-first century.[5] Both of these trends made questions of international relations within the church newly relevant.

During this era, the Church of the Nazarene and AME Church made significant changes in their polity in response to shifting trends in membership, with overseas membership increasing significantly and American membership growing more slowly. Policy choices that The Wesleyan Church made in an earlier era bore fruit in this era. The United Methodist Church, however, became preoccupied with American debates over sexuality during this period and did little to shift its global polity.

With this broad historical framework in mind, I turn now to the specific histories of each of the four denominations under study.

The Wesleyan Church

The Wesleyan Church is the result of a 1968 merger of two bodies: the Wesleyan Methodist Church, formed by founders who left the Methodist Episcopal Church in 1843, and the Pilgrim Holiness Church, which traces its roots back to founders who left the Methodist Episcopal Church in 1897.[6] Along the way, both groups absorbed a wide variety of other church bodies and missions (such as the 1946 merger of the Pilgrim Holiness Church and the Holiness Church), but The Wesleyan Church's polity remains distinctively Methodist. The Wesleyan Church is currently present in about 100 countries, the result of mission work in a wide variety of areas around the world starting in the nineteenth century. Across all these countries, it has more than 5,000 churches with over 560,000 members.[7]

5. See most notably Dana L. Robert, "Shifting Southward: Global Christianity since 1945," *International Bulletin of Missionary Research* 24:2 (April 2000), 50–58; Philip Jenkins, *The Next Christendom: The Coming of Global Christianity* (Oxford: Oxford University Press, 2007).

6. For a history of The Wesleyan Church, see Robert E. Black and Keith W. Drury, *The Story of The Wesleyan Church* (Indianapolis, IN: Wesleyan Publishing House, 2012). For additional information on the history of The Wesleyan Church outside the United States, see Robert E. Black and Wayne E. Caldwell, eds., *Reformers and Revivalists: History of The Wesleyan Church* (Indianapolis, IN: Wesleyan Publishing House, 1992).

7. "Global Update 2019," Global Partners, https://www.globalpartnersonline.org/about-us/global-update/global-update-2019/, accessed January 27, 2022.

The most basic group of churches in The Wesleyan Church is a district, roughly equivalent to an annual conference in other Methodist bodies. Wesleyan Church districts tend to be smaller than United Methodist annual conferences and are headed by district superintendents instead of bishops, but otherwise serve the same functions. There is one overall General Superintendent, but no bishops. Historically, the Wesleyan Methodist Church was governed by a General Conference, as in other Methodist traditions. Missions outside the United States and Canada were also organized into districts which related both to General Conference and the denominational mission agency.

The Wesleyan Methodist Church/Pilgrim Holiness Church merger in 1968 raised the question of what the role of churches outside the United States should be within the new denomination, as did the Methodist Church/EUB merger in 1968. Despite COSMOS entertaining a wider range of options, the United Methodist answer to this question eventually became that annual conferences outside the United States could either become completely autonomous or remain part of the UMC as a member of a central conference.[8] The Wesleyan Church took a different approach, however, one similar to possibilities raised in the COSMOS discussion by Latin American Methodists. The Wesleyan Church developed a system of different degrees of autonomy for groups of churches outside the United States with continued relationship between all Wesleyan churches everywhere. This plan was approved at their 1972 General Conference.[9] Under this plan, The Wesleyan Church kept the North American General Conference and districts within the United States the same. Outside the United States, it created several new options for groups of districts: national or regional conferences, Established Regional and National Conferences, and separate General Conferences.[10]

National and regional conferences continue to be governed by their originating General Conference and relate to the associated mission agency but can build national capacity for autonomous funding and governance.

8. See chapters in this volume by Joon-Sik Park and Philip Wingeier-Rayo.

9. *The Discipline of The Wesleyan Church 2016* (Indianapolis, IN: Wesleyan Publishing House, 2016), Part I: Basic Principles, Chapter 1: History, G. The Development of the World Organization.

10. *Discipline of The Wesleyan Church 2016*, Part 5: World Organization.

As that capacity grows, the North American General Conference can approve the creation of Established Regional and National Conferences and eventually separate General Conferences. With each step, a group of districts gains more autonomy. Established National or Regional Conferences write their own Books of Discipline, subject to General Conference approval, and still relate to their founding General Conference.[11] There are currently three: South Pacific, Canada, and Ibero-America (i.e., Latin America).[12] Separate General Conferences are fully autonomous, write their own Books of Discipline, and are headed by their own General Superintendent.[13] In addition to the North American General Conference, there are also General Conferences in the Philippines and the Caribbean.[14]

At the same time, the system adopted by The Wesleyan Church includes measures to preserve connection between these increasingly autonomous national and regional branches. The first of these measures is a delegated meeting of all Wesleyan Church bodies throughout the world, initially called the Wesleyan World Fellowship, but since 2004 called the International Conference. The International Conference includes representatives from all General Conferences, Established National and Regional Conferences, and mission units in additional nations, even though this last group is also represented at their associated General Conference. The International Conference's primary purposes are fellowship and coordination, since it does not directly control any bureaucracy or substantial budget, nor does it approve Books of Discipline. It must, however, approve the creation of new Established National and Regional Conferences and General Conferences.[15]

The second unifying measure is a common set of statements binding on all branches of The Wesleyan Church everywhere, called "The Essen-

11. *Discipline of The Wesleyan Church 2016*, Part 5: World Organization, Chapter 2: General Conferences and Established National/Regional Conferences.

12. "Global Update 2019."

13. *Discipline of The Wesleyan Church 2016*, Part 5: World Organization, Chapter 2: General Conferences and Established National/Regional Conferences.

14. "Global Update 2019."

15. *Discipline of The Wesleyan Church 2016*, Appendix A: Charter of the International Conference of The Wesleyan Church.

tials." This short, twelve-page writing consists mainly of 21 statements of faith. It can only be modified by a two-thirds vote of constituent General Conferences. The International Conference can sanction regional bodies that it deems are not living out The Essentials, but that is mostly a theoretical power.[16]

Thus, The Wesleyan Church and other Methodist bodies have taken different approaches to understanding what constitutes the most important elements that should be shared by denominational compatriots around the world. For The Wesleyan Church, the answer is that what's absolutely essential for everyone in the denomination to share is some basic theological affirmations and an understanding of how they will relate to each other. For The Wesleyan Church, this comes down to about two dozen pages of material contained in the "Charter of the International Conference of The Wesleyan Church." By contrast, other Methodist bodies, including the Church of the Nazarene, AME Church, and the UMC, share a much more substantial body of polity. Even a future UMC General Book of Discipline, on which work is ongoing, will still likely come to over 200 pages.

There are advantages and disadvantages to both The Wesleyan Church's system of honoring the autonomy of Christians outside the United States while preserving ties among Christians of different nations. Overall, The Wesleyan Church has emphasized autonomy (as has the Free Methodist Church), whereas other traditions including the Nazarenes, AME Church, and UMC (along with other groups such as the AME Zion and CME) have emphasized connection. Still, while The Wesleyan Church's system is set up to honor autonomy, it nonetheless privileges in some ways North Americans as the "parent" body of new Wesleyan churches in other countries, especially those that have not reached the level of establishing their own General Conference; by contrast, UMC Central Conferences' ability to adapt the *Book of Discipline* and the Nazarenes' emphases on self-support allow for a degree of autonomy in all regions.

---

16. *Discipline of The Wesleyan Church 2016*, Appendix A: Charter of the International Conference of The Wesleyan Church.

The Church of the Nazarene

The historical roots of the Church of the Nazarene are many and complex, but they include early leaders such as former Methodist Phineas Bresee, along with others who were part of the diverse holiness movement in late nineteenth-century America as well as abroad.[17] The Church of the Nazarene sees itself as a Wesleyan body in the Methodist tradition.[18] It strongly emphasizes the Wesleyan doctrine of sanctification, and although there are congregational influences on its polity as well (pastors are called by local churches, not appointed), on the whole, its polity is distinctively Wesleyan/Methodist.

Today, the Church of the Nazarene is the largest Wesleyan holiness denomination in the world. The church has over 2.6 million members across 164 "world areas" (countries or substantially distinct portions of countries, such as Guam).[19] That makes the Church of the Nazarene an extremely well-distributed church globally, much more so than the UMC. Among its membership, 30 percent reside in Africa, 23 percent in the United States & Canada, 17 percent in Mesoamerica, 13 percent in Eurasia (Europe, the Middle East, and South Asia), 12 percent in South America, and 5 percent in Asia-Pacific.[20]

The approach to being a global church that the Church of the Nazarene has taken does not emphasize contextual adaptation of polity so much as thorough implementation of Anderson/Venn "three-self" theory: that the goal for new mission churches should be to become self-led by indigenous pastors, financially self-supporting, and self-propagating through the ability to start new churches themselves. The roots of this approach in the Church of the Nazarene go all the way back to founder Hiram Reynolds, who as a mission executive and then General Superintendent sought to make this approach to mission standard policy for Nazarenes.[21]

---

17. For a complete history of the Church of the Nazarene, see Stan Ingersol, *Past and Prospect: The Promise of Nazarene History* (Eugene, OR: Wipf & Stock, 2014).

18. For instance, it is a member of the World Methodist Council.

19. "Homepage," Church of the Nazarene, https://www.nazarene.org/, accessed January 27, 2022.

20. "Annual Church Statistical Reports 2020," Church of the Nazarene, https://resources.nazarene.org/index.php/s/rYPMYe35ft9Nm9Z#pdfviewer, accessed January 27, 2022.

21. Ingersol, *Past and Prospect*, chapter 5.

This emphasis on creating three-self churches which remain part of a worldwide denomination (rather than become autonomous) has led to a long history of self-reflection by Nazarenes on what it means to be a global denomination. There are many milestones on this path, including the important decision in favor of "internationalization" in 1980, a self-conscious choice to remain an international denomination rather than breaking into a series of autonomous national churches.[22]

The Church of the Nazarene is structured into three legislative/deliberative levels: local congregations, districts (roughly equivalent to annual conferences), and General Assembly (equivalent to General Conference in other denominations). Districts are overseen by district superintendents, and the denomination as a whole is led by six General Superintendents, who have individual responsibilities for specific parts of the denomination as well as shared responsibility for the entire denomination.

The Church of the Nazarene groups districts into six continental "regions," which are not legislative but instead allow for contextually relevant administrative structures and upon the basis of which some denominational representatives are elected. Thus, the regions are somewhat analogous to jurisdictions or central conferences in the UMC, though there is no distinction between the USA/Canada region and other regions, in the same way that differences do exist between the UMC jurisdictions and central conferences.

The regions facilitate some level of contextualization. Nevertheless, like the AME Church and the UMC, but unlike The Wesleyan Church, there is one standard policy book for the entire denomination. The Church of the Nazarene's *Manual* is about 400 pages long and binding on churches everywhere, including a standard set of committees that are expected to exist in all districts and congregations.[23] The *Manual* does stipulate contextualization in places, such as the development of educational standards for pastors.[24]

---

22. Ingersol, *Past and Prospect*, chapter 5.

23. *Church of the Nazarene Manual 2017–2021* (Kansas City, MO: Nazarene Publishing House, 2017).

24. *Nazarene Manual 2017–2021*, Part VI: Ministry and Christian Service, IV: Education of Clergy. See especially ¶529.1.

An emphasis on three-self churches is still part of Nazarene policy, though. Nazarenes make distinctions between three types of districts: Phase 1, Phase 2, and Phase 3. Phase 1 districts are for new mission work. Phase 2 corresponds to a certain growth in size. A district doesn't become a Phase 3 district, however, until it is "100% self-supporting in regard to district administration."[25]

This means that once a district becomes a "Phase 3 district," no matter where in the world it is, it is able to take its place as a full equal to other Phase 3 districts throughout the rest of the world. A Phase 3 district in Africa is not financially dependent on districts in the United States, in the same way that many AME or UMC annual conferences in Africa still subsist on donations from the United States to cover basic programmatic expenses and even, in some instances, pastors' salaries. American Nazarenes may donate to charitable work in Africa or elsewhere,[26] but as far as the basic operations of the church, those are fully in the hands of locals.

Of course, the process of internationalization is ongoing work in the Church of the Nazarene. Questions about use of the English language and delegate visas for General Assembly remain. General Assembly is always in the United States, as is the denomination's headquarters. The Church of the Nazarene has three denomination-wide agencies covering the areas of education, mission, and Sunday School/discipleship. They are all based in the United States, though intended to serve all Nazarenes throughout the world. Most of the General Superintendents have been white American men, though recent elections have brought in more diversity. Since elections in 2017, the majority of the six General Superintendents of the Church of the Nazarene have been born outside the United States.[27] While the Church of the Nazarene still has work to do in its process of internationalization, it is well on its way. Indeed, it may well deserve the title of the most global Methodist/Wesleyan denomination.

---

25. *Nazarene Manual 2017–2021*, ¶200.2.

26. Nazarene Compassionate Ministries exists as an official denominational channel for doing so.

27. See profiles at "Board of General Superintendents," Church of the Nazarene, https://www.nazarene.org/who-we-are/organization/leadership/board-general-superintendents, accessed January 27, 2022.

The African Methodist Episcopal (AME) Church

The AME Church was founded in 1816 in Philadelphia, primarily by black members of St. George's Methodist Episcopal Church.[28] Within eight years, it started societies in Haiti. Work in Canada was added in 1840. Additional work in the Caribbean and South America started in the mid-nineteenth century. The AME Church expanded to Africa in the 1890s, where the church has grown substantially. Work in India and Europe started in the 1960s.[29] Today, the AME Church has members in 39 countries on five continents.[30]

Bishops play a significant role in the AME Church, and thus a central organizing principle in the AME Church is episcopal districts, which are similar to but more important than episcopal areas in the UMC. Representation in church-wide committees and other organizations (other than General Conference) is primarily based on episcopal districts.[31] Each episcopal district contains approximately a half dozen annual conferences, which tend to be smaller in geographic scope and membership than UMC annual conferences, since several annual conferences share a bishop. There are 20 episcopal districts, seven of which are entirely outside the United States (six in Africa, one in the Caribbean). Additional work in the Bahamas, Bermuda, Canada, and India is part of predominantly U.S. episcopal districts.[32]

Bishops are elected and assigned by the AME General Conference. Bishops must rotate between episcopal districts at least once every eight

---

28. For a complete history of the African Methodist Episcopal Church, see Dennis C. Dickerson, *The African Methodist Episcopal Church: A History* (Cambridge: Cambridge University Press, 2020).

29. This history is recounted in the denomination's *Doctrine and Discipline* book. See *The Doctrine and Discipline of the African Methodist Episcopal Church 2016* (Nashville: The African Methodist Episcopal Church AME Sunday School Union, 2017), Introduction, Section V: Global Expansion.

30. See "Bishops of the Church," African Methodist Episcopal Church, https://www.ame-church.com/leadership/bishops-of-the-church/, accessed January 27, 2022.

31. See, for instance, *Doctrine and Discipline 2016*, Part XII: The General Board.

32. For a complete listing of the areas covered by each episcopal district, see *Doctrine and Discipline 2016*, Part XIV: Conferences, Section II: The Annual Conference, Q. Annual Conferences and Their Boundaries within the Episcopal Districts, 275.

years, and there are no restrictions on where a bishop can be moved.[33] The downside of episcopal election by General Conference is that Americans, constituting a majority of delegates at General Conference, stand a much better chance of being elected bishop. Historically, most of the bishops serving outside of the United States have been Americans, and the AME Church has struggled since the 1960s with the issue of indigenous leadership in Africa.[34] Currently, bishops from outside the United States lead only two out of the 20 districts. Americans lead five districts outside the United States.[35] In contrast, Wesleyan, Nazarene, and UMC structures all provide for indigenous leadership in branches of the church outside the United States.

In contrast to the struggle for indigenous leadership, however, is the progress the AME Church has made in considering non-U.S. views through the Global Development Council and the Commission on Global Development.[36] African members of the AME Church began to agitate in the early 1980s for greater inclusion in what they perceived to be a predominantly U.S.-centric body. The bishops of the denomination took such pressures seriously. While overwhelmingly American, because the AME Church had retained the principle of general superintendency, the AME bishops were aware of what was going on in the church outside the United States, since many of them had served episcopal terms in Africa or the Caribbean.

The effort to address African concerns led to some new initiatives in the early 1980s such as partnership-in-mission agreements between American and international branches of the church. These agreements not only facilitated development work outside the United States but also sought to

33. See *Doctrine and Discipline 2016*, Part XI: Duties and Authority of Bishops and General Officers.

34. Dickerson, *The African Methodist Episcopal Church*, 488–500.

35. See "Bishops of the Church."

36. See *Doctrine and Discipline 2016*, Part XV: Global Witness and Development in Africa, the Nations of the Caribbean, Europe, South America and India.

develop deeper "mutual understanding" and "more meaningful dialogue and interaction" among AME members from different countries.[37]

Real changes in the global polity of the AME Church, however, awaited the late 1990s and early 2000s. Starting in 1996, the church undertook a primarily African-led process of self-study that led to the formation of the Global Development Council. Its duties include to "develop a structure to address the needs, aspirations, beliefs and cultures of the global context," "promote deeper understanding, collaboration, and cohesion among the AME Churches in Africa, the nations of the Caribbean, South America, Europe, and Canada with those in the United States," "determine methods to address the unique challenges of the Districts outside of the United States," and "propose legislation in the General Conference to move the process beyond the Global Development Council."[38] This is a broad scope of work, much beyond what the UMC's Standing Committee on Central Conference Matters is commissioned to do. The Global Development Council is a high-powered group, with all bishops, the General Board, and heads of administrative departments involved, as well as representatives from all episcopal districts. Such work is then further supported by the Commission on Global Development, part of the church's General Board.[39]

This process resulted in substantial changes to the denomination's *Doctrine and Discipline* book. These changes included adding a section on "Global Witness and Development in Africa, the Nations of the Caribbean, Europe, South America, and India" that includes a recounting of the history of greater global inclusion in the AME Church.[40] The *Doctrine and Discipline* also includes assertions such as "The budgets of the Episcopal Districts 14–20 of the AME Church [those outside the United States] shall be included in both the responsibilities and benefits of every activity

---

37. See *Doctrine and Discipline 2016*, Part XV: Global Witness and Development in Africa, the Nations of the Caribbean, Europe, South America and India.

38. *Doctrine and Discipline 2016*, Part XV: Global Witness and Development in Africa, the Nations of the Caribbean, Europe, South America and India, Section I: Preamble, B; Global Development Council, 297–301.

39. *Doctrine and Discipline 2016*, Part XII: The General Board, Section V: Commissions, 201.

40. *Doctrine and Discipline 2016*, Part XV: Global Witness and Development in Africa, the Nations of the Caribbean, Europe, South America and India.

of the church. Districts 14–20 shall not be treated separately or differently in any way, personal or financial. They shall also participate in the decision-making processes of the church."[41]

There are limits to this work. The AME Church's General Board remains U.S.-centered. The various departments of the General Board are headquartered in the United States, and the General Secretary/Chief Information Officer is required to have an office in either Washington, DC, St. Louis, Nashville, or Memphis.[42] The departments and the General Secretary are, however, required by the *Discipline* to have "voluntary" field representatives in episcopal districts outside the United States.[43] The AME Judicial Council is also predominantly American in membership,[44] though a South African laywoman, Thabile M. Ngubeni, was elected to the Judicial Council in 2021. She is the first African layperson elected to church-wide office.[45]

The AME Church also does not have separate General Conferences, as in The Wesleyan Church, or Central Conferences, as in the UMC, as a means of adapting polity to local circumstances outside the United States. Yet, through the Global Development Council and revisions to the Doctrines and Disciples, it has been successful in embracing internationalization and enshrining this value in their polity. While the Wesleyans and the UMC have emphasized local contextualization, the AME Church has emphasized international inclusion. While there are undoubtedly many factors behind this difference, the retention of a more fully itinerant general superintendency in the AME is likely an important one.

---

41. *Doctrine and Discipline 2016*, Part XV: Global Witness and Development in Africa, the Nations of the Caribbean, Europe, South America and India, Section II: The Budgets for Districts 14–20, 302.

42. *Doctrine and Discipline 2016*, Part XI: Duties and Authority of Bishops and General Officers, Section IV: General Officers, F. Duties and Responsibilities, 1. General Secretary/Chief Information Officer, 175–8.

43. *Doctrine and Discipline 2016*, Part XI: Duties and Authority of Bishops and General Officers, Section IV: General Officers.

44. See "Judicial Council," African Methodist Episcopal Church, https://www.ame-church.com/leadership/judicial-council/, accessed January 27, 2022.

45. Kathryn Post, "Four new bishops—and first biracial bishop—elected to AME Church," *Religion News Service*, July 12, 2021, https://religionnews.com/2021/07/12/four-new-bishops-and-first-biracial-bishop-elected-to-ame-church/.

The United Methodist Church

The United Methodist Church is the direct successor of the Methodist Episcopal Church, the first American Methodist body from which the above denominational traditions split. It is also the result of a series of mergers, most recently the 1968 merger of The Methodist Church and the Evangelical United Brethren Church, each of those the product of previous mergers. Through these various predecessor bodies, the UMC inherited a significant heritage of mission work in a large number of countries around the world.[46] Currently, the denomination has 12.5 million members in 58 countries across four continents.[47]

In earlier periods and again in the 1960s, United Methodists and their predecessors focused on domestic merger rather than crafting international polities. As indicated elsewhere in this volume,[48] while the COSMOS process considered extensive reformations to the international structure of The Methodist Church, this process was sidelined by The Methodist Church/EUB merger. This and previous decisions to pursue merger have had implications not only for the global nature of the church but also organizational consequences that have affected the church regardless of location. Other scholars have suggested that ecumenical motives were not the only ones at play in past Methodist mergers. There was also a desire to build a bigger and hence more influential church.[49] This desire for influence was a desire for cultural and political power in the United States and thus U.S.-focused. The consequences of such a desire for size and influence have affected the UMC, and not entirely in positive ways.

---

46. For a history of The United Methodist Church and its predecessors in the United States, see Russell E. Richey, Kenneth E. Rowe, and Jean Miller Schmidt, *American Methodism: A Compact History* (Nashville: Abingdon, 2012). For a history of select branches of the UMC outside the United States, see Amos Nascimento and Elaine A. Robinson, *Global United Methodism: Telling the Stories, Living into the Realities* (Nashville: Wesley's Foundery, 2019).

47. "2020 Delegate Calculations," The United Methodist Church, http://s3.amazonaws.com/Website_Properties/news-media/press-center/documents/2020_Delegate_Calc_by_AC_with_2016_comp.pdf, accessed January 27, 2022; "Central Conferences Directory," The United Methodist Church, https://www.umc.org/en/content/central-conferences-directory, accessed January 27, 2022.

48. See chapters in this volume by Joon-Sik Park and Philip Wingeier-Rayo.

49. See, for instance, Morris L. Davis, "The Methodist Merger of 1939: 'Successful' Unification?" in *Unity of the Church and Human Sexuality: Toward a Faithful United Methodist Witness* (Nashville: United Methodist General Board of Higher Education and Ministry, 2018).

As a result of the COSMOS process, all branches of the UMC in Latin America and most of the branches of the church in Asia became autonomous, a process that drained much of the impetus to rethink internal international relations from the denomination. That process of autonomy continued through the mid-1980s. A smaller wave of accepting African groups into the denomination that began in the 1980s and continued through the accession of Cote d'Ivoire in the early 2000s produced limited interest in reconsidering issues of internal equity within the church, though Darryl Stephens has argued that the 2008 Cote d'Ivoire merger deserved much more thorough attention than it was accorded.[50]

The growth in UMC membership in countries outside the United States, however, was more successful in raising questions about the U.S.-centered nature of the denomination, especially after the turn of the century. The UMC has changed the mandates of some of its general boards and agencies and adjusted formulas for membership on boards of directors to better reflect the interests of United Methodists outside the United States, but thus far has not made the same sort of significant changes that the AME Church has to its structures.

While significant changes have been proposed and even passed by the UMC General Conference, major changes have been sidelined by ongoing conflicts about human sexuality (which has been much less a topic of debate in the other traditions). A plan to create a U.S. Central Conference that was passed by the General Conference in 2008 was voted down by the annual conferences on the fear that it would allow the church in the United States to change its standards on gay ordination and gay marriage.[51] Extensive international conversations on the worldwide nature of the church leading up to the 2000, 2008, 2012, and 2016 General Conferences were overshadowed by continuing conflicts over sexuality and

50. Darryl W. Stephens, "A Widening Stream: Comparing and Contrasting United Methodism's 1968 and 2008 Mergers," *Methodist History* 58:3 (2020), 165–76.

51. Linda Green and Elizabeth Guye, "U.S. conferences disapprove structure proposal," *UM News*, July 29, 2009, http://archives.gcah.org:8080/bitstream/handle/10516/700/7261009.htm; "Maxie Dunnam, Eddie Fox release videos on proposed amendments," *MethodistThinker.com*, April 17, 2009, https://methodistthinker.com/2009/04/17/maxie-dunnam-eddie-fox-release-videos-on-proposed-amendments/.

U.S.-led plans to reorganize denominational agencies.[52] Thus, The United Methodist Church remains the one major American-originated Methodist denomination to not make significant revisions to its international polity since the early period of missionary expansion.

Conclusion

It would be possible to continue looking at other churches as examples of international Methodist polity (the Free Methodist Church, the AME Zion Church, the Salvation Army, the Methodist Church of Southern Africa, etc.). Nevertheless, the churches examined cover significant and distinct examples of how Methodist/Wesleyan churches have approached being a global denomination. One takeaway from this exercise in comparative polity is that there are several ways to be a global Methodist/Wesleyan body, and they all have their advantages and disadvantages.

The Wesleyans, the Nazarenes, the AME Church, and the UMC have each taken distinct approaches to trying to craft a global denomination that is not just dominated by U.S. Americans but fully supports and recognizes the gifts, ministries, and voices of members around the world. The Wesleyan Church allows the creation of separate General Conferences with separate Books of Discipline, united into one International Conference with a common kernel of shared doctrine and polity. The Church of the Nazarene emphasizes three-self theory and the creation of self-supporting, self-led, and self-propagating "Phase 3" districts around the world. The AME Church has denominational bodies (the Global Development Council and Committee on Global Development) with significant power to make changes in the denomination to better accommodate non-U.S. members. The United Methodist Church has elements of the AME approach (in the Standing Committee on Central Conference Matters) and the Wesleyan approach (in the provision for central conference

---

52. For the substance of those reports, see "Worldwide Nature of the Church: General Conference Reports," The United Methodist Church, http://ee.umc.org/who-we-are/worldwide-nature-church-general-conference-reports, accessed January 27, 2022; "Worldwide Nature of the Church: Executive Summary," The United Methodist Church, http://ee.umc.org/who-we-are/worldwide-nature-of-the-church-executive-summary, accessed January 27, 2022.

adaptation of the *Book of Discipline*) but has not gone as far as these other denominations.

Yet each denomination also faces struggles in addressing the ongoing impacts of American empire and U.S.-centrism in their denominations. The Wesleyan Church in the United States still exerts control over other branches of the church that have not yet become autonomous General Conferences. AME bishops still come mostly from the United States, and it remains difficult to elect indigenous leadership for the church elsewhere. All four denominations face questions about denominational leadership and agencies headquartered in the United States and international meetings that happen exclusively in the United States and predominantly in the English language.

Money also remains a significant force for perpetuating U.S. control of other branches of the church in each denomination. I have shown elsewhere how U.S. funding makes up a significant percentage of the budget of branches of the UMC in Africa, Eastern Europe, and the Philippines.[53] In some places, the church would not be able to function, at least on its present model, without U.S. funding. That level of funding gives U.S. interests significant leverage over denominational sisters and brothers elsewhere. Nazarene emphases on self-support and the self-support involved in autonomous Wesleyan General Conferences go a long way to mitigate the power of money as a form of imperial control, and AME attention to budgetary issues as central to the question of global development show an awareness of the power of money in international relations. Yet even in the Church of the Nazarene, mission spending by U.S.-funded and U.S.-located denominational boards still has an impact on relationships between various branches of the church. This caution about the impact of money is a reminder that, while there are many pathways to becoming a less U.S.-dominated denomination, there are also many ways in which U.S. imperial dominance expresses itself within the church. It is a phenomenon not easily dismantled through a single approach.

---

53. David W. Scott, "The Economics of International Mission," in *The Practice of Mission in Global Methodism: Emerging Trends from Everywhere to Everywhere*, ed. by David W. Scott and Darryl W. Stephens (New York: Routledge, 2021), 41–55.

The need to look beyond a single approach makes ecumenical histori-cal analysis relevant for the UMC today. Unlike its sister denominations, the UMC missed the last two windows for making changes to its struc-ture as a global denomination. Yet, given the current push for rethink-ing the denomination, the UMC finds itself on the precipice of another window of opportunity to make changes. There is still a chance for The United Methodist Church to join with its Methodist and Wesleyan sib-ling denominations to try to live into the goal of more fully being a global church that unites members from around the world while recognizing and enabling the variety of vital ministries each engage in. As of the writ-ing, proposals such as the Christmas Covenant[54] and the General Book of Discipline[55] provide possible pathways for the UMC to find its own path toward becoming a less U.S.-dominated denomination, though these remain up in the air amid a messy split over views on sexuality. This ecu-menical survey shows there are other options as well. What has been lack-ing thus far is not promising models, but the humility and willingness on the part of the U.S. church to try them.

---

54.   Homepage, Christmas Covenant, https://www.christmascovenant.com/, accessed January 27, 2022.

55.   *The Book of Discipline of The United Methodist Church, 2016* (Nashville: The United Methodist Publishing House, 2016), Part II: General Book of Discipline, ¶101.

Section 2

CONTEMPORARY PERSPECTIVES

4

THE UMC DISCIPLINE

A Parallel Power Structure to the American Administration of the Nation

Jørgen Thaarup

United Methodists who live outside the United States find themselves within a denomination that often functions in a foreign way. In my view, this tension has impacted the denomination in profound ways, and it partly explains the current schism of The United Methodist Church. In this chapter, I build from my experience as a United Methodist pastor and district superintendent in Denmark and as a delegate to General Conference. My argument is that the governance system of the UMC imitates the U.S. government system. I insist that this model has inhibited the growth of independent and incarnational Methodist theologies in the central conferences. Moreover, the American bias of United Methodist polity accentuates the impact of American social tensions in the life of the church as General Conference, as the denomination's law-making body, is organized in a way that makes its American delegates more comfortable than their central conference counterparts.

This issue is particularly pressing among United Methodists due to the fact that our historical ecclesial documents were shaped in the peculiar context of the aftermath of American independence. John Wesley never had a "Book of Discipline," and he never attempted to create one or anything similar. Wesley was an elder of the Anglican Church, and he was loyal to the theology and the ecclesiastic structure and administration of this church all his life. Frank Baker has shown how Wesley's thinking and his lifelong function as a pastor, even a pastor with supervising responsibilities, was completely loyal to Anglican theology and praxis and to the structure of the church, even when he initiated the new independent Methodist Episcopal Church in America.[1] Methodism in England during Wesley's lifetime was a movement and an ecclesiastic structure within the Anglican Church, and not until a generation after the death of John Wesley did Methodism in England become independent from the Anglican Church and form its own ecclesiastic structure.[2]

But how did ecclesiastic structure and power function in Wesley's church? In the same way as most established churches in Europe. The Anglican church did not have a comprehensive and united text with a constitution, faith and order agreements, and laws with all regulations of the function of the church. In fact, very little principal and policy texts and administrative texts are written in the established churches in Europe. The reason for that is that all churches of the people have grown out of history, and the churches follow the praxis and the theology of the tradition. When disagreements arose or new questions demanded new decisions, the history of the church, the tradition, formed the basis of how to proceed.

Wesley wrote two major historical works, each of them five volumes,[3] in which he wrote the history of the church from ancient Christianity, through the Romans, French, Germans, and English peoples. This was meant to be a comprehensive church history that linked the Jesus movement in Israel to Wesley's own period. His final main chapter in these ecclesiastical history books was titled: "The people called Methodist." Wesley's writings do not identify Methodism as a church or a movement,

1. Frank Baker, *John Wesley and the Church of England* (London: Epworth, 1970).

2. Wesley was so keen on his loyalty to Anglicanism that, when the foundation of Wesley Chapel, City Road, London, was laid, he proclaimed that: "Whenever the Methodists leave the Church, God will leave the Methodists." *The Works of John Wesley*, Vol. 3, ed. by Albert C. Outler (Nashville: Abingdon, 1986), "Sermon 112," 589:30–31. Wesley repeated this statement several times to underline that schism, splitting in itself, is a sin. Wesley's attitude to the Anglican Church is also expressed in his statement: "the Church of England is the most scriptural national church in the World." *Wesley Works*, Vol. 9, "Farther Thought on Separation from the Church," 538:5–7.

3. John Wesley, *A Concise History of England* (London: Foundry, 1775); John Wesley, *An Ecclesiastical History* (London: City-Road, 1781).

but as a people, a people connected with Christian people of other nations and cultures, having the same one Christianity. Because history and tradition are authoritative in doctrinal matters, Wesley often made decisions about practical church life based on arguments from history. When Methodism emphasizes tradition in the so-called Wesleyan Quadrilateral, this position is underlined strongly by Wesley's writings of church history and how the collected knowledge of the life of the church is normative for decisions in the modern church.[4]

Beyond history or tradition, civil laws give some ecclesiastic framework for the life and governance of the church, whereas The Articles of Religion gives theological directions for the church. Concerning these articles, we need to say that they are not the complete doctrinal standard of the church. In the same way as the Augustana Confession and the Heidelberg Confession on the European continent, the Articles of Religion are strongly influenced and strongly limited to the issues relevant during the time of the Reformation, and they mostly address issues of conflict in the church. The Articles of Religion are bound to the history of Anglican independence from Catholicism. In the Anglican Church, the Book of Common Prayer may be the most powerful tool of doctrinal standard and discipline. In it, we find the main expressions of theology on regular worship services, membership, baptism, wedding, ordination, and many actions of the church. Liturgy is a main instrument to state the confessional standard of theology, including definitions of sacramental understanding, understanding of the ordained ministry, and the function of the episcopacy.[5]

Wesley's "Discipline" and the Founding of the Methodist Episcopal Church in America

Given this Church of England background, Wesley didn't have a Book of Discipline to base his decisions on before sending Dr. Thomas

---

4. John Wesley, *Christian Library*, Vols. 1–50 (Bristol: William Pine & Felix Farley, 1749–55). In these selected collections of texts from the entirety of church history, Wesley focused on tradition and how tradition is normative for theology, including ecclesiology.

5. *The Book of Common Prayer* (London: William Clowes & Sons, [varies]).

Coke to America with the task to form a church. We have Wesley's letter to Thomas Coke and Francis Asbury and "our Brethren in North-America," written in Bristol on September 10, 1784.[6] In that letter, Wesley gave instructions about what he understood as authorities and normative texts on ecclesiastic issues. You can say that here we find what Wesley held as his "Discipline." Wesley talked about "civil-laws" as the framework for a church institution, and because America was constituted as a secular state and thus had no civil laws concerning ecclesiastical structures, which is totally different from all European states, this created an opening for an independent, self-constituted church, different from Wesley's own church. Wesley quoted Lord Peter King for his history on the episcopacy and used this foundation in history to legalize his own right as an ordained elder to perform ordination of other elders and consecration of superintendents, the so-called elder-bishops. Wesley gave the new church his revision of the Articles of Religion and his revision of the Book of Common Prayer, named Sunday Service. And he gave the new church a sung liturgy, his A Collection of Psalms and Hymns. One cannot forget that Wesley's hymns were, first of all, theological texts, a catechism in poetry, and in this understanding also doctrinal standards. Finally, Wesley offered his Sermons. Wesley came from the Anglican tradition of standard homilies,[7] and he wrote sermons that clearly marked the center of Christianity, not the boundaries.

Thomas Coke came to America with a given task from John Wesley. He himself was consecrated superintendent and appointed to oversee the Methodist connection in America. The letter from Wesley stated that the given task was not only to Thomas Coke and Francis Asbury, but to "our Brethren in North-America." When the "Brethren," all the preachers, were called and gathered in Baltimore to the Christmas Conference in 1784 and continuing directly into conference in January 1785, they did not follow the directions given in Wesley's letter of instruction. Instead, Wesley's order was overruled with the decision to form a democratic body, the General Conference, different from the ecclesiastic structure that Wes-

---

6. *Minutes of Christmas Conference and General Conference*, Baltimore, January 1785. Lovely Lane Museum.

7. Anglican Article of Religion XXXV, "The 21 Edwardian Homilies."

ley was loyal to. And then the decision was made in the General Conference to consecrate Francis Asbury, first as deacon, then as elder, and finally as superintendent.[8] It was a major step that the General Conference was created and empowered as the leading body.

The new Methodist Episcopal Church in America followed most recommendations from John Wesley, but not all of them. Wesley was a reformer of Anglican tradition in the sense that he revised the Articles of Religion. From that perspective, the new Methodist Episcopal Church became a reformed version of the Anglican Church. In Wesley's revision, he deleted all references to loyalty to the king of England and his jurisdiction as the head of the Church. Most clearly, Wesley included no Article of Religion on state-church relations. But on this point, American Methodism soon approved a new paragraph, Article of Religion XXIII, which acknowledges the rulers of the United States of America. Was this article intended to say that Methodism in America is an American church, fully integrated into American culture and its political system?

Today, after the union in 1968, all agencies of the UMC, the Council of Bishops, the administration of General Conference, and the Africa University (Tennessee) Inc. entity have their headquarters within the United States, and therefore they are working under the state-church relation formulated in Article of Religion XXIII. But all their work outside the United States does not follow the state-church relation in the same Article of Religion.[9]

When American Methodism spread back to continental Europe because of migration, the context of new Methodist churches in Europe absolutely understood that here came an American Church. When the first Methodist church in Copenhagen, Denmark, was consecrated in 1865, it was the American Ambassador, Mr. Wright from Berlin, who came up

---

8. James K. Mathews, *Set Apart to Serve* (Nashville: Abingdon, 1985), 94–104.

9. In the Confession of Faith of the Evangelical United Brethren Church, Article XVI, we find a text about church-state relations, but here the state is not fixed to one specific nation or state, only the "civil government" in any place. The location of the American flag in front of many local United Methodist churches is yet another instance that gives the impression to newcomers that here we have a nationalistic American Church. The Stars and Stripes do not indicate a global church, a supranational church, or a multi-cultural church.

and did the full ceremony.[10] When the Danish Methodist Church applied to the Danish state for approval and the right to perform weddings, and the state was slow to answer, the American presidential candidate Ulysses Grant wrote the Danish state, and approval was given. Also, the first American ambassador in Copenhagen, Dr. Cramer, played an important role in inspiring the Danish state to accept Methodism as a church in Denmark. Ambassador Cramer was a brother-in-law to President Grant. My point is that, in many European countries, Methodism was understood as an American church, even an American-embassy church, in the same way as we here in Copenhagen have an English, a Russian, a Norwegian, and a Swedish church, all representing countries and states.

The Development of Bishops in American Methodism

The constitution of the United States reflects the formation of a secular nation built on the enlightenment philosophers' understanding of a balanced national administration with separate legislative, executive, and judicial powers. Russell E. Richey shows in his book *Early American Methodism* how the formation of the Methodist Episcopal Church in America developed parallel to this philosophy of the nation. The ongoing steps in building up the ecclesiastical structure of the church was as a mirrored parallel to the development of the democratic structure of the new nation, the new union of states.[11] How did this parallel history influence the structure and theology of American Methodism?

On the issue of superintendents, the first step in the development was that the General Conference in 1788 titled Coke and Asbury as bishops. When Wesley heard that, we have one of the harshest reactions ever from him: "How dare you suffer yourself to be called 'bishop'? For my sake, for God's sake, for Christ's sake put a full end to this!"[12] Wesley saw that the

10. A. Haagensen, *Den Norsk-Danske Methodismes Historie paa Begge Sider Havet* (Chicago: Norsk-Danske Boghandel, 1894), 287.

11. Russell E. Richey, *Early American Methodism* (Bloomington: Indiana University Press, 1991).

12. John Wesley, *Letters*, VIII, 91.

Americans tried to develop the episcopacy in the same direction as the Anglican bishops, not in Wesley's understanding that we have an elder-episcopacy. After Wesley passed away, the title bishop was fully used in American Methodism.[13]

Second, we find in American Methodism a tension between the power of the episcopacy and the power of conference. This tension Richey called the episcopal language of the church in conflict with the republican language of the church.[14] The first split in American Methodism came when James O'Kelly and his republican fellows, primarily in the state of Virginia, conflicted with Francis Asbury because they found that his leadership as bishop was too powerful compared to the conference.[15]

Third, the episcopacy developed over time to become the main executive power of the church. The bishops don't have the right to vote in General Conference, and they should not influence the law-making process. This structure changes the very common understanding of the episcopacy in the whole of church history that the ministry of the bishop is a teaching ministry, a ministry of doctrine. How can bishops hold the responsibility of keeping up correct Christian doctrines if they don't have the right to participate in the process of deciding new laws with doctrinal implications? The idea that the episcopacy has the executive power has pushed the role of bishops in the direction of being general secretaries of an NGO or executive directors of a company. And when recruiting new bishops, the ability of being a good manager and administrator, good knowledge of civil law, and fundraising abilities very easily take priority over abilities of good exegesis, systematic theology, and pastoral care.

Fourth, episcopacy in the UMC has developed to become very powerful within the church. As mentioned, the tension between episcopacy and conference was clear from the very beginning. In British Methodism, we find the same tension after the death of John Wesley. In British Methodism, the conference was the strongest part, and they decided to limit the power of the episcopal function. The way they did it was to elect a new

---

13. Matthews, *Set Apart to Serve*, 118–25.

14. Russell E. Richey, "The Four Languages of Early American Methodism," *Methodist History* 28:3 (April 1990): 155–71.

15. Fredrick A. Norwood, *The Story of American Methodism* (Nashville: Abingdon, 1974), 124–29.

presiding officer every year. The general superintendency of the church is one of the elders, who for one year chairs the conferences, leads the ordinations, and does other representative duties.

American Methodism went in the opposite direction. Lifetime episcopacy itself has over time made episcopal power very strong, especially when the *Book of Discipline* recommends that almost all other positions in the church shall be limited to some years, and when most elections are recommended to have new persons in the position. The bishops will always be the most powerful because they are the most experienced. Another development is that the power in many boards and institutions of the church is divided among three groups: the laity, the elders, and the bishops. This is the case in most General Conference agencies, boards, and committees. Why the bishops are a separate group from the elders is very difficult to understand given Wesley's insistence that bishops are elders in a specific administrative function and not a separate order of clergy.

Another specific issue is this: how did the church develop the structure of the Council of Bishops? The *Book of Discipline* sets the parameters for the function and roles played by the Council, but we have no theology of the ecclesiastic meaning and function of the Council of Bishops.[16] But it is very clear in the life of the UMC that the Council of Bishops is a very strong power structure, and that the council has a strong influence on legislation in the General Conference, contrary to the idea that bishops are the executive branch of the church, and because of that, they should not vote or influence the process of legislation.

A Federal and Democratic Structure of Conferencing

General Conference became more and more a legislative body similar to the House of Representatives, where American lawmaking takes place. This characteristic of the General Conference became evident after 1968, when The United Methodist Church was founded with a new structure and new content in the *Book of Discipline*. General Conference

---

16. UMC *Discipline* 2016, ¶47.

has delegates from each annual conference according to their size, the same system as the House of Representatives, where large states have more delegates compared to smaller states. The House of Representatives and Senate make the laws for the whole United States; the General Conference (influenced by the Council of Bishops) makes the laws for the whole global UMC.

Something new happened in the power structure of American Methodism when the church grew, and annual conferences were organized in each state, with most annual conferences having their own bishop. Annual conferences and the individual bishops became a decentralized federal structure. The Council of Bishops is constructed in the same way as the U.S. Senate, with one or two persons from each unit of the federation, providing for the same number of votes from large and small units.

John Wesley, in his letter to establish the Methodist Episcopal Church, was aware of the civil laws in America and the differences between national laws and state laws, with implications for the church. "A civil authority is exercised over them, partly by the Congress, partly by the State Assemblies," decentralized federal structures and a central national structure, with implications for ecclesiastical issues.[17] In modern times, we have new tensions between Congressional and state power around issues of abortion and climate policy, where strong voices polarize the whole culture in America. In The United Methodist Church, we have the same struggles between power given to the annual conferences and power given to the General Conference.

Judicial Administration:
A Third Branch of Governance

The philosophers of the Enlightenment saw the judiciary branch as the third independent power structure of the nation. American Methodism developed a similar power structure, now most concretely expressed in the Judicial Council of the UMC. All nations worldwide have a system

---

17. *Minutes of the Methodist Conferences 1773 to 1794 under the superintendence of John Wesley, bishop Asbury and Coke*, Lovely Lane Museum.

of judicial administration and especially a supreme court as a third court where decisions can be appealed. But in the United States, the Supreme Court has the right to cancel a piece of legislation if the new legislation conflicts with the constitution. We see in American political life that many issues from the civil legislation of the country are overruled by the Supreme Court. Because of this kind of judicial mandate, the court itself has become a battleground for the struggle between conservative and liberal political forces.

The United Methodist Church has a parallel system, a Judicial Council where so-called declaratory decisions can be made and legislation cancelled with a null-and-void decision. Furthermore, in the UMC, we see conservative and liberal positions in the Judicial Council. The Judicial Council is also influenced by church political conflicts. In most countries in Europe, the supreme court has no authority to declare a piece of legislation null and void. If a piece of new legislation conflicts with the constitution of the country, that legislation goes back to the parliament for correction. The judicial administration of the UMC is American in both philosophy and praxis.

Global Everything in the UMC

Quite often, the UMC quotes John Wesley's "The world is my parish," to find support for global mission, global evangelism, global ministry, global boards, and finally the global nature of the church. I do not see any other Protestant churches with this global thinking and this claim to hold a global nature and build a global structure of the church. I find more often the claim to be an *incarnational* church in a concrete culture; the claim to be incarnational is understood in opposition to being transnational, transcultural, and global.

As mentioned, John Wesley was loyal to the theology and structure of the Anglican Church of dividing the country and the ministry of its clergy into parishes. A parish is a geographically defined area with a number of inhabitants and a local church institution with the responsibility to be church to serve the people in the area. Most European countries have the parish system. An area of possible conflict in the parish system is when a pastor who is appointed to one parish recruits members to his or her own church from the neighboring parish, or more critically, if a pastor in one parish preaches and evangelizes in a parish where this pastor has no appointment.

John Wesley came into conflict with clergy colleagues several times when he was preaching around the country. He was a Fellow at Lincoln College in Oxford for 26 years, and in this capacity, he held a specific authority given only to College Fellows to preach in all parishes. But after his leave from Oxford University, Wesley continued to preach around the country. First, he gave the order that Methodists should not have worship services near a local Anglican Church and absolutely not at the time of ordinary services. Second, we find that Wesley's field preaching was in places where the Anglican Church didn't have a church building. Kingswood was a new, upcoming, industrial and mining area, and the Anglican Church had no building and no activity in that place. Wesley saw this place as the world different from the church. And so, all over the country, places where there was no church building and no church activities were considered the "world," different from the parish church. In this historical context, Wesley was criticized for interfering with the local Anglican parish church, and he stated, "The world is my parish," meaning, all places in England where the Anglican Church has no church building is the world, and Methodists are primarily working among people not attending the parish church. With the words, "The world is my parish," Wesley had no intention to spread Methodism to other countries, neither the European continent nor America. Methodism came to America and the European continent and Ireland without any decision taken by John Wesley.[18]

The United Methodist Church has used this quotation from Wesley to support its global church thinking and structure. British Methodism has never gone this way. In British Methodism we find that, from the very beginning, mission in other countries was linked to the British Annual Conference as long as needed until the new mission was big and strong enough to be organized as an independent church. And then, the structural connection to the mother conference in England was cut. So it was in the time

18. *Wesley Works*, Vol. 19, "Journal," 66–67.

of Wesley where the Irish annual conference was independent of the British annual conference, and so it was with Methodism in countries and colonies outside the British Isles. No structure binds the churches in different areas of the world together. British Methodism does not have a conference above the annual conference and no General Conference as a lawmaking body.

The United Methodist Church, however, has built a hierarchical conference system, and I think the reason is that, very early in the history of American Methodism, we find federal thinking within the structure of the church and the new nation. So, when American Methodism early on had a structure similar to one ruling body for the whole country and another ruling body for the smaller units, it was very easy to fit new missions, new annual conferences, and new bishops in countries outside United States into the American structure of church. In a way, the American ecclesiology was designed to be global and hierarchical because of its federal nature, but with a strong foundation of always being American in its culture, understanding of democracy, administration, and finances.[19]

For the first 75–100 years of American Methodism, the church developed in all its dimensions solely in the U.S. context before mission and migration brought American Methodism to countries outside America.[20] Of course, the new mission churches planted all over the world after 1833 brought the American understanding of ecclesiology, conferencing, and theology to the new places.[21] Is it possible to turn a national ecclesiology into one that is global? The only way is to go in a decentralized federal direction.

Central Conferences as Decentralized Federal Organizations

When the structures for central conferences started to develop in the General Conference back in 1884, there was no theology of the global

19. Thomas Edward Frank, *Polity, Practice, and the Mission of The United Methodist Church* (Nashville: Abingdon, 1997), 203–62.

20. 1840–1910 was the intensive period where migration brought Methodism to continental Europe.

21. Jack M. Tuell, *The Organization of The United Methodist Church* (Nashville: Abingdon, 1997).

nature of the church. Quite the opposite, and in full harmony with the theology of the new mission of all the Protestant, evangelical churches, the theology was incarnational with a strong focus on the cultures and different civilizations all over the world. The basic paragraphs in the 2016 *Discipline* on central conference independence, self-governing leadership, and writing their own *Books of Discipline* are more than 120 years old. If the central conferences had used these paragraphs to develop themselves and take responsibility for their own practical divinity (the Wesleyan method of theology developed out of the local praxis of the church), then I could have been a prophet saying, "The schism in the global UMC in 2022 over the issue of human sexuality would never had a chance to spread from some annual conferences in the United States to any of the central conferences."

The crisis we have now over the issue of human sexuality is to some extent rooted in the fact that the central conferences have not developed into independent and self-governing churches with strong incarnational identities, as it was intended in the original vision for the central conferences.[22] Why? I think the answer is different from continent to continent. In Europe, World War I and World War II totally damaged the work with church structures among the Methodist churches in the many annual conferences. And then the Cold War happened and Europe was divided, with an Iron Curtain between Communist countries and Western Europe. The Iron Curtain has been gone since 1989, but the conflict over the issue of homosexuality—in politics, culture, and religious institutions—mostly follows the same lines as the Iron Curtain. Very strange! Two of the European UMC central conferences will split over the same issue, almost following the same Iron Curtain. It shows that the conflicts over the issue of homosexuality follow different borders and philosophical arguments on the North American and the European continents, and one and the same discussion over the issue is not possible.[23]

My point is that the central conference structure in the UMC is a necessary decentralized federal structure, and the potential to develop is

---

22. In Africa, it is my understanding that the central conference structure and organization has never really been implemented, except for the function of electing bishops.

23. "'New House' of Europe," in *Book of Resolutions, 2000*, 740–43.

already given in the *Discipline*, but not used by the central conferences. Harry Wescott Worley, in his 1938 Yale University doctoral dissertation, gives good wisdom for the development of central conferences according to the theology of mission and incarnational church. The interesting title of the dissertation is: *The Central Conference of the Methodist Episcopal Church: A study in ecclesiastical adaptation, or a contribution of the mission field to the development of church organization.*[24] Maybe one can also say that the central conferences and their bishops have been too weak to develop the ecclesiastic structure given in the *Discipline*. If so, we must criticize the Council of Bishops regarding their responsibility to have general and global oversight of the church and ask: Why have bishops for more than a century accepted the dissatisfactory ecclesiastic structure in the central conferences? In any event, by doing so little, the central conferences also have some degree of responsibility; American-developed Methodist ecclesiastical structure and theology were adopted uncritically by the central conferences with no adaptions to local culture and civil administration and no will to be integrated into context. It is very problematic and a threat to all remaining central conferences to stay in unity with the UMC.[25]

In a private conversation in Denmark in 1995, with Emilio Castro, a Uruguayan Methodist and the General Secretary of the World Council of Churches from 1985 to 1992,[26] I asked why the Methodist churches in Latin America are no longer part of the UMC. His first critique was the UMC policy on alcohol and the claim on an abstinence lifestyle, espe-

24. Harry Wescott Worley, The *Central Conference of the Methodist Episcopal Church* (Foochow, China: The Christian Herald Mission Press, 1940).

25. A subject matter that I cannot fully address in this chapter is the issue of central conferences that have gained autonomy from The United Methodist Church in the United States. In my view, we could learn a lot about incarnational church and local formation of ecclesiastical structures if we focus on conferences no longer included in the UMC and then investigate if the struggle for ecclesial autonomy is related to American imperialism. For accounts of this in the official documents of the Methodist Church, see *Discipline* of The Methodist Church, 1939, ¶483 *The China Central Conference*, ¶484 *The Central Conference of Southern Asia*, ¶485 *The Latin America Central Conference*. According to Worley's dissertation from 1938, we have had central conferences in Southern Asia, Eastern Asia, South Africa, Latin America, Europe, China, India, Malaysia, and the Philippine Isles. For a recent study of church autonomy, see the chapters from Wingeier-Rayo and Park in this volume.

26. Emilio Castro, *Sent Free: Mission and Unity in the Perspective of the Kingdom* (Geneva: WCC, 1985).

cially for the clergy. How should this policy function in his home country of Uruguay and neighbors like Argentina and Chile with so many wine farmers and a different ethical standard? His second critique was that the mission engagement from American Methodism in Latin America was politically conservative, supportive of the shifting fascistic governments and evangelical "born again" theology, but Methodism in Latin America developed more in the direction of a Marxist theology of liberation,[27] social justice for the poor, and criticism against the conservative government.[28]

What will happen with the current central conferences now if future central conferences do not develop their own incarnational, ecclesiastical culture for replacement of the unexamined, imported culture of American Methodism?

A Parallel Structure to the Civil Administration of the United States

From 1744, Wesley called his preachers to annual conferences. The success of these conferences developed the theological understanding that the conference was a means of grace. The issues of the conferences and the focus areas were conversation about the life of the church, its mission, and how to preach and develop its work. Items for discussion came out of the praxis of the church. The results of these annual conferences were The Minutes, often written as questions and answers. What were the "minutes"? Minutes were not laws but notes to remember the history and how church work was done in the actual time and culture. After a number of annual conferences, Wesley organized all the minutes into the Large Minutes, where all the notes of history were organized into subjects. But still, the conference and the minutes did not turn into a lawmaking machine.[29]

---

27. José Míguez Bonino, "Reflections on the Church's Authoritative Teaching on Social Questions," in *What Should Methodists Teach?* ed. M. Douglas Meeks (Nashville: Abingdon, 1990), 58–68. José Míguez Bonino, "Wesley in Latin America: A Theological and Historical Reflection," in *Rethinking Wesley's Theology*, ed. Randy Maddox (Nashville: Abingdon, 1998), 169–82.

28. Thomas Langford, *Practical Divinity* (Nashville: Abingdon, 1983), 250–52; Néstor O. Míguez, "The Old Creation in the New, the New Creation in the Old," in *Wesleyan Perspectives on the New Creation*, ed. M. Douglas Meeks (Nashville: Abingdon, 2004), 53–72.

29. *Wesley Works*, Vol. 10: *The Methodist Societies, The Minutes of Conference*.

Preachers like Francis Asbury participated in Wesley's conferences and implemented the same system in the American colonies starting in 1773. We have the "Minutes of some conversations between the preachers in connection with the Rev. Mr. John Wesley, 1773 to 1785," where the first General Conference was organized. The General Conference in 1785 and the following years didn't change the character of conference work. It was still conversations about the practical work. All the items for discussion came out of the practical work of the preachers, and no legislation was made, only minutes to remember the history and the good practices.[30]

Methodists talk about "holy conferencing," an idea that comes from John Wesley and this way of doing conference: conversation and notes of our history. Wesley called church work in the present time and the notes of our history "practical divinity." We can call it practical theology or theology of experiences. In a way, it is the Anglican theology that history has doctrinal authority, because the development of theology comes from the life and the struggles of the church. But over time, and most clearly after 1968, when the UMC *Discipline* was formed with a constitution, a number of laws for church work, a Judicial Council, a separation of the power of legislation in General Conference from the executive power of bishops, and the strange construction of the Council of Bishops, we have a clear parallel structure to the state and national administration of the United States.

When General Conference is in session for lawmaking, the so-called legislative process, the conference follows Robert's Rules of Order. What are Robert's Rules of Order? It is the parliamentarian order of the two houses of Congress on Capitol Hill in Washington.[31] The way of working is this: first you formulate your petition, which must be done no later than 230 days before the first session of General Conference.[32] The preparatory work in legislative committees follows the same pattern as in Congress. When the petition is on the agenda, then the delegates can speak in favor or against the petition or amend the petition. The way of

---

30. *Minutes of the Methodist Conferences 1773 to 1794 under the superintendence of John Wesley, bishop Asbury and Coke,* Lovely Lane Museum.

31. *Daily Christian Advocate,* Vol. 1, 2020, 29–71.

32. UMC *Discipline* 2016, ¶¶505–7.

working is the political way for and against, with the focus being to create new legislation. This parliamentary procedure creates polarization from the very beginning of the process. And then there are the strict time limits of speeches: two minutes, one minute. Who can say anything important in two minutes? You can state the position you had before the conference. One cannot do what Wesley did in his conferences, where conversation started on a specific subject, and then the conversation could be developed in some specific direction. Maybe the conversation matured into a decision, and a note of the conversation was put into the minutes; if the conversation didn't mature or come to a final decision, the conversation could continue next time the conference gathered. This method did not polarize everything in the same way we see it in the General Conference now, and I think the polarization and the conflicts we experience at General Conference are influenced by the way we work. Why have we developed General Conference into a lawmaking process, and why must all items end up in a specific paragraph in the *Book of Discipline*?

It is my understanding that annual conferences, particularly in the central conferences, work very differently from General Conference, that they are similar to Wesley's conferences. But the General Conference has become something else.

Because General Conference is this lawmaking machine, different from how annual conferences work and also very different from how central conferences work, delegates from outside America have major problems, first to understand the system and then to function and contribute to the process of conferencing. This might be my own confusion about the system, but my impression is that American delegates control the system and are able to use the system in ways no delegates from outside America are able to do. American delegates sometimes also find themselves in confusing parliamentary situations over the legislative process at General Conference. So much time is lost over questions of right procedures and protests against the presiding officers. Sometimes annual conferences elect delegates with judicial competencies to help the delegation to operate in General Conference.

It is my understanding that many delegates from outside America have given up on contributing to the work of General Conference. I do not have any statistics about the petitioners and where they come from, but it is my impression that here also we have a major dominance of petitions from America. My experience as a delegate covers five General Conferences, two of them as sub-committee chair and member of the committee on the agenda. The first two times as a delegate, you learn the system of order of the conference; only after the third time can you understand the system and feel able to contribute. But most delegates do not serve three times or more. My experience is that a few delegates have been delegates many times, and they know the system and are in control of the democratic process, but most delegates struggle with the system and are not in control of their participation. My experience is that annual conferences function much better than the General Conference. The General Conference is experimental each time, and delegates have to learn every time. Is this different for American delegates compared with delegates from the central conferences? Yes, I think all central conference delegates find the General Conference very difficult to work with, because the system of conference work is so different from what they are used to in their home countries and also from the type of political work going on in their home countries' national parliaments.

When Things Go Wrong

For many decades, The United Methodist Church didn't have any problems with its structure. When things go smoothly and gently, nobody asks critical questions of our ecclesiastic conference system. It is always in times of crisis and difficult challenges that focus is put on our system and structure. The crisis we have in The United Methodist Church over the issue of human sexuality has shown how our system is not functioning. The idea to govern a church on the basis of a global *Book of Discipline*, and to think that we can solve the problems by the lawmaking process in General Conference has failed.

How have we ended up in a situation where the *Book of Discipline* states that "the practice of homosexuality is incompatible with Christian teaching," a statement true only in some limited groups in America, even though some groups outside America have adopted the same position? Seen in the perspective of ecumenical, Protestant, and even Roman Catholic theology through the whole history of Christianity, human sexuality has never been a subject of Christian teaching, Christian doctrine, or what Protestant theologians calls *status confessionis*. Human sexuality is a subject of ethics, biblical exegesis, human rights, and civil law. And it is a subject of our understanding of marriage. In my opinion, including a sentence that marks human sexuality as a subject for Christian teaching is a stupidity in the academic theological world outside some small groups in America. It seems to me that some American theologians have constructed their own definition of Christian teaching. According to Christian tradition and history, bishops hold the ministry of teaching, the responsibility of keeping the church to the creeds and basic doctrines, but in the UMC we have limited the bishops' power to influence the paragraphs in the *Discipline*, and by doing so, we have limited the bishops' ability to oversee even the *Book of Discipline* and to take away from the *Discipline* what is a theological stupidity.

The way we have organized Judicial Council also restricts bishops' power of ensuring that new legislation is not in violation of the Constitution, including our doctrinal standards. It is beyond debate that the sentence of homosexuality being incompatible with Christian teaching is not in conflict with our doctrinal standard because no creeds, no Article of Religions, nor other standards of Christian teaching have any paragraphs on human sexuality. There is no piece of text in our doctrinal standards that any human sexual praxis can be incompatible with. The Judicial Council has not succeeded in declaring this clearly wrong formulation null and void. The Denmark Annual Conference appealed to the Judicial Council to declare the formulation null and void, but Judicial Council decided, based on a very old decision (a typical American judicial principle different from European judicial praxis) that Judicial Council cannot rule in a case that is not concrete, even though it is clear that the formulation is in conflict with the Constitution.[33]

General Conference after General Conference has had petitions on human sexuality on the table, but no decisions can be made as long as some American delegates agree with the *Discipline* that "human sexuality is a subject of Christian teaching." Many other delegates find this formulation a stupidity and have stopped discussing the issue on these conditions many years ago, and are frustrated that our system—with Judicial Council's right to make declaratory decisions and the bishops' role to judge in doctrinal issues—has not solved this problem. Many European delegates have given up engaging in any changes in the *Discipline* on this critical issue.

One reason American delegates and delegates from the central conferences are functioning in disharmony with Methodist theology and ecclesiology is that no central conference follows the *Discipline* in the same way the UMC follows the *Discipline* in America. Even from central conference to central conference different parts of the *Discipline* and the ecclesiastical structure have been implemented. In Europe, we don't have the district organization, the local churches do not negotiate salaries for the pastors, the pension system and health insurance are in most places not an issue for the church but for civil society, and the ceremonies of marriage follow the tradition of the country rather than the *Book of Worship*. The annual conferences outside America focus on Article of Religion XXII, saying clearly "that rites and ceremonies should not in all places be the same; for they have been always different, and may be changed according to the diversity of countries, times, and men's manners."

American Methodism was first in using Article XXII to change the ceremonies of weddings from full integration in a church worship service to a very short ceremony that can take place in a secular place; this is very different from weddings in Europe. From America, this ceremony of weddings in secular places distant from an ecclesiastical context has spread to many countries outside America. Praxis is also theology!

The handling of finances, salaries, pension, health insurance, and human aid and money for mission work follow one system in America de-

---

33. UMC Judicial Council, *Memorandum* 1347.

scribed more-or-less in the *Discipline*. In all central conferences, other systems are used, and in these areas of administration the *Discipline* is almost not in use. The UMC apportionment system is part of our connectional obligations, but the system in America has never been implemented in the central conferences. Also, the general agencies play a very different role in America compared to the central conferences.

When the central conferences neither use nor implement quite a number of paragraphs and ecclesiastical structures, then the question is clear: Who decides which paragraphs in the *Discipline* shall be in function and which paragraphs are not important? Why should we follow the paragraph saying that practicing homosexuals cannot be ordained, when we never have followed all the paragraphs on the structure of districts or the paragraphs directing the flow of money in the church? Do our arguments from history, that human sexuality is not a question of Christian teaching, have the same kind of legality as John Wesley's argument from history—based on Lord Peter King's theology, that elders and bishops are the same—when he consecrated Thomas Coke to be a superintendent? It is very difficult to understand in the central conferences that all paragraphs have the same authority.[34]

Even the understanding of democracy is different. In many cultures, the leader is the first to speak on a new subject of discussion, and democracy is understood as voting loyally with the leader. In other cultures, this is considered dictatorship and overruling dominance. In other cultures, it is the democratic praxis that the leader listens to many voices, and when everyone has spoken, the leader can conclude the decision. As a delegate to General Conference, it is easy to see the differences between the delegations. In some delegations, all delegates are focused on the leader, who is the one to give his or her opinion first, then everyone votes in loyalty. It is even seen as a provocation if you speak up on a subject before the leader has marked his or her position. In other delegations, all members are in discussion, and the leader is more silent and more of a listener. Democracy is different in different places of the church. At General Conference, the chair is always asking: "Do we have a second?" "Second!" And before

---

34. *Book of Discipline, 2016 Supplement* (Copenhagen: Northern Europe and Eurasia Central Conference, 2017).

you get an answer, the vote is taken. What happened? In Europe, no chair will ever ask that question, and no member knows what a second is. In General Conference committees, it is the normative praxis that the chair does not vote. In Europe it is the praxis, when you have a tie vote that the chair's vote determines the final outcome, so the chair is always voting. How can anyone think that the General Conference can function according to homogeneous ideas of democracy and only one version of the *Discipline*, when the fact is that the use of the *Discipline* is different from region to region, and the very fundamental understanding of democratic praxis is not the same?

A Way Forward

When General Conference 2016 failed totally to find an acceptable way forward in the ongoing crisis, the decision was made to ask the Council of Bishops to appoint a "Commission on the Way Forward." It was a solution for the General Conference 2016. But it was a strange solution, one that shows the problems of General Conference and its weak ability to govern the church. The General Conference transferred its own task and ability to the Council of Bishops.

General Conference 2019 totally failed again. It was nearly an absurd situation, when the conference-approved Commission on A Way Forward presented a very good One Church Plan, and the majority of bishops openly supported the plan, but it was not approved in General Conference plenary session. A number of other legislations were approved by the plenary session, even though the session was well informed about the unconstitutional character of the petitions, and immediately the approved legislation was declared null and void by the Judicial Council. General Conference 2019 was close to the collapse of the UMC ecclesiastic power structure.

Fine. We need to go forward. I have no power to lead the UMC forward into the future. But if I had the power, my suggestions would be these: Reorganize the church in the direction of a federation of self-governing units. Give priority to the ecclesiastic structure of the church in regions so they can be an incarnational church in that region, and give up the American praxis and culture of the church, including the "global church thinking." Limit the general *Book of Discipline* to the Constitution and a new major part with our history and Our Theological Task. Delegate all decisions on organization and guidelines for the work of the church to the annual conferences and the central conferences. Let the central conferences develop their right to adapt and amend the Social Principles. General agencies are functioning well in America, but I suggest organizing new agencies in each of the central conferences to work in their own area.

Then change the balance of power between the Council of Bishops and General Conference. Elect all bishops for limited terms, and let bishops go back to elder status when their term has ended. Change membership rules so that all elders and bishops are members of a local church and do not hold church membership in annual conferences or the Council of Bishops. Give the bishops the power of the teaching ministry on doctrinal issues. Give the bishops the power of supervision, not only over pastors and congregations, but also over the *Book of Discipline* and the institutions of the church.

Finally, change the Judicial Council so that it can stop being the battleground of conservative and liberal church politicians. Take away the Judicial Council's right to make Declaratory Decisions. Let all issues of constitutionality go back to General Conference. Let the General Conference work with a consensus method and not the Robert's Rules system, as in the synods of other churches and the World Council of Churches.

I think this will bring The United Methodist Church more in harmony with what Wesley understood as *conference* and the *elder-episcopacy*. And I think it will take The United Methodist Church away from the framework of having the parallel structure of the American administration of the nation, with its strict division of the branches of legislative power, executive power, and judicial power. My vote is for transforming The United Methodist Church in the federal direction and empowering the annual conferences to be more incarnational in their context of culture, politics, and history. I think it would stimulate the mission of the church.

Concerning the whole issue about imperialism and the ecclesiastical structure of the UMC in the present time, it is very helpful to use Wesley's agenda from the first Methodist conference: "What do we meet for? To consider before God: 1. What to teach? 2. How to teach? 3. What to do? i.e., doctrine, discipline, and practice."[35] Using this agenda, the conference would focus on the work and mission of the church, and then the ecclesiastical issues as an empiric experience could be left over to the church historians.

---

35. *Wesley Works*, Vol. 10: *The Methodist Societies. The Minutes of Conference*, 120.

5

A GLOBAL ETHIC FOR A DIVIDED CHURCH

Darryl W. Stephens

On May 17, 2016, the highest legislative body of The United Methodist Church (UMC) re-approved a motion to rewrite this church's primary statement of social teachings. The petition read as follows: "The General Board of Church and Society will continue to give priority to developing Social Principles for a worldwide church and will refer this work to the General Conference 2020."[1] Intended to address the long-standing problem of U.S.-centrism in this church's social witness, this initiative had "the goal of making [the Social Principles] more succinct, theologically founded and globally relevant."[2] The same day, General Conference ground to a legislative halt over the issue of homosexuality, pleading for help from its bishops to find a way forward for this deeply divided denomination.[3] Facing the real possibility of imminent schism, the Council of

---

1. World-wide Social Principles (60062-CA-NonDis-G), as amended by the legislative committee "Church and Society 1," at "2016 Legislation Tracking," http://ee.umc.org/who-we-are/legislation-tracking (accessed May 21, 2022).

2. These goals were articulated in legislation from the prior General Conference—the work that the General Board of Church and Society would "continue" in 2016–2020. "Revise Social Principles" (20986-CA-Non-Dis), referred to the Connectional Table, at "General Conference 2012: Legislation Tracking," http://calms2012.umc.org/Menu.aspx (accessed May 3, 2022). For background of U.S.-centrism, see Darryl W. Stephens, "A Cross-Cultural Dialogue of Social Principles," *Methodist History* 54:2 (Jan 2016): 102–16.

3. Kathy L. Gilbert and Sam Hodges, "Conference pleads with bishops for leadership," *UM News*, May 17, 2016. https://www.umnews.org/en/news/conference-pleads-with-bishops-for-leadership (accessed May 3, 2022).

Bishops proposed a study commission and subsequently issued a call for a special session of its normally quadrennial General Conference to meet in February 2019.[4] The presenting issue was whether this church should maintain its prohibitions against same-sex marriage and the ordination of homosexuals, proscriptions based on the Social Principles. Unresolved internal divisions aside, the UMC's General Board of Church and Society (GBCS) proceeded to draft a document for public comment in April 2018.[5] After the 2019 General Conference, it completed work on the "United Methodist Revised Social Principles" and submitted the 2020 draft for consideration at the next General Conference.[6]

The Social Principles document offers a window into how United Methodists understand their faith in relation to each other and the world beyond this church. It functions as not only a public statement but also a practice, a site of intradenominational contestation about the character and identity of the UMC.[7] Homosexuality and the global nature of this church are but two of many issues contested within this arena. The discourse about homosexuality has been overt and openly divisive; the discourse about U.S.-centrism abutting this church's increasingly international character has been less prominent though no less politicized.[8] However, the Social Principles provides a record only of the majority opinion, not the debate itself. It thus illumines neither homosexuality nor U.S.-centrism with the "persuasion and reasonable discourse" that David Hollenbach identified as "the proper mode of public participation by religious believers."[9] Absent reason and per-

---

4. Heather Hahn, "Bishops set date for special 2019 General Conference," *UM News*, April 25, 2017. https://www.umnews.org/en/news/bishops-set-date-for-special-2019-general-conference (accessed May 3, 2022).

5. GBCS, "The United Methodist Social Principles: Working Draft 1, April 11, 2018," https://ntcumc.org/English_Draft_of_the_Revised_Social_Principles.pdf (accessed March 27, 2023).

6. GBCS, "Social Principles 2020: United Methodist Revised Social Principles," https://umcsocial-principles2021.org/ (accessed March 28, 2023).

7. Darryl W. Stephens, *Methodist Morals: Social Principles in the Public Church's Witness* (Knoxville: University of Tennessee Press, 2016), 6.

8. Darryl W. Stephens, "A Widening Stream: Comparing and Contrasting United Methodism's 1968 and 2008 Mergers," *Methodist History* 58:3 (April 2020): 165–76.

9. David Hollenbach, SJ, *The Global Face of Public Faith: Politics, Human Rights, and Christian Ethics* (Washington, DC: Georgetown University Press, 2003), 14.

suasion, what are the possibilities and potential for this document to function as a global ethic for a divided church?

The UMC's attempt to revise its social witness while navigating denominational schism reveals tensions between global relevance and what divides this church. In evidence is a struggle with empire, defined by Joerg Rieger as "large and ever-changing conglomerates of power that are aimed at controlling all aspects of our lives."[10] This church has difficulty acknowledging its history of empire and predominant mindset of White racism, and its Social Principles has little to say directly but much to imply about this topic. Amid the rise of nationalism across global politics and long-simmering intradenominational division about homosexuality, a shared statement on human rights and cross-cultural critique, among other issues, would be an important counter-witness to the moral animosity shaping current political discourse: within the UMC, the United States, and the world. Does the Social Principles discourse contain a "theological surplus," to use Rieger's phrase,[11] sufficient to overcome this denomination's tendency toward empire, whether it be based on nationality, race, or sexuality?

This chapter explores the potential of the 2020 draft Social Principles to serve as a global ethic for a divided church. It identifies two significant sites of ideological division within the UMC: competing views on homosexuality and an implicit perspective of White, U.S.-centrism. A pervasive Anglo-American mindset within the UMC highlights the need for articulating a global ethic of human rights and enabling cross-cultural dialogue through this church's Social Principles. Rieger's notion of surplus, "anything that points beyond the status quo," provides glimpses of grace beyond the structures of empire.[12] This chapter argues that the theological surplus of the 2020 draft Social Principles is found not in its assertions of moral stances but in its capacity to enable moral deliberation and transform relationships of power.

---

10.   Joerg Rieger, *Christ and Empire: From Paul to Postcolonial Times* (Minneapolis: Fortress, 2007), vii.

11.   Joerg Rieger, *No Rising Tide: Theology, Economics, and the Future* (Minneapolis: Fortress, 2009), 162.

12.   Rieger, *Christ and Empire*, 9.

A Divided Church

The UMC claims a membership diverse in traditions and moral frameworks. This church counts among its founders not only John and Charles Wesley, both Anglican priests, but also preachers from the German Reformed, Mennonite, Lutheran, and Free Church traditions. Geographically, United Methodism spans four continents: North America, Africa, Europe, and Asia. Culturally, Methodism in the United States reflects multiple ethnic and racial groups, including the diversity and divisions of White Protestantism. White, U.S. Methodists gathered at camp meeting revivals and sat together as trustees of hospitals and universities; they also found themselves on opposite sides of many cultural rifts, including slavery vs. abolition, evolution vs. creationism, and fundamentalism vs. modernism. Political divides between Trump-supporting Republicans and progressive Democrats are no exception. George W. Bush, Dick Cheney, Jeff Sessions, and Hillary Rodham Clinton all share membership in this denomination. United Methodists can be found on all sides. The difficulty, past and present, occurs when this diversity can no longer be accommodated within one ecclesial polity.

Ideological Division: Competing Views on Homosexuality

Debates over homosexuality have served as a significant arena for ideological contestation in the UMC since its establishment in 1968. Some Methodists argue that homosexuality is a U.S.-based problem that liberals and progressives are imposing on African delegates and annual conferences and that Christian sexual ethics has nothing to do with culture. For example, the Social Witness statement of the newly formed Global Methodist Church assumes a "consensus vision transcending cultures" when interpreting and "affirming a scriptural view of sexuality and gender."[13] Other Methodists, who hold the view that homosexual activity is not universally

---

13. Global Methodist Church, *Transitional Book of Doctrines and Discipline* (updated October 10, 2021), ¶¶201–202, https://globalmethodist.org/wp-content/uploads/2022/04/Transitional-Discipline.2022041257.pdf (accessed May 3, 2022).

sinful, argue that conservatives and traditionalists are imposing their own cultural and historically located values on others through church law, rejecting sources of knowledge that might complicate this depiction.

The conservative movement in the UMC traces its political beginnings to an article by Charles Keysor, originally published in 1966, in which he spoke out for Methodism's "silent minority . . . variously called 'evangelicals' or 'conservatives' or 'fundamentalists.'"[14] Keysor spoke out against a reigning theological liberalism in Methodism's church structures, leadership, and seminaries. As the UMC took up the issue of homosexuality, Keysor's silent minority found its voice. In 1972, General Conference declared "the practice of homosexuality . . . incompatible with Christian teaching" even as it advocated for the "human and civil rights" of gays and lesbians.[15] Subsequent General Conferences built on this foundation in the Social Principles, forbidding the ordination of "self-avowed practicing homosexuals,"[16] celebration of same-sex marriages or unions, and the use of general church funds to promote the acceptance of homosexuality.[17] Conservative caucuses within the UMC became increasingly more organized and powerful, voicing their theological convictions through a series of declarations. For example, the Houston Declaration, written in 1987, asserted "three crucial truths" for the church: 1) primacy of scripture; 2) the Trinity; and 3) heterosexuality for ordained ministers.[18] It is no accident of history that this declaration was written barely six months after then-retired Houston area Bishop Finis Crutchfield died of AIDS—

---

14. Charles W. Keysor, "Methodism's Silent Minority," *Christian Advocate*, July 14, 1966, https://web.archive.org/web/20220517132650/https://goodnewsmag.org/2017/01/24/methodisms-silent-minority-4/ (accessed March 28, 2023).

15. *The Book of Discipline of The United Methodist Church, 1972* (Nashville: The United Methodist Publishing House, 1972), ¶72.C. See discussion in Stephens, Methodist Morals, 38–39.

16. *The Book of Discipline of The United Methodist Church, 1984* (Nashville: The United Methodist Publishing House, 1984), ¶402.2.

17. Ashley Boggan, "Human Sexuality and The United Methodist Church: Timeline 1964–2014," May 2015, https://s3.amazonaws.com/Website_Properties/connectional-table/documents/Human-sexuality-and-united-methodist-church-timeline.pdf (accessed May 3, 2022).

18. The Confessing Movement within the UMC, "The Houston Declaration," December 15, 1987. https://docs.wixstatic.com/ugd/6dcfa3_dcb0487b20b940caa065dc79b0b05f42.pdf (accessed May 3, 2022).

his sexual "orientation" and "practice" posthumously contested.[19] In their concern about appropriate sexuality (and also abortion, to some extent), conservative United Methodists have mirrored a larger, U.S. political discourse led by the so-called "religious right."

United Methodists in 2023 must look back more than thirty years to find the most recent church-wide study of homosexuality. From 1988–1992, under a mandate from General Conference, a committee of theologically diverse United Methodists studied, conducted interviews, and held listening sessions across the UMC. While the committee could not arrive at a consensus on the issue, they agreed on lists of things the church can and cannot responsibly teach regarding homosexuality.[20] The majority report asserted:

> The present state of knowledge and insight in the biblical, theological, ethical, biological, psychological, and sociological fields does not provide a satisfactory basis upon which the church can responsibly maintain the condemnation of homosexual practice.[21]

For many conservatives, beginning with "the present state of knowledge" was itself evidence of the problematic division within the church.

United Methodist conservatives argue that Scripture and tradition, not evolving scientific knowledge, should be the basis of the church's stance on homosexuality. A 22-page document produced by the Wesleyan Covenant Association's Task Force on Sexual Brokenness in December 2021 makes clear an understanding of sexuality and gender having nothing to do with science.[22] This document affirms, along with the Global Methodist Church, "a scriptural view of sexuality and gender."[23]

---

19. "Bishop Who Died of AIDS Called Gay," *The Washington Post*, June 6, 1987, https://www.washingtonpost.com/archive/local/1987/06/06/bishop-who-died-of-aids-called-gay/0bbaf688-f53c-4740-a15a-152ca3d2550e/ (accessed May 3, 2022).

20. *The Church Studies Homosexuality: Study Book* (Nashville: Cokesbury, 1994), 29–33.

21. Boggan, "Human Sexuality," 8.

22. Wesleyan Covenant Association, WCA Task Force on Sexual Brokenness, "Sexual Holiness, Wholeness, and Brokenness Task Force Report," December 2021, https://wesleyancovenant.org/wp-content/uploads/2021/10/Human-Sexuality-Report-2.pdf (accessed May 3, 2022).

23. Compare: Wesleyan Covenant Association, "Sexual Holiness"; Global Methodist Church, *Transitional Book*, ¶202.8.

To address "sexual brokenness," the document posits a "Christian sexual counterculture" rooted in the kingdom, in contrast to the culture of our "earthly surroundings."[24] Both the Sexual Brokenness document and the *Transitional Book of Doctrines and Discipline* seek to conserve a particular, immutable view of human nature, including sexuality and gender, as intended by God and appropriate to discipleship—complicated neither by the diversity of witness within Scripture, its history of interpretation, nor changes in culture, society, and medicine over the past 2,000 years.

Thus, before the 1992 General Conference had a chance to consider the church-wide study, a group of conservative United Methodists objected to the committee's majority report. Their "Memphis Declaration" commanded its intended readers, "Let us cease to debate homosexual practice as if the witness of the Scripture and the tradition of the Church were not clear from the beginning."[25] Having already discerned their position, they were no longer interested in engaging in discussion with those who disagreed. Their influence was significant. While General Conference adopted a new statement in the Social Principles on "Rights of Homosexual Persons" at the committee's recommendation, the rest of their report was rejected.[26] The 1992 General Conference did not alter the UMC's prohibitive language within church structures. Furthermore, subsequent General Conferences repeatedly refused to amend the Social Principles to acknowledge any disagreement in this church about homosexuality. Disagreement, itself evidence of a theological surplus beyond the control of church law, was too much of a threat to the power structures for it to be officially acknowledged.

A shutdown of discourse prevents productive argumentation and learning within a church discerning how to live with disagreement. Two sub-

---

24. Wesleyan Covenant Association, "Sexual Holiness," 8–10.

25. The Confessing Movement within the UMC, "The Memphis Declaration," January 25, 1992. https://docs.wixstatic.com/ugd/6dcfa3_5e7c1833374341bcae02d11834e4b67d.pdf (accessed May 3, 2022).

26. *The Book of Discipline of The United Methodist Church, 1992* (Nashville: The United Methodist Publishing House, 1992), ¶71.G.

sequent church-wide consultations notwithstanding,[27] divisions within the UMC after the 1992 General Conference devolved into political infighting rather than the "holy conferencing" Methodists are so keen to claim as a distinctive means of grace. The Houston Declaration, Memphis Declaration, and other foundational documents of the Confessing Movement within the UMC might be considered constructive contributions to the ongoing moral argument that animates this church. However, their authors' refusal to continue debate revealed a deep rift in this denomination, one that has only grown larger over the years. Despite passing a resolution in "Opposition to Homophobia and Heterosexism" in 2008, this church has long-ceased healthy discourse on the issue of homosexuality.[28] Although conflicts over homosexuality pose the most obvious threat of schism, this is not the only or even the most significant source of division within the UMC.

Ideological Division: Ecclesial Identity and the Presumptions of White Christian America

Despite inaction on a level of polity and a declared end to debate on homosexuality by conservatives, the UMC could not insulate itself from internal and external change. Since Keysor's clarion call to orthodox Methodists, the share of members residing outside the United States increased dramatically. In 1986, membership outside the United States accounted for no more than 5 percent of the total. Every subsequent decade showed dramatic shifts toward internationalization. By 1996, this share had risen to 12 percent, by 2006, 30 percent, by 2016, 45 percent, and by 2022, 53 percent of the total membership of the UMC resided

27. General Board of Discipleship and General Commission on Christian Unity and Interreligious Concerns, "Report on the Consultation on Scriptural Authority and the Nature of God's Revelation," http://gbod.org.s3.amazonaws.com/legacy/kintera/entry_1873/17/SCRIP_AUTHORITY_REPORT.PDF (accessed May 21, 2022); United Methodist Commission on Christian Unity and Interreligious Concerns, "In Search of Unity: A Conversation with Recommendations for the Unity of The United Methodist Church Dialogue on Theological Diversity within The United Methodist Church, Nashville, November 20–21, 1997; Dallas, February 19–20, 1998," http://www.umaffirm.org/cornet/unity.html (accessed May 21, 2022).

28. *The Book of Resolutions of The United Methodist Church, 2008* (Nashville: The United Methodist Publishing House, 2008), 132–33.

outside the United States.[29] Concurrently, the non-White racial and ethnic composition of this church's U.S. membership almost doubled, from less than 5 percent in 1996 to nearly 9 percent in 2016.[30] This trend is due both to an numerical increase in Black, Hispanic, Asian American, Pacific-Islander, and Native American membership as well as a 21 percent decline in White membership during the twenty-year span.[31] These numbers mirror the broader trends characterizing the end of what Robert P. Jones named "White Christian America," suggesting that the UMC mirrors the cultural power struggles of the United States.[32] While the UMC is no longer composed of the overwhelmingly White, U.S. constituency presumed in past generations, the presumptions of White Christian America still permeate its polity and practice.

For many decades, U.S. Methodism tried to maintain both its White U.S. power structure and a desire for worldwide influence. In Rieger's language, U.S. Methodism participated and still participates in "the spirit of empire."[33] Methodist missionaries in the nineteenth century traveled from the United States to many countries to share their version of the gospel. As these initiatives took root, the Methodist Episcopal Church allowed for some degree of local autonomy while still maintaining U.S. control, designating "central conferences" to carry out "the work of the Church outside the United States of America."[34] Similarly, the "Central Jurisdiction" created in 1939 was designed to ensure racial separation among U.S. Methodists, allowing for some degree of autonomy for African Americans while maintaining White control of church structures. Methodists elimi-

---

29.   Data provided by William Furones, Data Management Specialist, based on data submitted to and processed by the General Council on Finance and Administration (personal emails dated July 16, 2018, and June 14, 2022). See also The Connectional Table, *The Mission Is Yet Alive: 2018 State of the Church Report* (Nashville: United Methodist Communications, 2018), 10, http://web.archive.org/web/20221102023747/http://ee.umc.org/who-we-are/state-of-the-church-report (accessed May 3, 2022).

30.   David W. Scott, "American UMC Decline Is a White People Problem," *UM & Global*, March 9, 2017, www.umglobal.org/2017/03/american-umc-decline-is-white-people.html (accessed May 3, 2022).

31.   Scott, "American UMC Decline."

32.   Robert P. Jones, *The End of White Christian America* (New York: Simon & Schuster, 2016), 51.

33.   Néstor Míguez, Joerg Rieger, and Jung Mo Sung, *Beyond the Spirit of Empire: Theology and Politics in a New Key*, Reclaiming Liberation Theology (London: SCM Press, 2009).

34.   Methodist Episcopal Church, *Doctrines and Discipline of the Methodist Episcopal Church 1924* (New York: Methodist Book Concern, 1924), ¶95.2(6).

nated this church's racially segregated structures during the merger of The Methodist Church and The Evangelical United Brethren Church in 1968 when forming the UMC. In fact, the constitution of this new church included an article on racial justice. However, the structural inequities of central conferences remained.

The UMC includes seven central conferences spanning three continents: Congo, Africa Central, West Africa, Central and Southern Europe, Germany, Northern Europe and Eurasia, and the Philippines. Central conferences are authorized to amend and adapt the General *Discipline* "as the conditions in the respective areas may require."[35] Thus, there are multiple versions of the *Discipline* adapted for use around the world, in many different languages, all of which operate within the UMC.[36] Thus, central conference delegates attend General Conference, which, as of 2023, has always been held in the United States, legislate the *Discipline*, and return home with the ability to alter the *Discipline* to fit their contexts. This ability to adopt the *Discipline* is evidence of the kind of theological surplus that the White, U.S. empire could not fully contain. In a previous publication, I described this surplus as a mask, enabling difference within a supposed unity.[37]

This unusual legal arrangement has a precedent in the Anglican Church. A resolution by the 1867 Lambeth Conference explained the relation of the "Mother-Church" to its overseas outposts in this way:

> That, in order to the binding of the Churches of our colonial empire and the missionary Churches beyond them in the closest union with the Mother-Church, it is necessary that they receive and maintain without alteration the standards of faith and doctrine as now in use in that Church. That, nevertheless, each province should have the right to make such adaptations and additions to the services of the Church as its peculiar circumstances may require. Provided, that no change or addition be made inconsistent with

---

35. *The Book of Discipline of The United Methodist Church, 2016* (Nashville: The United Methodist Publishing House, 2016), ¶¶28 and 31.5; see also ¶543.7.

36. For discussion of central conference adaptations, see Stephens, *Methodist Morals*, chapter five.

37. Darryl W. Stephens, "Face of Unity or Mask over Difference? The Social Principles in the Central Conferences of The United Methodist Church," *Thinking About Religion* 5 (2005), http://web.archive.org/web/20201027170912/http://organizations.uncfsu.edu/ncrsa/journal/v05/stephens_face.htm (accessed May 3, 2022).

the spirit and principles of the Book of Common Prayer, and that all such changes be liable to revision by any synod of the Anglican Communion in which the said province shall be represented.[38]

While U.S. Methodists have never explicitly embraced the language of "Mother-Church" and "colonial empire," the effect and reality of this asymmetrical arrangement of power within church structures remains. U.S. Methodists have assuaged their mild discomfort with these power relations through near-continuous studies of central conference relations to the U.S. church since 1948, all the while maintaining structural asymmetries between U.S. and non-U.S. membership within this church's polity. For example, in 2018, United Methodist conferences in Africa accounted for 46.78 percent of the denomination's membership but paid only 0.11 percent of total apportionments.[39] The structures of empire persist.

The exceptional and often secondary status of central conferences within the UMC is an expression of an ingrained, imperialistic attitude present among White, U.S. Methodists from very early in the movement.[40] For example, in a study of Methodist involvement in the Sand Creek Massacre of 1864, historian Gary Roberts identified a combination of civic theology and sense of cultural superiority among White Methodists as an enabling factor in this tragic and violent incident.[41] An Anglo-American mindset of superiority seemed to justify domination of native peoples by Whites, including this massacre led by a Methodist clergyman and enabled by a Methodist politician. Although the Sand Creek Massacre was widely condemned at the time, the Methodist Episcopal Church

---

38. Compare UMC *Book of Discipline, 2016*, ¶31.5 to Anglican Consultative Council, "The Lambeth Conference: Resolutions Archive from 1867," Anglican Communion Office (2005), 3, http://www.anglicancommunion.org/media/127716/1867.pdf (accessed May 3, 2022).

39. "2018 Membership and Apportionments Data for the Africa Central Conference," https://www.gcfa.org/media/1921/5b-2018-africa-cc-membership-and-apportionments-data.pdf (accessed May 21, 2022).

40. This paragraph is condensed from Darryl W. Stephens, "Sand Creek: Repenting of an Imperialistic Mind-set Then and Now," *United Methodist Insight*, April 7, 2016. http://um-insight.net/general-conference/2016-general-conference/sand-creek-repenting-of-an-imperialistic-mind-set-then-and-n/ (accessed May 3, 2022).

41. Gary L. Roberts, "Remembering the Sand Creek Massacre: A Historical Review of Methodist Involvement, Influence, and Response," in the *Daily Christian Advocate Advance Edition* (The United Methodist Publishing House, 2016), 1235–1408. http://ee.umc.org/who-we-are/gc2016-advance-edition-daily-christian-advocate.

remained silent.[42] A nationalistic mission driven by a sense of Manifest Destiny created a self-fulfilling circumstance in which White Methodists understood their faith through the lens of their nation and the progress of their nation as evidence of the truth of their faith.[43] "Methodism had become an establishment church," according to Roberts, embracing "American exceptionalism and destiny as tenets of Church policy and ministry."[44] As Methodism continued to grow, becoming the predominant sect in U.S. Christendom, every incremental achievement of greater domination fed back into an even greater sense of divine favor. These examples of White Methodist relations with Native Americans exemplify the kind of imperialistic attitudes and structures at work throughout the multinational and multicultural UMC.

White, U.S. United Methodists are still coming to terms with this imperialistic mindset. The UMC has made strides toward addressing these aspects of its past through official acts of repentance. General Conference engaged in an Act of Repentance for Racism in 2000 and an Act of Repentance toward Healing Relationships with Indigenous Peoples in 2012, which precipitated Roberts's historical account. The ceremony in 2012 included testimonies and reports by Native American United Methodists as well as a worship service featuring Native Americans with indigenous garb and musical instruments.

General Conference's wholehearted embrace of native drums and headdresses, however, did not sit well with some African delegates to General Conference. Early Methodist missionaries to Africa taught that these things were pagan: their indigenous clothing, music, and practices were considered incompatible with Christian teaching. For example, in many parts of Africa today, a "Christian" wedding requires that the bride wear a Western-style white bridal gown. The offense felt among African delegates to General Conference was understandable. Their parents, grandparents, and great-grandparents had been taught to abandon their drums and traditional practices to become Methodist only for later generations to

---

42. Roberts, "Remembering the Sand Creek Massacre," 1378, 1393, 1397.

43. Roberts, "Remembering the Sand Creek Massacre," 1287.

44. Roberts, "Remembering the Sand Creek Massacre," 1395.

travel to the United States for a General Conference celebrating and worshipping with these very things. Vestiges of the U.S. colonial empire and its "Mother-Church" of Methodism, not to mention charges of cultural appropriation, present a continuing conundrum for articulating a global ethic of human rights and cross-cultural critique through this church's Social Principles.

Silence and Disagreement

As the UMC continues its experiment of global polity spanning many different languages and nations, it is even more imperative that this church's Social Principles encourage and nurture faithful and thoughtful cross-cultural dialogue and critique. This task involves more than just translating the Social Principles into ten different languages.[45] To invite theological surplus, it must be more than a consensus document articulating the lowest common denominator of agreement. To address disagreement within this "worldwide" church, the Social Principles must not only assert shared morality but also equip church members to name where and how they disagree.

The 2020 Social Principles draft is much more forthright about the need to live together amid disagreement than any previous statement of Social Principles. Where the 2016 Social Principles Preamble "affirm[s] our unity in Jesus Christ" and "acknowledge[es] differences in applying our faith in different cultural contexts," the 2020 draft "respect[s] differences within Christ's Body," such as "life experiences . . . shaped by . . . sexual orientation and gender," and considers "differences . . . a precious gift and daunting challenge."[46] The 2020 draft Preamble asserts that "faithful Christians need to face their disagreements . . . and not cover differences with false claims of consensus or unanimity."[47] However, neither the 2018 nor the 2020 draft document lived up to this aspiration.

---

45. GBCS, https://umcsocialprinciples2021.org/translations (accessed May 3, 2022).

46. Contrast UMC *Book of Discipline, 2016*, 106, to GBCS, "Social Principles 2020," 6.

47. GBCS, "Social Principles 2020," 7.

Both drafts silence rather than face disagreement within the UMC. The 2018 draft omitted statements on human sexuality and rights in relation to sexual orientation, noting, "This section will be drafted after the 2019 Special Session of the General Conference."[48] If the Social Principles is understood as both a site of and a participant in the moral deliberation of the UMC, it would have been helpful for the drafters to contribute to the conversation leading up to General Conference 2019. However, the 2018 draft's silence on the issue ceded participation in this discussion. Did the drafters envision the Social Principles as only a documentation of the results of debate at General Conference? If so, can the Social Principles be reimagined as a catalyst and resource for productive dialogue on contentious issues within the church?

After the 2019 General Conference, GBCS continued its work revising the document. In a statement of "basic rights and freedoms," the 2020 draft rejected discrimination based on sexual orientation, a commitment unambiguously asserted six times in the document[49]—despite the "Traditionalist Plan" adopted by General Conference in 2019, which tightened the strictures and punishments against LGBTQ persons and their allies in the UMC. The 2020 draft Social Principles based its assertions on the "inherent dignity and worth" of every individual and the "basic rights and freedoms" due every person as part of "God's gracious act in creation" and "revealed fully in Jesus's incarnation of divine love."[50] Thus, the 2020 draft clearly declared, "we are committed to supporting the equal rights, liberties and protections of all people, regardless of sexual orientation or gender identity."[51] Absent in the 2020 draft were the contentious and long-standing statements in the Social Principles declaring "the practice of homosexuality . . . incompatible with Christian teaching"[52] and

---

48. GBCS, Social Principles Working Draft, 21. Contrast UMC *Book of Discipline, 2016,* ¶¶161.G and 162.J to GBCS, "Social Principles: Working Draft," 13, 21. The 2018 draft also omitted any definition of "marriage as the union of one man and one woman"; contrast UMC *Book of Discipline, 2016,* ¶161.C to "Social Principles: Working Draft," 12.

49. GBCS, "Social Principles 2020," 36; see also 34, 37, and 39.

50. GBCS, "Social Principles 2020," 35–36.

51. GBCS, "Social Principles 2020," 39.

52. *Book of Discipline, 2016,* ¶161.G.

defining marriage as "between a man and a woman."[53] Also absent was any acknowledgment, much less repentance, of the UMC's longstanding proscriptions. Eliding the church's stances on same-sex marriage and gay ordination, the 2020 draft fails to perform as a means by which United Methodists can uncover and face up to their disagreements. The 2020 draft, while asserting essential rights for LGBTQ persons in society, does little to adjudicate these rights within UMC polity. Rieger's theological surplus is found not in assertion or silence but rather in the new relationships forged through deliberation about these rights.

Rights and Deliberation

The language of human rights is an indication of moral contestation within a community. According to Jon P. Gunnemann, "Rights language is the language of dispute."[54] Rights language becomes necessary in social situations where the moral presuppositions of various actors differ, especially when there is not a common moral framework shared by all parties.[55] Recourse to rights becomes important when the tacit moral assumptions shared by a community no longer suffice to guide action, that is, when the assumptions of one moral agent conflict with another. Although this situation can happen within a moral community, with otherwise shared assumptions, it happens most often between different moral communities, with differing moral assumptions. "To claim to 'have a right' . . . is to claim participation in a moral community . . . that either differs from or transcends the morality of the community with which one has the conflict."[56] In a church that includes many different cultures and communities, the language of rights serves both to assert shared understandings and to indicate that these assertions have been or continue to be contested within and beyond the church. These sites of contestation reveal differen-

---

53. *Book of Discipline, 2016,* ¶161.C.

54. Jon P. Gunnemann, "Human Rights and Modernity: The Truth of the Fiction of Individual Rights," *Journal of Religious Ethics* 16:1 (1988): 171.

55. Gunnemann, "Human Rights and Modernity," 163–65.

56. Gunnemann, "Human Rights and Modernity," 165–66.

tials of power and a resultant theological surplus freed, if only momentarily, of the logic of empire.

The concept of human rights is a central aspect of Methodist social witness. Not only were Methodists heavily involved in creating and supporting the Universal Declaration of Human Rights (UDHR), the UMC and its predecessors have displayed an unwavering public commitment to human rights.[57] As a matter of doctrine, the UMC asserts within its Confession of Faith, "We believe . . . governments should be based on, and be responsible for, the recognition of human rights under God."[58] Furthermore, the Social Principles document shares substantive commitments with much of the UDHR and the International Covenant on Civil and Political Rights.[59] Thus, it is no surprise that the draft 2020 Social Principles also voices support for a wide variety of individual human rights.

Assertions of rights in the 2020 draft Social Principles are based on seeing others as bearers of the image of God—an equalizing premise amid differences of power. Consistent with prior editions of the Social Principles, the 2020 draft "affirm[s] the important work of the United Nations"[60] and upholds the UDHR as a definitive explication of basic rights.[61] The 2020 draft grounds "basic human rights and freedoms" in "God's gracious act in creation" and pledges "to protect these rights and freedoms within the church" and society.[62] The "dignity and worth" of every person is mentioned eleven times in the 2020 draft,[63] functioning as a shorthand for the UMC's commitment to human rights grounded in God's good creation. This connection is made explicit in the section on

---

57. Numerous resolutions by the UMC establish a solid tradition in support of human rights, for example: "Statement Concerning Church Participation in Public Affairs"; "The United Methodist Church and Peace"; and "Globalization and Its Impact on Human Dignity and Human Rights," to name only a few. UMC *Book of Resolutions, 1968* (Nashville: The United Methodist Publishing House, 1968), 38–41; UMC, *Book of Resolutions, 2016* (Nashville: The United Methodist Publishing House, 2016), 634–49, 528–29.

58. *Book of Discipline, 2016*, ¶104.

59. Stephens, *Methodist Morals*, 82–92.

60. GBCS, "Social Principles 2020," 32.

61. GBCS, "Social Principles 2020," 35, 38.

62. GBCS, "Social Principles 2020," 35.

63. GBCS, "Social Principles 2020," 6, 16, 17, 25, 27, 32, 33, 36, 37.

Basic Rights and Freedoms: "We condemn all attempts to deny individuals their basic rights or freedoms or to strip human beings of their inherent dignity and worth."[64] Then follow ten subsections asserting rights pertaining to various groups and contexts, including women and girls, men and boys, "indigenous, native, and aboriginal communities," and "sexual orientations and gender identities."[65] However, while asserting support for many human rights, the draft fails to guide the reader in understanding when or how the language of rights applies.

Does the concept of rights apply to race, for example? The 2020 draft upholds basic rights and freedoms for all individuals but does not employ the language of rights to address race. The 2020 draft condemns "racism, ethnocentrism, and tribalism" and rejects laws and practices that discriminate on these bases,[66] but it does not use the word race at all. How is one to understand the 2020 draft's subsection against environmental racism, for example, in the absence of any definition or discussion of race? In contrast, the robust statement of "Rights of Racial and Ethnic Persons" in the 2016 Social Principles clearly defines personal and systemic racism, "recognize[s] racism as sin," encourages "oppressed people . . . to demand their just and equal rights as members of society," and supports affirmative action.[67] The 2020 draft does none of these things. Admittedly, the label "racial and ethnic persons" does not translate well from the United States to a global context. However, eliminating this subsection in the 2020 draft leaves the problem of racism inadequately addressed.

Given Methodism's past complicities with empire in the form of White supremacy, particularly by condoning slavery and supporting racially segregated structures in church and society, a steadfast commitment to the rights of persons regardless of race cannot be taken as a given. The draft statement on Basic Rights and Freedoms asserts, "in the face of historic wrongs perpetrated against indigenous peoples, enslaved African peoples and other marginalized groups, we call for forthright confession and re-

---

64. GBCS, "Social Principles 2020," 36.

65. GBCS, "Social Principles 2020," 36–39.

66. GBCS, "Social Principles 2020," 29.

67. *Book of Discipline, 2016,* ¶162.A.

pentance as well as concrete acts of reparation to redress past and present forms of social injustice."[68] However, this call raises more questions than it answers. Why is the called-for "forthright confession" left unstated in this draft of Social Principles, particularly when it was so elaborately stated in the 2016 Social Principles? How does this call to repentance differ from the UMC's prior act of repentance for racism? Which current resolutions support reparations, as envisioned here? Why are the "past and present forms of social injustice" against "enslaved African peoples" not named as racism? Antiracist commitments could have been communicated with references to the UMC's constitutional commitment to racial justice, its Act of Repentance for Racism (adopted in 2000 and renewed in 2008), and its numerous resolutions on race relations and racial justice. Speaking out against discrimination is not a sufficient substitute for asserting human rights.

In contrast to race, the rights of indigenous peoples and the context for the UMC's repentance are more evident in the draft Social Principles. The 2020 draft invokes the language of rights for "indigenous, native, and aboriginal communities," appealing to the UDHR for an articulation of basic human rights.[69] The 2020 draft condemns genocide, calls for enforcement of treaties, recognizes indigenous land rights, and supports the revitalization of indigenous languages and cultures.[70] The 2020 draft also recognizes the disproportionate impact of environmental degradation on indigenous peoples, affirming their wisdom and need for self-determination in these matters.[71] However, the 2020 draft romanticizes indigenous peoples and their "traditional wisdom" of "living in harmony and balance with the earth."[72] Such idealization "denies Indian personhood" and actually "contributes to the exploitation of Natives."[73] Thus, the uncritical affirmation of "traditional

68. GBCS, "Social Principles 2020," 36.

69. GBCS, "Social Principles 2020," 38.

70. GBCS, "Social Principles 2020," 38.

71. GBCS, "Social Principles 2020," 10–11.

72. GBCS, "Social Principles 2020," 12–13.

73. Jace Weaver, "Introduction," in *Defending Mother Earth: Native American Perspectives on Environmental Justice*, edited by Jace Weaver, 1–28 (Maryknoll, NY: Orbis, 1996), 4.

wisdom" serves to "other" indigenous persons rather than encountering them as complicated moral agents and equal members of the UMC.

More subtly, by identifying indigenous communities as the bearers of certain rights, the draft Social Principles implies both their belonging and their otherness in relation to the UMC. Gunnemann presented rights language as an invention made necessary by modern scales of community. Rights are a tool for addressing contestations over moral membership, a way to voice moral dispute about who is counted as a full moral agent in a community. Within differentiated and pluralistic communities, rights address distorted power relations and exclusivity.[74] Rights are also indispensable for moral interaction with strangers—persons of a different moral community with different moral assumptions.[75] Thus, rights are a critical tool for evaluating and rectifying human moral community in the context of empire. By asserting the rights of indigenous peoples, the draft Social Principles both asserts their belonging and draws attention to exclusions within the UMC as a moral community. Contested rights reveal differentials of power. The theological surplus in this assertion of rights is the extent to which indigenous persons find voice and agency within the UMC—an exercise of power.

In light of the UMC's rejection of gambling, the right to self-determination of native peoples in the 2020 draft yields an interesting dilemma. The 2020 draft acknowledges that some native communities have established gambling resorts "as an act of self-determination and a crucial step toward economic survival."[76] What should be done when these rights collide with a principled moral stance against gambling? In this case, "rather than condemning such actions," the 2020 draft views this as an opportunity for the church "to encourage dialogue and education" with and within these indigenous communities.[77] This statement is consistent with the 2016 Social Principles, which "acknowledges the dichotomy that can occur when opposing gambling while supporting American Indian

74. Gunnemann, "Human Rights and Modernity," 171–2.

75. Gunnemann, "Human Rights and Modernity," 174.

76. GBCS, "Social Principles 2020," 26.

77. GBCS, "Social Principles 2020," 26.

tribal sovereignty and self-determination" and asserts, "the Church's role is to create sacred space to allow for dialogue and education that will promote a holistic understanding of the American Indians' historic quest for survival."[78] The UMC's attempt to navigate conflicting interests in the context of historical injustices evidences honest deliberation. This is the kind of sacred space necessary for moral debate within a divided church and society.

Seeing the Complexity of Our Connections

By enabling dialogue across difference, the Social Principles has the potential to help United Methodists seek paths through institutional division and moral dilemmas. Rieger concluded his book, *No Rising Tide*, by observing the existence of an unexpected theological "surplus" emerging from "alternative relationships among people who are brought together . . . often against their will."[79] This observation pertains not only to economic systems but also to situations of institutional connection. While Rieger referred to class differentials, the UMC is an ecclesial body that brings together people from different positions of power, including but not limited to class. The UMC of 2023 seems so hopelessly divided that its members are often brought together, seemingly against their will, to negotiate what this church is and will become. Yet, Christ promised to those who seek agreement, "where two or three are gathered in my name, I am there among them" (Matthew 18:20, NRSV). Might a global document of Social Principles yield an unexpected surplus of grace, allowing United Methodists to see the "complexity of our connections to other people" and to God, even amid oppressive relationships shaped by structures and histories of racism, LGBTQ oppression, and colonialism?[80]

Truth-telling and honesty are the foundations of this sacred space, and the 2020 draft of the Social Principles provides a remarkable example in a

78. *Book of Discipline, 2016*, ¶163.G.

79. Rieger, *No Rising Tide*, 162.

80. Rieger, *No Rising Tide*, 162.

statement on "Colonialism, Neocolonialism, and their Consequences."[81] Never before has the Social Principles mentioned colonialism, although the *Book of Resolutions* includes many discussions of this topic. The 2018 draft did not address colonialism, either. Yet, the 2020 draft courageously acknowledges "the tangled and complex legacies of colonialism and neocolonialism [that] hang heavily over the global fellowship of United Methodists."[82] Here, both colonialism and neocolonialism are defined and the complexity of relationships within the UMC described:

> Some of us belong to countries and groups that have richly benefited from the subjugation of whole peoples and from the seizure of lands and other resources. Others of us live in countries or are a part of communities that continue to struggle with the ongoing history and impacts of all forms of colonialism.[83]

Yes, United Methodists occupy all sides of this oppressive dynamic. Furthermore, the draft calls the UMC to account for its complicity: "We recognize that far from being innocent bystanders, the church has often been deeply involved in colonialism and neocolonialism."[84] What, then, are United Methodists to do? The 2020 draft calls for education, repentance, and reparation.

This proposed statement cannot solve the problems of colonialism and neocolonialism, nor can it make up for centuries of oppression. However, the "potential for alternative relationships," as Rieger puts it, is palpable. "These relationships," claimed Rieger, "can lead to new kinds of solidarity."[85] In the wake of the Traditionalist Plan adopted by the 2019 General Conference, United Methodism has experienced *blowback*, which Rieger described as "the unintended consequences of the politics of empire."[86] The ensuing resistance, ecclesiastical disobedience, disaffiliations, and debate in the UMC manifested a tangible blowback against

---

81. GBCS, "Social Principles 2020," 24.

82. GBCS, "Social Principles 2020," 24.

83. GBCS, "Social Principles 2020," 24.

84. GBCS, "Social Principles 2020," 24.

85. Rieger, *No Rising Tide*, 162.

86. Rieger, *Christ and Empire*, 1.

the otherwise invisible structures of empire binding United Methodists to each other and to systems of inequity and control. Alternative relationships, "developed in solidarity with real people whose lives are being destroyed," emerged from a surplus of grace.[87] Despite this church's structures of empire, liberating forms of power began to find expression.

Toward a Global Ethic

The surplus in the 2020 draft Social Principles is not in what the document proclaims but in the moral deliberation and disruption of oppression that it enables. By "seeing this complexity of our connections to other people," United Methodists open themselves to God's transformation of those relationships and "have a better chance of becoming fully human," to use Rieger's framing.[88] The power is not in the words of the Social Principles but its capacity to allow new forms of relationship. Thus, a global ethic requires more than majority ratification by a legislative assembly to be morally persuasive and grace-filled.

At a time when the very idea of "social justice" is under attack within many church bodies, the UMC cannot effectively proffer a statement of Social Principles that does not ground itself in a theology and practice of social engagement. While the 2020 draft Social Principles emphasizes human rights of individuals and communities, it offers little guidance for adjudicating moral disagreements rooted in cultural differences. This deficiency is especially apparent in the way the draft speaks about indigenous peoples and traditions. Suffering from a lack of general theological or moral principles to ground cross-cultural critique and discernment, the document fails to address the most pressing issues dividing this denomination, raising questions about the possibilities and potential for the Social Principles to function as a global ethic for a divided church.

It is no small task to develop a denomination-wide social witness statement for a church that spans many different cultures and societies. The UMC, as an aspiring "global" church, transcends national and soci-

---

87. Rieger, *No Rising Tide*, 155.

88. Rieger, *No Rising Tide*, 162.

etal boundaries. The UMC's social setting includes its present and historical Anglo-Saxon mindset, White racism, and colonial mission enterprises
as well as the liberating voices emanating from within communities oppressed, discriminated against, and colonized by this same church. Unacknowledged, these factors hinder this church's ability to address the wide
cultural diversity encompassed within it; acknowledged, the very words
of witness spill over in a surplus making room for the activity of the Holy
Spirit. However, a social witness that does not provide resources for addressing divisions within this church's membership undercuts its own va-
lidity.

The 2020 draft Social Principles needs more internal truth-telling to
address the challenge of empire. A global ethic—especially for a divided
church—must "take [the] risk of cultural dialogue," asserted Hollenbach.[89] To be liberative, this cultural dialogue must also exceed the spirit
of empire, allowing for new, more equitable relationships of power. This
risk is apparent in both the 2016 Social Principles and the 2020 draft's call
for dialogue and education about the dilemma of gambling and tribal sovereignty as well as the UMC's legacies of colonialism and neocolonialism.
Acknowledging the discrepancies between its moral commitments and
practices, the UMC witnesses to a theological surplus beyond its control.
The 2020 draft Social Principles provides, in a few key places, a glimmer
of this witness.

---

89.   Hollenbach, *The Global Face of Public Faith*, 11, 165.

6

ECCLESIASTIC EMPIRES

American Conflict and the UMC in Africa

Taylor Denyer

The dominant rhetoric in The United Methodist Church (UMC) to-day is that irreconcilable views on human sexuality are tearing our denomination apart, that underneath this conflict is a larger conservative/progressive theological divide, and as such the fight is between these two opposing perspectives. Church leaders in the United States tend to operate with the assumption that this divide spans the entire denomination, such that each geographical region of the UMC (or groups within those regions) can be accurately labeled as being "conservative" or "progressive" in the way these words are used in the United States. Because of this limited, U.S.-centric perspective, these leaders fail to comprehend the complexity of the conflicts in our denomination's central conferences and the effects that actions taken by U.S. leadership are having on them, especially the damage that has been done to the thousands of United Methodist ministries across the three African central conferences (ACCs).[1]

Contrary to the prevailing American narrative, the labels of "conservative" and "progressive" have little meaning in most of the ACCs, which have not abandoned Wesleyan theology and social holiness practices. By the standards of their contexts, the ACCs are, like John and Charles Wesley, traditional in their doctrine and progressive in their ministries. The pri-

1.   West Africa Central Conference, Congo Central Conference, and Africa Central Conference

134

mary division lines in the ACCs are not about theological debates; they are about power struggles with roots that predate the UMC's current identity crisis. Thus, the commonly accepted UMC conflict narrative does more to distort the reality of the UMC in Africa than it does to illuminate it.

United Methodists from the United States bring their false assumptions into the African continent to detrimental effect. The infusion of American conflicts into these power struggles through the strategic distribution of project funding, employment, networking, and other resources has raised the stakes and raised the lengths to which people will go to ensure that their side wins. This has had the effect of throwing gasoline on several fires, and the results have been explosive, with life-or-death consequences for African United Methodists and their communities. The fallout of bringing the U.S. fight about human sexuality to the ACCs includes sabotaged ministries, slander campaigns that have impaired the church's witness of the gospel, government intervention in church polity, and credible death threats—even documented poisonings—made against United Methodist leaders.

The damage being done to the UMC in Africa calls into question the motivations of Americans who treat the ACCs as merely another battlefront in their war. Viewed from an African perspective, the injection of American concerns into local African conflicts looks less like an effort to uphold right religion and more like a conspiracy to build/control ecclesiastic empires. In *Evangelism After Pluralism*, Bryan Stone condemns these sorts of imperial impulses of church leaders and writes that "the question for practicing evangelism in a postcolonial context can no longer be the imperial question of how we can reach more people, grow our churches, or expand our influence. The more fundamental question is whether the church can relearn how to bear public witness on the Spirit's terms rather than the empire's terms, recapturing some of the ancient church's counter-imperial deviance while imagining ever new forms of faithfulness."[2] Sadly, Stone's words of wisdom are not being heeded by those escalating the war within the UMC; the building and protecting of a global empire is being

---

2. Bryan Stone, *Evangelism After Pluralism: The Ethics of Christian Witness* (Grand Rapids, MI: Baker Academic, 2018), 29.

treated as more important than the Wesleyan mandate to bear faithful witness to the gospel and avoid doing harm. It seems that the lust for power and dominion are the real primary forces at play on both continents. U.S. United Methodists are, regardless of whether they see it as such, engaged in building a colonial empire rather than collaborative mission partnerships.

In this chapter, I will describe how this power struggle has thus far played out in the North Katanga Episcopal Area (DR Congo), with which I am most familiar, and in other locations across the ACCs. Although born in the United States and raised in the former South Indiana Annual Conference, I have been a friend of North Katanga since 1991, when my late father, the Rev. Dr. "Biking Bob" Walters, was given a chance to witness the church's work in the region and returned home with a love for Katanga so intense that it changed the life path of our entire family.[3] As a result, I eventually moved to North Katanga and was ordained an elder in that conference. This chapter also draws on my scholarly study of missiology and international partnerships between Americans and Congolese. My published ThD dissertation, *Decolonizing Mission Partnerships,* analyzes the evolution of relational dynamics between UMC leaders in North Katanga and the United States.[4]

Since the deeper we study the past the better we understand the present, this chapter's historical account begins long before the 1968 creation of The United Methodist Church. Instead, it begins at the beginning of Methodism's battles for dominion over Africa.[5]

Historical Background

3. See Bob Walters, *The Last Missionary* (Eugene, OR: Wipf and Stock, 2020); Bob Walters and Kate Koppy, *Pastors, Chiefs, and Warlords: The Ministry of Being With* (Eugene, OR: Wipf and Stock, 2022).

4. Taylor Walters Denyer, *Decolonizing Mission Partnerships: Evolving Collaboration between United Methodists in North Katanga and the United States of America.* American Society of Missiology Monograph Series, vol. 47 (Eugene, OR: Pickwick, 2020).

5. For more on the (neo)colonial dynamics of these interactions, see my dissertation or my chapter on "Decolonizing Methodist Mission Partnerships," in *The Practice of Mission in Global Methodism: Emerging Trends from Everywhere to Everywhere,* edited by David W. Scott and Darryl W. Stephens, Routledge Methodist Studies Series (New York: Routledge, 2021).

Treating Africa as a territory for American Methodists to conquer is nothing new, as can be seen in the vest pocket edition of *A Centenary Survey of Methodist Episcopal Missions*, published in 1919. In it, Africa is described as having three "battle fronts," and readers are urged to send financial support for the Methodist campaign to push back the "Mohammedan advance."[6] Vestiges of these battlefronts can still be clearly seen by simply looking at a map or statistical reports of The United Methodist Church's territories and Advance[7] projects.

During the colonial period, U.S. and European-funded mission stations working in cooperation with local evangelists led to rapid expansion of the denominations they represented. In the nearly 200 years since missionaries from the Methodist branches that now form the UMC arrived on the African continent, the denomination has grown so large—numerically and geographically—that in the last official published count in 2018 the ACCs boasted thirty-two annual conferences (three provisional), thirteen active bishops, 9,025 ordained pastors, and 5,118,749 recorded professing members.[8]

Inevitably, over the years the annual conferences within the ACCs have faced and overcome disagreements and conflicts.[9] Conflict is a natural part of the human experience, and few people like having their dirty laundry aired in front of others. Thus, United Methodists in the ACCs, as

---

6. See, *A Centenary Survey of Methodist Episcopal Missions* (New York: Joint Centenary Committee, Methodist Episcopal Church, 1919), 14.

7. "*Advance*" is the name of the United Methodist program to fund global missionary activity. Note that the UMC has not yet removed the empire and war imagery from the name of its primary U.S.-based system for raising funds for ministries outside of the USA. In the February 1949 issue of *The Christian Advocate*, this system was its featured cover story and marketed as "The Advance for Christ and His Church, From Crusade to Conquest." See: *The Christian Advocate* (New York: The Methodist Episcopal Church, February 17, 1949).

8. Published statistics used for calculating delegate numbers for General Conference 2020, released in 2018: http://s3.amazonaws.com/Website_Properties/news-media/press-center/documents/2020 _Delegate_Calc_by_AC_with_2016_comp.pdf.

9. See, for instance, Peter Marubitoba Dong, A. J. Filiya, Mary Samuel Bambur, John Pena Bambur, and Ayuba Ndule Bambur, *The History of The United Methodist Church in Nigeria* (Nashville: Abingdon, 2000), Chapter 6, "Schism in the Muri Regional Church"; Levi C. Williams, *A History of The United Methodist Church in Liberia* (Denver: Outskirts, 2014), Chapter 11, "A Time for Healing"; Michael Kasongo, *History of the Methodist Church in the Central Congo* (Lanham, MD: University Press of America, 1998), Chapter 6, "The Decline and Fall of the Central Congo Episcopal Area, 1960-1996." I am not endorsing the views of any of these authors on the conflicts they write about but merely offering a sense of the breadth of conflicts of local origin in the African church.

elsewhere, have tended to avoid discussing any unpleasant internal politics or discord with outsiders or writing about such things in internationally published documents, those sources cited in the previous footnote notwithstanding. Further contributing to the dearth of information available to most outsiders about ACCs has been the massive barriers to communication (e.g., need for translation, lack of functioning postal system, transport/visa, access to phone/internet technologies, etc.). For generations, foreign missionaries were the sole conduits of information between African Methodists and those in the United States and Europe, and these missionaries had strong financial incentives to downplay any problem/scandal that might discourage donors; often, the foreign missionaries themselves were not aware of the dynamics at play. Even today, with the game-changing impact of the internet and affordable smartphones, the fear of the potential consequences/retribution resulting from sharing too candidly, combined with the politics of who is granted permission to act as a conference spokesperson, has created a reality where United Methodists not directly involved in any of the ACCs know very little about what goes on there. This is true to the point where they have been unaware of the biggest organized attack on the African episcopal areas to date. In contrast, African delegates to the General Conference sessions not only know of but have been forced to witness the dominating fights between leaders of the U.S. branch of the denomination.

What further makes the ACCs' political battles different from those in the UMC jurisdictions in the United States is the presence of a large number of powerful outsiders in Africa, mainly in the form of American *missionaries* and American *mission partners* of various sorts. I use the former term to describe those who live in the region for some length of time and the latter term to describe those who collaborate on church-related projects and may visit, but do not stay. Over the past several decades, the number of long-term missionaries has been declining and the number of short-term (or entirely at-a-distance) mission partners has been increasing.

The problem with missionaries and mission partners is that they have access to resources (money, education, life opportunities, etc.) that most local leaders do not. This puts them in positions of tremendous power.

Most African societies—especially rural ones—are patronage systems, in which those with the most power serve as the community's patrons. Patronage, as missionary-missiologist Bob Walters explains, is "[t]he social-economic system in which all the resources are controlled by a single person, a patron—for instance, a chief or a missionary. As a community and as individuals, clients petition the patron for needs and favors."[10] In an ideal patronage system, the patron coordinates the collection and redistribution of the community's resources for the benefit of the entire population and also brings in goods and skilled persons from outside of their territory. In the UMC across Africa, those elected to the episcopacy (or those with aspirations of being elected) are under great pressure to be effective patrons, acquiring money and needed materials, mediating quarrels, and functioning as the conference's ATM whenever a crisis strikes. United Methodists from the United States who arrive as missionaries or partners are also expected to serve as patrons and/or conduits of resources for the primary patron—the bishop—to distribute. Regardless of whether foreigners understand or accept this role, they cannot escape it. If they choose to continue the relationship, their three options are to channel resources through the bishop, finance someone with aspirations of supplanting the bishop, or, as has often been the case with long-term missionaries, set up their own organization/mission-station with them acting as its primary patron.[11]

In their role as patrons, missionaries and mission partners are frequently asked to intervene in local church conflicts. As I have written about missionaries to North Katanga, "Often Americans would become triangulated into a conflict, where less powerful church leaders would come to them complaining about the actions of a higher ranked church leader. Such conflicts tended to involve accusations of the misappropriation of funds/resources, nepotism, or some other misconduct that nega-

---

10. Walters, *The Last Missionary*, vi.

11. For more on patronage and American/Congolese relationships, see Denyer, *Decolonizing Mission Partnerships*, 67–68, 175–81. Note also why the departure of foreign missionaries resulted in the collapse of numerous mission stations that had been built upon a system requiring a missionary to serve as the collector and distributor of resources.

tively impacted others."[12] United Methodists operating out of a patronage system where Americans function as patrons have sought to pull Americans into their conflicts, and American missionaries and mission partners have all too often been willing to have their power leveraged in this way, especially when participation in such a conflict has allowed them to advance their personal agendas or interests.

What the coalition of conservative U.S.-based caucus groups has done in recent years is take this dynamic to a destructive extreme by not only building and heavily funding a rival patronage economy (i.e., the Wesleyan Covenant Association, the Africa Initiative, and now the Global Methodist Church) but appointing as its regional leaders those with open ambitions of becoming bishops. Some of these appointments have happened with disregard for the reasons why these persons had lost previous elections or been suspended or even defrocked (for gross misconduct, in some cases involving criminal actions), and the Wesleyan Covenant Association has not held their selected leaders accountable for using unethical methods while attempting to topple the United Methodist bishops of their regions of origin.

The Human Sexuality Debate and American Interest in Africa

For decades, American United Methodists' involvement in African conflicts was largely confined to missionaries, who were the only group of Americans that had extensive interactions with African United Methodists. That began to change in the 2000s as denominational debates over human sexuality intensified. While the UMC's General Conference has been voting on opposing statements about human sexuality for decades, the use of African delegates as political pawns in this fight is a relatively recent development triggered by a rapid rise in membership numbers reported by episcopal areas across the African continent. In 1992, only 11 percent of General Conference delegates were from anywhere outside the

---

12.   Denyer, *Decolonizing Mission Partnerships*, 139–40.

United States, including Africa, Europe, and the Philippines together.[13] By 2004, however, 11 percent of General Conference delegates were from Africa alone,[14] and this number has risen considerably since then.

At the UMC's 2004 General Conference in Pittsburgh, strategists across the theological spectrum realized that denominational membership statistics in Africa had grown so large that the African delegations to the General Conference now determined the outcomes of contentious votes. Caucuses that were in the minority among U.S. delegates could become the majority with the support of these delegations from African nations. Suddenly, numerous groups and agencies wanted to befriend these delegates, and new funding and visitors started streaming toward the continent. In a dramatic pivot, African United Methodism went from being relatively untouched by the denominational in-fighting in the United States to becoming a strategic battleground.

This change initially seemed to be a beneficial thing for African central conferences. African leaders were encouraged to speak their minds on the denomination-level stage and share about their ministries and the challenges they faced. Yes, there was the occasional overt partisan move—such as when in 2008 a conservative caucus handed out free cell phones to Congolese and other central conference delegates and then texted them instructions on which way to vote on various resolutions[15]—but such actions were not directly harming the church in Africa and did not (yet) appear to be significantly impacting their voting decisions.

Most African delegates whose cultural beliefs agreed with the denomination's official stance on human sexuality did not initially understand the politics at play or the potential ramifications of the legislation they voted on. African bishops were also unaware of the threats to their regions, seeing no reason to object to delegates befriending whomever they wanted or attending caucus group gatherings. What caucus groups were doing through these interactions, however, was seeking to identify and recruit

---

13. "A Profile of the 1992 General Conference Delegates," *Daily Christian Advocate*, May 5, 1992, 11.

14. "General Conference 2004: Number of Delegates," The United Methodist Church, http://ee.umc.org/who-we-are/general-conference-2004-number-of-delegates.

15. Linda Green, "Doubts arise following gifts of cell phones," *UM News*, April 25, 2008.

key leaders of the UMC in Africa to their organizations, focusing on conferences that had the highest number of delegates, and especially on their potential future bishops.[16]

Large waves of conservative American United Methodist groups looking to cultivate reliable voters in their fights over human sexuality showed up in Africa, where they were warmly welcomed as wealthy patrons. Individuals recruited by the conservative caucuses were especially showered with gifts: scholarships, unregulated project money, large personal loans, and the sending of their children to expensive private schools and even universities in the United States. In the DR Congo, Liberia, and Sierra Leone, these gifts were especially well-timed, as these countries were emerging from devastating wars. Those wars had both disrupted previous flows of American money through missionary channels and increased the need for resources to rebuild war-torn churches and ministries.

Yet these gifts were not freely given; they came with strings attached, and they were given without oversight or honesty about those strings. To prevent episcopal leadership from protesting these actions, American caucuses were strategic at financing the construction of churches and various conference ministries. These teams made many trips to Africa under the guise of building conference partnerships all while hiding their long-term goals (i.e., controlling the messaging, leadership, and therefore voting in these regions) from the bishops and many of their recruits.

The System of Ecclesiastic Empire Solidifies

The system of American patronage in exchange for African votes took another significant step forward with the formation of the Africa Initiative (AI), which held its first gathering in 2012. Despite its name, the AI was launched not by Africans, but by a coalition of conservative groups based in the United States, the primary one being the Wesleyan Covenant

---

16. Many ACC bishops were approaching the mandatory retirement age, and election campaigns had quietly or not-so-quietly begun for their possible replacements.

Association (WCA).[17] The AI was highly effective at recruiting and galvanizing General Conference delegates through its gatherings, which were used to discuss proposed legislation. In most cases, though, it was the AI's financial sponsors—not Africans themselves—dictating what proposals to discuss and support. The effectiveness of the AI's strategy could be seen by all at General Conference 2012, and thus centrist and progressive U.S.-based caucus groups tried to do the same with their recruits, but those behind the AI had much larger financial resources and were significantly more advanced organizationally.

Most UMC leaders from Africa initially thought that the AI was a wonderful idea. For the first time, African delegates to the General Conference were able to unite, meet, and strategize; they could understand the nature of petitions and craft ones that advocated for African issues. They could also build networks and communication lines between leaders across the continent. In 2016, Global Ministries General Secretary Thomas Kemper offered to help the AI become an official UM caucus group so it could receive funding from the denomination. AI leaders such as Rev. Dr. Jerry Kulah (Liberia) and Rev. Forbes Matonga (Zimbabwe) were invited by Global Ministries for planning meetings. However, after Kulah and Matonga returned home and spoke with their financial sponsors, they decided that they didn't want the AI to become an official caucus of the UMC. If the AI were to become a recognized and funded UMC caucus group, the coalition that financed its launch would risk losing control of its leadership.

Gradually, the African bishops themselves became concerned about some of the practices of the AI. The first warning sign the bishops saw was that the majority of those being recruited for leadership positions in the AI and WCA were either bitter former rivals for the episcopacy or those with open ambitions of becoming a bishop.[18] Since these leaders had not been successful in their attempts to be elected to serve as bishops

---

17. For more on this history, see chapter in this volume by Lloyd Nyarota. As Nyarota notes, other groups such as Good News, the Confessing Movement, and the Institute for Religion and Democracy were part of this coalition of conservative groups.

18. Jerry Kulah, Kimba Evariste, and Forbes Matonga have all held leadership positions in the Africa Initiative (and other Traditionalist groups such as the WCA), and all are former episcopal candidates.

or to receive a financially profitable role within the patronage system of the official structure of the church, they sought to establish themselves as leaders in the alternative patronage system offered by the AI. In this way, they could still have the prestige and financial resources they had sought through episcopal elections.

Thus, certain African leaders' search for patrons to help them pursue their political ambitions connected with certain American leaders' search for allies who would support their political projects. The AI and the WCA (and other conservative U.S.-based groups) discovered that they could aid each other's political goals, with American patronage as the cement to bind these interests together. This is pure empire politics—attempting to seize power and resources in foreign lands by destabilizing established leadership structures and co-opting power-hungry rivals. This is the neocolonial basis upon which such American/African partnerships were established. They would not be possible if it were not for the economic inequalities that exist between the United States and African countries and Americans' continued (neo)colonial thirst for establishing ecclesiastic empires.

The Problems of Ecclesiastic Empires in Africa

Again, this is not a benign pattern. The creation of a separate power structure by the WCA through the AI has not supplemented or existed alongside the official structures of the denomination; it has actively undermined them. In an October 2020 report from their meeting the previous month, the African bishops asserted that there is "a lot of interference in African conferences by people from the United States who are causing confusion and hatred among Africans in the church. Effort should be made to stop such people from coming and sowing seeds of hatred among the Africans."[19] The elected bishops of the UMC's central conferences in Africa were excluded from many AI conversations and came to be concerned that the AI was emerging as a separate and destructive power struc-

---

19. Council of Bishops, The United Methodist Church, "African Bishops: Let's Make Our Own Choices," October 30, 2020, https://www.unitedmethodistbishops.org/newsdetail/african-bishops-let-s-make-our-own-choices-14367017.

ture within African Methodism, one propped up by its American funders and the patronage they were dispensing.

Operating outside of our denomination's regulations, the AI and the WCA have neither accountability in their finances nor transparency in what happens in their meetings. This makes it impossible to monitor the income sources of the AI, how WCA funds are being used in Africa, or what plans are being made behind closed doors. Under the auspices of COVID response, the WCA has channeled large amounts of unregulated funds to its recruits in Africa.[20] This money went directly through its own patronage channels rather than operating through the official channels of the denomination.

One revealing glimpse behind the curtain of the AI occurred in late 2020, when videos filmed at its October and November 2020 meetings were leaked and uploaded onto YouTube. Links to these videos were quietly shared and viewed by many UMC bishops, general agency employees, and other church leaders before they were taken down. In the recordings, contempt toward the UMC, its general agencies, and a large number of its bishops was expressed without filters. For example, Bishop Joaquina Nhanala was referred to as "the lady from Mozambique," and a prominent AI leader from Liberia expressed pleasure that Bishop John Yambasu had unexpectedly died, thus creating another episcopal vacancy. Large parts of the meeting were spent not only strategizing how to promote their candidates for upcoming episcopal elections but also how to undermine the efforts of rival candidates. No ethical guidelines were discussed concerning methods used to obtain these political goals nor were reprimands given to those present who had been sabotaging ministries, leaders, and episcopal candidates in their annual conferences (e.g., loudly asserting, in a country where being found guilty of exhibiting same-sex attraction carries the death penalty, that a major UMC-led local construction project was being funded by homosexuals).

Increasingly, the AI's African members have taken a multi-pronged approach, striving to destabilize and take control of the official structures

20. "WCA Awards Grants to Twelve Ministries in Central Conferences," Wesleyan Covenant Association, November 13, 2020, https://wesleyancovenant.org/2020/11/11/wca-awards-grants-to-twelve-ministries-in-central-conferences/.

of the UMC while at the same time hedging their bets by aligning themselves with the founders of the newly launched Global Methodist Church
(GMC). Whenever there is a vacancy in a powerful denominational position (such as in the case of the episcopacy in Sierra Leone following
Bishop John Yambasu's death in August 2020), the AI has pushed to have
their candidate elected, although thus far most of their candidates have
been rejected by voters,[21] and the AI fought hard to have episcopal elections in Africa in 2022 in order for their candidates to fill positions well in
advance of the next General Conference.[22] One of the factors creating this
sense of urgency in holding regional elections and General Conference is
that unregulated funds have already been given to those whose votes the
AI and WCA need in order for their proposed legislation and candidates
to win. Waiting too long reduces the influence those funds provide.

In January 2022, instead of following denominational protocols that
state that it is the Commission on General Conference that responds
to logistical problems of General Conference delegates, the WCA announced that it was wiring large sums of money for vaccinations for General Conference delegates.[23] These funds were not sent through official
UMC channels, but through their local WCA employees in Africa. The
funds were distributed without oversight or coordination with the official General Conference delegation leaders, and they were given to people
in places where COVID vaccines were either free or not even available.
Bishops from the impacted central conferences labeled this funding by
how it functioned on the ground—bribery to join the WCA and its new
denomination[24]—and they wrote an open letter denouncing the action,

---

21. Rev. Prof. Edwin J. J. Momoh is a member of the Africa Initiative and was an episcopal candidate
in Sierra Leone following Bishop Yambasu's death, though the Sierra Leone Annual Conference nominated
Rev. James Boye Caulker instead. "Sierra Leone United Methodists nominate Rev James Boye-Caulker,"
West African Writers, March 6, 2022, https://www.westafricanwriters.org/sierra-leone-united-methodists-
nominate-rev-james-boye-caulker/.

22. Africa Initiative, "Envisioning the Next Methodism in Africa," June 3, 2022, https://
juicyecumenism.com/wp-content/uploads/AFRICA-INITIATIVE-PRESS-RELEASE-
ENVISIONING-THE-NEXT-METHODISM-IN-AFRICA-FINAL.pdf.

23. Keith Boyette, "Access to Covid Vaccines Offered to All General Conference Delegates," Wesleyan Covenant Association, January 7, 2022, https://wesleyancovenant.org/2022/01/07/access-to-covid-
vaccines-offered-to-all-general-conference-delegates/.

24. Heather Hahn, "Bishops, Others Denounce WCA's Vaccine Plan," *UM News*, January 18, 2022,
https://www.umnews.org/en/news/bishops-others-denounce-wcas-vaccine-plan.

saying, "Offering vaccines to General Conference delegates or covering the cost of delegates to travel to places where they can be vaccinated is not an expression of vaccine equity. Rather, it appears as an attempt to benefit those who have been given a special responsibility, and who the donor wishes to fulfill a certain purpose."[25] They continued, "The unfortunate thing about the entire process by WCA is that it has all the marks of colonialism which our countries went through some years ago. The tactics of divide-and-conquer have created chaos and division on the African continent and should not be allowed in our churches."[26]

Misinformation has been a major tactic used in the attacks on the African central conferences. One of the counterfactual arguments being used by the AI, the WCA, and the GMC to persuade Africans to leave the UMC is the claim that once the conservatives leave to join the GMC, the UMC and thus the ACCs will immediately officially affirm and include in all levels of leadership openly LGBTQ+ persons. The perceived threat is not merely about church law conflicting with one's personal views on human sexuality, but the persecution a person in many parts of Africa would face being a member of a denomination with policies that break the laws of their home country. However, this fear comes from a deliberate misrepresentation of the denomination's polity. Outside of the Articles of Religion and the denomination's Constitution, central conferences have the authority to adapt the *Book of Discipline* to their context, thus preventing the problem of having policies that are rejected or illegal in their regions. In short, the *Book of Discipline* that is voted on at General Conference is not the same *Book of Discipline* that has authority in the ACCs, as they have jointly created their own version that holds authority in Africa.

As previously touched upon, the deliberate misrepresentation of UMC polity is not the only unethical tactic being used by AI and WCA leaders in Africa. The open secret in the ACCs that bishops have only recently begun saying aloud is that the AI and WCA leaders have been using slander, intimidation, and extortion against bishops and rival can-

25. "Statement from Central Conference Bishops on Vaccine Offers," January 17, 2022, https://www.unitedmethodistbishops.org/files/websites/www/pdfs/statement+from+central+conferences+bishops+on+vaccines+jan+17+final.pdf.

26. "Statement from Central Conference Bishops on Vaccine Offers."

didates for the episcopacy over the past few years. They also use personal gifts and money to gain favors. They have been doing this aggressively in DR Congo, Zimbabwe, Angola, and other areas. These tactics have made the political situation in the UMC in Africa highly volatile, as AI leaders have demonstrated that they will use any means available to take control of the UMC in Africa. What is not clear, however, is whether the AI's members have fully thought through their long game. Do they want to burn down the ACCs, rule them, or pillage and supplant them with the Global Methodist Church?

Empire-building is not just about domination; it is driven and sustained by the exploitation of resources. What reasons do the African defectors to the Global Methodist Church have to believe that their newfound patrons will remain loyal once the power to vote on General Conference bills that would channel money and property to the GMC has been lost? While it is doubtful that all the protagonists have deeply considered what the endgame will look like or what pathways to peace remain, ACC bishops have been discussing such things with one another intensely, as the mounting pressure to relent to the WCA has forced them to consider, not only the sacrifices they are prepared to make, but what precisely they pledged on the day they were consecrated as United Methodist bishops. The sacrifices and risks many of them have already faced in this U.S.-financed war merit badges of honor, yet until recently they have suffered in silence in a failed attempt to not further sully the denomination's reputation. What follows is just the tip of what they have endured.

Open Attacks on African UMC Bishops

While a few African bishops initially joined the WCA, most have refused and continue to do so, not as a rejection of its belief statements, but due to the character of its leaders, particularly their unscrupulous methods. Throughout the ACCs, the AI and regional WCA leaders have been using their personal social media accounts (especially Facebook) as well as

WhatsApp[27] to relentlessly slander the UMC and bishops who refuse to submit to them. These actions do not merely damage the bishops' reputations; they have put their very lives in danger, with credible death threats regularly sent to them. The smear campaigns are not limited to their episcopal areas either. Tom Lambrecht, one of the leading members of the WCA's council, has published articles through Good News that charge Congolese bishops with dishonest treatment of their members, and he deliberately misrepresents their views on human sexuality, disregarding their public statements about their views.[28]

WCA leaders are also attempting to financially punish any bishop who stands up to them by destroying established mission partnerships with those bishops' conferences. Not only has the WCA worked to cut off defiant bishops from the financial support of its longtime conservative partners in the United States, they have also damaged the partnerships with non-aligned, mixed, and progressively leaning conferences in the United States and denominational agencies by spreading the narrative that African conferences that partner with these groups are themselves pro-homosexuality. The messages their leaders are blasting out through social media platforms mischaracterize U.S. partner conferences and general agencies, especially Global Ministries and Church and Society, claiming that these are agents of the LGBTQ+ agenda.

One partnership that has been strained by these mischaracterizations is the decades-old friendship between the West Ohio Annual Conference in the United States and the North Katanga Annual Conference in the DR Congo. In building its partnerships, North Katanga has never imposed a litmus test regarding who is centrist, liberal, or conservative. It has partnered with any conference wanting to collaborate regardless of how their members lean theologically. West Ohio has members from across the theological spectrum, yet now the narrative being widely disseminated is that North Katanga's relationship with West Ohio is proof that the North

---

27.   An extremely popular application used across Africa and other regions of the world for disseminating written messages, videos, web links, and photos directly to smartphones. One feature of this platform is the ability to create what are essentially large-scale "private" group texts. WhatsApp groups function as a major form of (mis)information in the ACCs.

28.   See David W. Scott, "The Traditionalist Bid for Africa," *UM & Global*, August 5, 2020, http://www.umglobal.org/2020/08/the-traditionalist-bid-for-africa.html.

Katanga Annual Conference supports gay marriage. Through such campaigns, ACC bishops are put in impossible situations. As bishops, they are expected to be the lead fundraisers for ministries in their episcopal areas, yet they cannot receive funding from conservative groups without handing over financial control to individuals selected by the WCA, and if they try to raise funds from any group not sanctioned by the WCA, they are branded as liberals, thus giving their political rivals additional leverage when recruiting members to defect and join the Global Methodist Church.

Tragically, the people most harmed by this financial warfare have been the most vulnerable populations: those whose lives could have been saved—even transformed—by the local church ministries (e.g., nutrition centers, medical programs, disaster relief, etc.) that have been devastated by the exodus of funding streams. After years of hoping and praying that these attacks would fizzle out once the U.S.-based wing of the UMC ended its war—what many thought would happen at the 2019 General Conference and then at the session that was scheduled for May 2020 but has yet to meet—ACC bishops concluded that it was up to them to take the lead in mediating a Christ-centered peace agreement.

The Breaking Point

As they have elsewhere in The United Methodist Church, the conflicts associated with ecclesiastic empire-building in Africa have escalated over the past several years. In 2019, Bishop John Yambasu, Bishop Mande Muyombo, and Bishop Christian Alsted decided together to invite representatives from traditionalist, centrist, and progressive UMC caucuses to meet and negotiate a peaceful path forward. This initiative sought to resolve conflicts in the United States, thus dampening the spread of those conflicts to other areas of the church. From this gathering was born what was named the Protocol of Reconciliation and Grace through Separation, also known as The Protocol.[29] While it was primarily African bishops

---

29. "Protocol of Reconciliation and Grace through Separation FAQ," *UM News*, January 3 2020, https://www.umnews.org/en/news/protocol-of-reconciliation-and-grace-through-separation-faq.

who initiated the conversation that created The Protocol, the WCA later hijacked it and fought against having African bishops on the mediation team.[30] This action further eroded the African bishops' relationship with the WCA and led most of them to retract their support of The Protocol.[31] Thus, the intensity of attacks against ACC elected leadership worsened.

In September 2022, the Africa College of Bishops met at Africa University in Zimbabwe, with the crisis facing the denomination being one of their primary discussion topics. Out of this meeting came an official open statement endorsed by all active United Methodist bishops in Africa except for Bishop John Yohanna of the Nigeria Episcopal Area. This statement asserted that "whereas the Africa Initiative is now working with Wesleyan Covenant Association to destroy our United Methodist Church" and is "working with and supporting the Global Methodist Church," the "Bishops of the UMC in Africa . . . will dissociate from any activities of the Africa Initiative and will not allow any activities of the Africa Initiative in our areas," "will not allow or entertain any activities of the Wesleyan Covenant Association who are wrongly influencing God's people in our areas," and "will not tolerate anyone giving false information about The United Methodist Church in [their] areas."[32]

This statement, which was covered by multiple news outlets, including the Religion News Service,[33] an agency outside of the denomination, made waves throughout the UMC, as it disrupted the narrative that all of Africa would be aligning itself with the WCA and GMC in the UMC's schism. Not long after the bishops' statement was made, the Africa Initiative published a press release, which was distributed via the WCA's Facebook page.[34] The AI's response incorrectly claimed that only seven of the

30. For more, see chapter by Lloyd Nyarota in this volume.

31. See Council of Bishops, "African Bishops: Let's Make Our Own Choices."

32. Africa College of Bishops, "Statement from the Africa Colleges of Bishops," September 8, 2022, https://www.unitedmethodistbishops.org/files/statement+from+africa+colleges+of+bishops+-+sept+8.pdf.

33. Emily McFarlan Miller, "UMC Bishops in Africa Break with Africa Initiative, Wesleyan Covenant Association," *Religion News Service*, September 14, 2022, https://religionnews.com/2022/09/14/umc-bishops-in-africa-break-with-africa-initiative-wesleyan-covenant-association/.

34. Africa UMC Initiative, "Africa Initiative's Response to African Bishops' Accusation," September 12, 2022, https://www.facebook.com/wesleyancovenant/photos/pcb.5441756589203837/5441754702537359.

thirteen active bishops had endorsed the original statement and, without offering names, falsely claimed that some of those bishops have written to disassociate themselves from the document. The response also failed to directly address the primary accusations made by the bishops: that the AI is attempting to destroy the UMC in Africa, deliberately spreading misinformation and working closely with the Global Methodist Church in its agenda to seize control of the membership and assets of the UMC in Africa. The AI called the bishops' statement "a declaration of war." Yet, as this chapter has demonstrated, the war started long before then.

The political impact of the bishops' unified statement was swift and dramatic. The giant had stood up, and the timing could not have been worse for the WCA, as jurisdictional conferences across the United States were preparing to meet, and they all resulted in a sweeping loss for WCA-aligned candidates,[35] signaling a resounding rebuke from both sides of the Atlantic.

Going Forward with Hope

How does one speak the truth, stand one's ground, *and* de-escalate a war? What does it mean to lead a multitude with a shepherd's crook, to be a servant-leader in an age of empire, or to become a post-empire bishop? These are complex questions facing United Methodist bishops that merit ongoing deep reflection, but, in the meantime, there is reason to be hopeful that the WCA and others funding the AI may, in the face of the events of September-November 2022, decide to cut their losses and redirect their energies elsewhere, as there has recently been a reduction in public attacks on ACCs and their bishops.

One possible post-empire leadership model for the church is described in the 2014 viral blog post "Methodism 2.0," in which Rev. Jeremy Smith uses the metaphors of operating system upgrades and spider vs. starfish

---

35. Jeremy Smith, "Bishop Elections Show #UMC Future Despite Unjust Laws." *Hacking Christianity*, Nov. 14, 2022, https://hackingchristianity.net/2022/11/bishop-elections-show-umc-future-despite-unjust-laws.html.

(headless) organizations[36] to envision a future of the UMC that involves increased connections, autonomy, and agency at the grassroots/regional level.[37] Smith's January 2023 follow-up post, "On the Success of Methodism 2.0," asserts that starfish Methodism—a headless organism that can regrow and even multiply when its limbs are cut off— is now in charge of The United Methodist Church in the United States.[38]

While the next General Conference is not until 2024, in many ways the traditionalist vs. progressive battle for control over the UMC in the United States has already reached its end. Over 2,000 traditionalist congregations in the United States have recently exited the denomination, and at the 2022 jurisdictional conferences, each of the five jurisdictions made statements and/or took steps toward widening inclusion of LGBTQ+ persons in the church.[39] In the ACCs, there is a heightened sense of agency and autonomy, as ACC bishops have demonstrated that they and their conferences will no longer tolerate the abuse and paternalism they have endured for so long. Not every outcome of this conflict has been fully determined, however. Since the 2022 jurisdictional conferences, the AI has ramped up its efforts to persuade GC 2024 delegates to support The Protocol, which, if passed, could give twenty-five million dollars to the Global Methodist Church. Liberia and Nigeria are currently being targeted by the AI as the areas of the church with the highest chances of winning political allies, but the odds are rapidly shrinking that the remaining U.S.-traditionalists in the UMC will manage to pass any of their legislation at GC 2024, even with votes from the ACCs.

By the time this book is published, much may have changed in the UMC in Africa and in the overall denomination. What the reader most needs to take away from this account of recent events is that the destructive empire mindset—seeking power and dominion without account-

---

36. Smith was inspired by Brafman and Beckstrom's *The Starfish and the Spider: The Unstoppable Power of Leaderless Organizations* (New York: Portfolio (Penguin Group), 2006).

37. Jeremy Smith, "Methodism 2.0." *Hacking Christianity*, Jan 2, 2014, https://hackingchristianity.net/2014/01/the-release-of-methodism-2-0.html.

38. Jeremy Smith, "On the Success of Methodism 2.0," *Hacking Christianity*, January 3, 2023, https://hackingchristianity.net/2023/01/on-the-success-of-methodism-2-0.html.

39. Heather Hahn and Sam Hodges, "Taking Stock after a Season of Disaffiliations," *UM News*, Dec. 15, 2022, https://www.umnews.org/en/news/taking-stock-after-a-season-of-disaffiliations.

ability and regardless of the damage done—remains an active force in our church, that the underlying conflict in our denomination is not, in actuality, about human sexuality, and that as such it will inevitably eventually reignite over another litmus test issue unless the empire dynamics and mentalities are proactively identified and replaced by a system that is impossible to dominate.

The dynamic of ecclesiastic empire working through the means of patronage is one that the church will need to work to dismantle for some time. That work will involve all United Methodists, regardless of their identification as progressive, centrist, or traditionalist. To the average WCA member who had no idea what their leaders have been doing in their name: demand accountability and a new model. To the "centrists" and "progressives": don't be fooled by the myth that you and your leaders don't engage in or profit from empire politics. Greed, lust for power, and even patronizing savior complexes are equal opportunity sins. To the Methodists exiting the denomination: If you want to build a new church, focus on reaching those who do not have a faith community instead of pillaging existing ministries. Don't pressure United Methodists to leave a church they love—one that has raised them, trained them, and helped them in times of war and disease. To all those intending to remain in The United Methodist Church, whether American or African, conservative or progressive: I plead that you engage in the hard conversations—the holy conferencing—necessary to envision a means of being the church together across national boundaries, one that creates an alternative to ecclesiastic empire. Given the history of Western colonialism, Methodists in the United States must be particularly committed to dismantling rather than perpetuating the systems and structures of empire in all their manifestations.

The resources for such work are there in our Methodist heritage. Joerg Rieger has written about the means of grace as an alternative to empire and the "theological surplus" in Methodism that points beyond empire.[40] In particular, Methodist theology has always emphasized love: God's love

---

40. Joerg Rieger, *Grace Under Pressure: Negotiating the Heart of the Methodist Traditions* (Nashville: United Methodist General Board of Higher Education and Ministry, 2011).

for us and, in response, our love for God and for others. This is not a superficial love or a cheap grace, but one that requires us to open our eyes to sin in the world, humbly confess our role in it, and strive for the freedom and prosperity for all people as much as we seek it for ourselves. As the late scholar and social activist bell hooks reminds us, "awaking to love can happen only as we let go of our obsession with power and domination."[41] As United Methodists, we must enact this kind of love in our congregations, in our local annual conferences, and in our partnerships with our UMC siblings around the world.

---

41.   bell hooks, *All About Love: New Visions* (New York: William Morrow, 1999), 159.

7

THE STRUGGLE OF AFRICAN VOICES IN THE UNITED METHODIST CHURCH

Lloyd Nyarota

The expansion of the European empires across Africa came entangled with Christianity. This can be witnessed by how denominations experienced growth following the influence of European powers. The same tactics or strategies used by Europe to occupy Africa were also used by the churches in their evangelization programs in the mission field. John Wesley Z. Kurewa wrote, "The missionaries and the colonists shared a common interest in eradicating anything that was viewed as African, either in perception or practice."[1] Imperialism and Christianity are cojoined in the formation of modern Africa with repercussions that are very much still alive today.

Colonists and missionaries also agreed on the necessity of dividing Africa. To this day, Africa is divided into three European language zones or blocks: Anglophone, Lusophone (Portuguese), and Francophone, a legacy of its colonial past. Many countries in Africa are also divided into zones of denominational influence. In Zimbabwe, it is almost certain that, when

---

1. John Wesley Zwomunondita Kurewa, *An African Pilgrimage on Evangelism: A Historical Study of the Various Approaches to Evangelism in Africa (100-2000 CE)* (Salt River, South Africa: Salty Print, 2011), 70.

one tells their denomination, the hearer can correctly guess their tribe/ clan or region of the country they come from. The churches employed the same concept that was used during the partition of Africa at the Berlin Conference of 1884, where European empires divided the continent among themselves to exploit its resources.[2] Using the same concept, the churches under the London Missionary Society partitioned countries into areas of influence through evangelization.

The purpose of the partitions was to influence and control their subjects and converts. As Kurewa wrote, "Each missionary society ended up with a territory within which it was to develop its missionary work, leaving the people with no option to choose which brand of denominational church they would want. They had to accept the denomination that was assigned to its area."[3] This was the widely used practice of comity agreements, a phrase that has, ironically, come back into play because of its inclusion in the United Methodist *Book of Discipline* ¶2548.2, which the Wesleyan Covenant Association (WCA) has tried to use to exit the denomination,[4] though ultimately to no avail.[5] This same colonial strategy has been repackaged in modern day Methodism.

This chapter will show how United Methodist conflicts in the United States were exported to Africa as part of the expansion of empire by those who held on to neocolonial ideas of influence and control over Africa. It will explore how groups like the Wesleyan Covenant Association and Good News, in their attempts to expand their influence and control of The United Methodist Church, looked at African votes as raw materials that could be used to take control of the denomination. These groups sought to mine African delegates to General Conference like colonies, where they would extract much needed votes to fight the power battles of taking control of the denomination. Generally, Africans ended up falling

2. John Mackenzie, *The Partition of Africa, 1880-1900: And European Imperialism in the Nineteenth Century* (New York: Routledge, 1983).

3. Kurewa, *An African Pilgrimage on Evangelism*, 68.

4. Lawrence E. Hillis, "What is Comity, really? Debunking the WCA's 'Loophole' around the UMC Trust Clause," *United Methodist Insight*, May 31, 2022, https://um-insight.net/in-the-church/umc-future/what-is-comity-really-debunking-the-wca%E2%80%99s-%E2%80%9Cloophole%E2%80%9D-around-/.

5. Heather Hahn, "Church court clarifies property-transfer rules," *UM News*, August 23, 2022.

to imperial techniques of exploitation, and in the process acted against their own interests as they participated in imperial projects. Some of the U.S. caucuses used American imperialistic strategies to try to take over leadership of the African United Methodist Church by using their surrogates as candidates in elections.

The Reform and Renewal Coalition

A case in point came sometime after the 2000 General Conference. The Reform and Renewal Coalition—a coalition of Good News, the Confessing Movement, the WCA, and other related groups—realized how the terrain in the United States was changing. They came up with a grand plan by which they intended to implode The United Methodist Church from within to create a breakaway denomination over which they would have total control.

One of the major challenges in executing this plan was the growth of the African Church, which was heading toward having the largest numbers and representation in the denomination's decision-making processes. The Reform and Renewal Coalition saw that growth as potential raw material that could be exploited to cause trouble in the denomination. They had to develop a strategy for how to exploit and extract this raw material in the form of votes at denominational meetings. This was an important means they needed to use to achieve their greater goal of imploding the denomination from within through fanning the fires of divisions.

The Reform and Renewal Coalition needed to identify an issue that would make Africans emotional and gullible to their machinations. They accurately identified homosexuality as an emotional subject for Africans; they had already been using it as the presenting issue in organizing in the United States as well. It is clear that this game plan was not shared with the Africans.

The Africa Initiative

The Reform and Renewal Coalition created what amounted to a *puppet* caucus in Africa, which they named the Africa Initiative. The name was carefully chosen to appear as an African-initiated caucus. This venture started with Rev. Jerry P. Kulah in 2012 under the guise of the Sustainable Economic Development Plan for Central Conferences in Africa.[6] This new group was initiated with an eye toward convening at the 2012 General Conference. It was around then that the Reform and Renewal Coalition started the pre-General Conference gatherings of African delegates.

After the 2012 General Conference, African bishops began to question how African delegates had gathered in Atlanta for a pre-General Conference orientation without their knowledge. As a response to the bishops' questions, Kulah wrote a letter to the African bishops on July 18, 2013, presenting a proposal for the so-called Sustainable Economic Development Plan.[7] The document articulated all the issues that are now part of the Reform and Renewal Coalition messaging. The document stated:

> Many leaders of the Church have simultaneously been caught in a state of shock, disbelief, and disappointment, unfortunately, over the rapid decline of the UMC in some other parts of the world which were once strong pillars for propagating the Gospel of Jesus Christ and sending out missionaries to the rest of the world. For example, it is estimated that the United Methodist Church in the U. S. has lost 3.5 million members within four decades and is losing about 100,000 members annually. Consequently, also, many annual conferences there are struggling financially, and the General Church agencies are reducing budgets, and likely will continue to do so in the future. . . . Also, the Central Conferences of Africa having close to 30% of the General Conference vote while currently contributing very little to the funding of the General Church raises genuine arguments against our rights to voting on the General Church's budgets and allocation of funds.[8]

Note in this statement the focus on the decline of the church in the United States, financial cuts to the general agencies, and the growth of the African vote, all issues that became part of the WCA's rhetoric.

This communication with the bishops was now building toward the 2016 General Conference, as it pointed to the 30 percent African vote at

---

6. This is a document that was written in 2012 by Rev. Jerry P. Kulah and circulated to Africa central conference bishops proposing a gathering of African central conferences.

7. Letter, Rev. Jerry P. Kulah to Bishop Eben K. Nhiwatiwa. This letter was sent through my email to print and forward to Bishop Nhiwatiwa in his role as president of the Africa Central Conferences College of Bishops.

8. Jerry P. Kulah, "Sustainable Economic Development Conference for the Central Conferences of Africa: A Proposal to Secure the Economic Future of the Central Conferences of Africa," 2013, p. 3.

General Conference. At the 2016 General Conference, the African Initiative organized its first gathering and prayer service on the sidelines of General Conference. There was, however, no harmony between the Africa Initiative leadership and the African bishops. The tensions continued for years until 2022, when the African bishops released a statement disassociating themselves from both the African Initiative and WCA, accusing both of spreading false information about the UMC in their areas. The bishops went further, stating they will not allow activities of these groups in their episcopal areas. They claim that the WCA and Africa Initiative were wrongly influencing God's people in African episcopal areas.[9]

As we approached the 2016 General Conference, Rev. Kulah had started to recruit some members in his annual conference with a particular focus on General Conference delegates, which tells a lot about the caucus. It was clear that its focus was basically on how to exploit the Africans and their needed votes, which had to be managed at General Conference.

An interesting point to note is that this initiative targeted Liberia as the entry point for the Americans to exploit Africa. Although the Liberia Conference is historically the oldest branch of United Methodism in Africa, they are far from the biggest in Africa. There are ten times as many United Methodists in the Democratic Republic of Congo as in Liberia.[10] We need to take note of the history of Liberia, which is quite interesting in relationship to the American history of imperialism. Liberia is part of land that was bought by America to which freed slaves who wanted to return to the land of Africa were sent. Liberia has a history of being ruled by presidents who were born in and had connections to the United States. The first indigenous president of Liberia was Samuel Doe, who came to power through the April 12, 1980, coup.

Because of the strong imperial ties between Liberia and the United States, the Liberian church had stronger ties to the UMC in the United

---

9. Africa Colleges of Bishops, "Statement from Africa Colleges of Bishops, Thursday, September 8, 2022, Africa University, Mutare, Zimbabwe," https://www.unitedmethodistbishops.org/files/statement+from+africa+colleges+of+bishops+-+sept+8.pdf.

10. General Commission on Finance and Administration, "2020 Delegate Calculation by Annual Conference," http://s3.amazonaws.com/Website_Properties/news-media/press- center/documents/2020_Delegate_Calc_by_AC_with_2016_comp.pdf.

States than to most of the African conferences.[11] It is, therefore, not a coincidence that the Reform and Renewal Coalition chose a Liberian and the Liberia Conference as an entry point to expand American imperialism in the African United Methodist Church.

This plan to use the Africa Initiative to line up votes on behalf of the Reform and Renewal Coalition fits with the 2004 Good News strategy document, "Options for the Future, With Some Strategic Implications, Summer 2004."[12] That document lays out the possibility of "amicable separation" and "voluntary departure." In discussing the "tactics" to achieve these and/or other ends, the document emphasizes the importance of networks and notes, "If there comes a time when a specific goal is decided upon, we could launch a new formal network in support of that goal." The Africa Initiative is just such a formal network, launched to support the Reform and Renewal Coalition's goals.

This Reform and Renewal Coalition plan to amicably separate the UMC was finally achieved at the General Conference special session of February 2019, which imploded the denomination.[13] Although the special General Conference was intended to resolve conflict in the denomination over human sexuality, the conference proceedings and the narrowly passed Traditional Plan merely added fuel to the fires of conflict in the denomination.

Protocol of Reconciliation and Grace through Separation

After the Reform and Renewal Coalition achieved their goal of passing the Traditional Plan, The United Methodist Church was left fractured. Africans became victims because of how their votes were exploited and ended

11. For a history of The United Methodist Church in Liberia, see Levi C. Williams, *A History of The United Methodist Church in Liberia* (Denver: Outskirts, 2014).

12. Mark Dicken, Scott Field, Phil Granger, and Tom Lambrecht. "Options for the Future: With Some Strategic Implications, Summer 2004, "https://web.archive.org/web/20050306020025/http://faithfulchristianlaity.org/options_for_the_future.htm.

13. Jeremy Smith, "The Betrayal of Good News: How a 2004 Blueprint Created the #GC2019 Endgame," *Hacking Christianity*, February 6, 2019, https://hackingchristianity.net/2019/02/the-betrayal-of-good-news-how-a-2004-blueprint-created-the-gc2019-endgame.html.

up shouldering the total blame for what happened at the 2019 General Conference.[14] The Reform and Renewal Coalition, however, saw a window of opportunity to be exploited in creating their own denomination. There were efforts to negotiate a deal that would give those who planned to break away a chance to do so in a way that would give them leverage over properties and denominational funds.

Once the church was fractured at General Conference 2019, efforts were made to split it up, including the so-called Protocol of Reconciliation and Grace through Separation and the formation of the Global Methodist Church (GMC). These efforts to divide the church, however, were imagined as purely American initiatives and ventures where Africans had no stake. The Protocol of Reconciliation and Grace through Separation was a fancy name for an agreement that offered nothing substantial that related to the title. There is no reconciliation, and there is no grace in that agreement. It may be that *separation* was the only word related to the agreement, which should have been named, "A Protocol of American Schism." This was purely an American agreement to resolve an American problem and conflict.

The negotiating team was composed of fifteen people representing the three opposing groups in the United States. In seeking to resolve their conflict by crafting The Protocol document, the United States had twelve members on the team, though they represent less than 50 percent of church membership and are experiencing the fastest membership decline in the denomination.[15] Although Africans compose a significant percentage of the denomination's membership,[16] the only African present in the negotiating room was Bishop John K. Yambasu, who was not part of the negotiations but rather a facilitator. He was later replaced by Kenneth Feinberg, an American, when it came to the finer details. Those of us who have been involved in negotiations and conflict resolution or transformation processes know very well that, in negotiations, facilitators do not speak their view-

---

14.   Lloyd Nyarota, "Africa's Great Betrayal: A Harvest of Thorns," *United Methodist Insight*, June 18, 2019, https://um-insight.net/perspectives/africa-s-great-betrayal-and-a-harvest-of-thorns/.

15.   Heather Hahn, "US dips below majority of membership," *UM News*, November 25, 2019.

16.   Africans comprised 42% of church membership as of 2018, though this percentage has likely grown since then. See General Commission on Finance and Administration, "2020 Delegate Calculations by Annual Conference."

points, as it is up to the conflicting parties to agree on the terms and decide outcomes.

This means that Africa had zero representation at the negotiating table. I want to emphasize the point that facilitators are not negotiators and have no control over the outcome. Looking at The Protocol from this perspective, Africa becomes the only region that had zero representation in negotiating and crafting the so-called Protocol, even though, to repeat, we represent 50 percent of the denomination's membership and the fastest growing part of The United Methodist Church. One European bishop, Christian Alsted, one bishop from the Philippines, Rudolfo Rudy Juan, and one Filipino clergyperson, Rev. Egmedio "Jun" Equila Jr., were part of The Protocol negotiation team, meaning that those two regions, even though they have fewer members than Africa, were represented, although Africa was not.[17]

Even Rev. Jerry Kulah, the Renewal and Reform Coalition's face in Africa and founder of the Africa Initiative initially opposed The Protocol as being colonialist. As soon as The Protocol was announced, the Liberia Conference passed a resolution opposing it on February 14, 2020, because they noted that Africa was not part of the negotiations.[18] It says a lot that even Rev. Kulah, who has been the staunchest African ally of the Reform and Renewal Coalition, thought that the plan was bad for Africans. Note that, after the Reform and Renewal Coalition called a meeting in Johannesburg on February 24–27, 2020, where they had to pressure him and other coopted African WCA council members, he later came around, but his initial reaction is telling.[19]

To calm the storm of the initial resistance from the Africa Initiative, the WCA organized a hypocritical non-event in Johannesburg. The Africa Initiative suggested amendments to The Protocol and even sent them to the Liberia Annual Conference for voting, but they were not told that renego-

---

17. For a full list of members of The Protocol mediation team, see Reconciliation and Grace Through Separation, "Mediation Team," https://www.gracethroughseparation.com/who-we-are. Bishop Mande Muyombo, an African, is listed as having "participated in the initial meeting convened by Bishop John Yambasu and other Central Conference Bishops in July 2019 and consulted with the mediation team during the process," but was not a member of the mediation team itself.

18. E. Julu Swen and Sam Hodges, "Liberia wants changes in Protocol," *UM News*, February 24, 2020.

19. Hahn Heather, "Key African group supports Protocol plan," *UM News*, February 27, 2020.

tiation wasn't possible. One of the points raised by the Africa Initiative was to keep The United Methodist Church's logo. The Africa Initiative were told lies and offered false hope of consideration for their amendments, just as the GMC was launched without consideration of the proposals from the Africa Initiative. If the WCA and the Reform and Renewal Coalition supported the changes proposed by the Africa Initiative in Johannesburg in February of 2020, why did they name their new denomination the GMC without accommodating the proposed amendments to The Protocol from the Africa Initiative? This disregard for Africans' stated concern for the United Methodist name and logo indicates that the WCA/GMC was simply telling lies to their colonial/coalition partners, the Africa Initiative.

Patricia Miller, a member of The Protocol negotiating team, said something interesting about the splinter group. On July 17, 2021, during a Zoom meeting, she told Zimbabweans that, even if The Protocol fails, the Global Methodist Church will go ahead with its established structures. This means that the proposals of the Africa Initiative were insignificant and of no value to shaping the structure, discipline, and doctrine of the GMC. It is now time for the leadership of the Africa Initiative to see the true posture of this neocolonial coalition. The Africa Initiative should tell the WCA to take their knee off their necks and let them breathe, or else they will be dead.

When one studies The Protocol, one must conclude that what The Protocol wanted to achieve are the very things Africans do not support. For example, the intent of The Protocol as stated in the preamble is, "We further envision that the post-separation UMC will repeal the Traditional Plan and remove all restrictive language related to LGBTQ persons."[20] This is totally against what Africa is advocating for the future of the UMC. There is nothing in The Protocol that reflects anything about the African United Methodist Church. Even the Africa Initiative agreed that The Protocol does not express anything African. The Protocol was an embodiment of everything Africans stand against. The Protocol wants to divide the church; Africa stands for unity. The Protocol wants to change the language in the current *Book of Discipline* on homosexuality; Africa stands for maintaining it, as they voted in February 2019.

---

20. The Protocol of Reconciliation and Grace through Separation: Preamble.

164

This approach to negotiating The Protocol can only be explained by the neocolonial mentality of those Americans who purported to be representing Africans as self-appointed spokespersons at the negotiating table. On one hand, the Reform and Renewal Coalition realized that the majority of Africans are generally conservative in theology and scriptural interpretation; their mistake was to think that Africans can be so stupid as to always accept decisions made on their behalf. On the other hand, the Progressive coalition understands how the majority of Africans are generally tolerant and hospitable by nature, but they may be missing the point that Africans are not foolish.

More and more African delegates have self-respect and want to honor the struggles of our ancestors: those who survived in ships, packed like sardines in chains; those who rose against colonialism in Africa; those who have struggled against segregation and humiliation; those who have taught us that we are equal human beings, all created in the image of God, and that we have a simple task. To honor and respect them and our history, African delegates and people of African descent began to distance themselves from the so-called Protocol and planned to vote against it at the General Conference. This vote was intended to tell the Americans that they should move away from the centuries-old position that they were masters and Africans were slaves to be dictated to and told what to do. Africans began to see through the cynical agreement that was made without us, but some Americans wanted to whip Africans into line to support it. Having seen through these machinations, the African bishops voiced the exclusion of Africa in The Protocol negotiations and found it difficult to support an agreement that excluded the growing African church.[21]

The Global Methodist Church

Unfortunately, the Wesleyan Covenant Association presented itself as an organization that thinks and speaks on behalf of Africans. This is an outdated practice that some Africans denounced, as it undermines the

---

21. "African Bishops: Let's Make Our Own Choices," *UM News*, October 30, 2020.

equality of all humans and denies people their basic dignity.[22] The worst example of this disingenuous nature of the relationship was where they said one thing and did something else. The WCA told Africans that passing the Traditional Plan will resolve all the problems in The United Methodist Church, when they knew that it would worsen the conflict. They condemned the One Church Plan, yet they built the Global Methodist Church *Transitional Book of Doctrines and Discipline*, ¶337, around the One Church Plan model.[23] To enhance the appearance of cooperation, the organization engaged in coopting a few Africans to deny claims of exclusion when these people were not even consulted when decisions were made. Only talking points decided in the United States were given to people in Africa.

After General Conference and a vote on The Protocol were delayed again to 2024, the WCA formed a splinter denomination, the Global Methodist Church, which they tried to impose upon Africans and upon Africa as a continent. Just like they did with The Protocol negotiations, they never even talked to their so-called coalition/colonial partners, the Africa Initiative, whom they continued to use as an avenue through which influence was extended to promote American imperialism. However, when the Global Methodist Church was announced, just like when The Protocol was announced, Africans, including the Africa Initiative leadership, were shocked to hear the WCA associating Africa with these ventures. The Africa Initiative was never consulted. In a statement released on February 12, 2022, Bishop Kasap Owan of Congo, who has been a member of the WCA, lamented that the announcement of the Global Methodist Church was a sign that African voices are not listened to.[24] There were lots of expressions of shock and surprise on social media, and the Africa Initiative

---

22. Albert Otshudi Longe, "Beware the 'Berlin Conference' Model of the Protocol of Separation," *United Methodist Insight*, April 21, 2021, https://um-insight.net/in-the-church/umc-future/beware-the-berlin-conference-model-of-the-protocol-for-sep/.

23. Jay Therrell, "Ten Reasons Why I Will Join the Global Methodist Church," Wesleyan Covenant Association, July 8, 2022, https://wesleyancovenant.org/2022/07/06/ten-reasons-why-ill-join-the-global-methodist-church/. Reason #8 is "Greater Autonomy for Local Churches."

24. Kasap Owen Tshibang, "Bishop Kasap Owen's Greeting Message to the 226 Pastors of the South Congo Annual Conference this Saturday, February 12th, 2022, in Jerusalem Church/Lubumbashi, DRC."

continued to say they will wait for the 2024 General Conference to make their final decisions.[25]

There has been a façade of inclusion of Africans in the WCA leadership, but when one pays close attention, one can see who the decision makers are. The WCA coopted Rev. Jerry P. Kulah, Rev. Forbes Matonga, and Kimba Evariste as WCA council members to represent the three central conferences in Africa, but all the decision-making bodies in the WCA have included no African representation. If this is how decision making is done in the WCA, the question then becomes, who is in charge in the GMC, and how will future decisions be made in this splinter group? This American-dominated approach sends a clear message to Africans who may be lured by and entertaining the remote idea of joining the Global Methodist Church. This is an American venture where Africans will be mere guests, always treated like children who must be told when to speak and how to behave and only receive whatever the masters decide. It is the replication of a pattern visible in American political dynamics. If a decision doesn't come from those who see themselves as in charge, it must be undermined by placing a knee on our neck to suffocate any energy; they can't comprehend that something good may come from those they deem as inferior.

One can clearly see through and read such an attitude in everything the WCA says and writes. For example, Good News and the WCA have published several articles attacking the Christmas Covenant, a proposal written by central conferences leaders and delegates, most of whom are from Africa.[26] (See more on the Christmas Covenant in the next chapter.) They also attacked the African bishops when they stated they would not support any proposal to dissolve or split The United Methodist Church.[27] Whenever we try to contribute to the future of The United Methodist

25.   Albert Otshudi Longe, "Dual Membership or Duplicity: African United Methodists and the Global Methodist Church, *United Methodist Insight*, June 1, 2022, https://um-insight.net/in-the-church/umc-future/dual-membership-or-duplicity-african-united-methodists-and-t/.

26.   Tom Lambrecht, "Understanding the Christmas Covenant," *Good News Magazine*, November 16, 2020, https://tomlambrecht.goodnewsmag.org/understanding-the-christmas-covenant/.

27.   Walter Fenton, "African Bishops and the Protocol for Reconciliation and Grace through Separation," Wesleyan Covenant Association, November 20, 2020, https://wesleyancovenant.org/2020/11/17/african-bishops-and-the-protocol-for-reconciliation-and-grace-through-separation/.

Church as Africans, they press their knees on our necks. The concerted effort by the WCA to undermine a proposal from the central conferences follows this thought process of maintaining colonial hegemony that dictates what to do, and when, and how. To them, African delegates are only a source of votes to be mined like raw materials used to achieve their American-centered agenda, not partners to be treated with mutuality in crafting the future of the church.

Africans have no stake in the splinter Global Methodist Church. This should be observed from the simple understanding that the GMC *Transitional Book of Doctrines and Discipline* was written without involvement of the Africa Initiative.[28] Some of their members were not even aware of what the GMC *Transitional Book of Doctrines and Discipline* says and didn't have a copy. A group of Africans, including me, made efforts to obtain the GMC *Transitional Book of Doctrines and Discipline* and share electronic copies with some Africa Initiative members, even though they were supposedly coalition/colonial partners of the WCA.

The GMC *Transitional Book of Doctrines and Discipline* does not include the Traditional Plan, which is something Africans strongly want to be included.[29] The hypocrisy became visible when the GMC and WCA abused the confidence of their allies who voted for the Traditional Plan at General Conference 2019 by abandoning it and asking them to join a new splinter group. This is true betrayal. The GMC *Transitional Book of Doctrines and Discipline* is totally silent on homosexuality; they do not even have the incompatibility paragraph, though they do refer to marriage as between a man and a woman.[30] For the Africa Initiative, which considers these stances as non-negotiables, there is a need to clearly question the level of trust that must be afforded to versatile groups that change based on their interests. Why then should Africa have anything to do with the GMC? Africa is not a stakeholder in the GMC; it is an American venture.

---

28. David W. Scott, "Where Are the Central Conferences in the WCA's New Denomination?" *UM & Global*, November 15, 2019, http://www.umglobal.org/2019/11/where-are-central-conferences-in-w-cas.html.

29. Global Methodist Church, *The Transitional Book of Doctrines and Discipline*, https://global-methodist.org/wp-content/uploads/2022/09/Transitional-Discipline.20220912-Final.pdf.

30. See Global Methodist Church, *The Transitional Book of Doctrines and Discipline*.

The lack of clarity on many social concerns that afflict African peoples should raise an alarm as to the core beliefs of these colonial/coalition partners. The GMC will have a very limited set of social principles, but many African leaders have been very clear that the social witness of the church is important to the African churches and communities. At the same time, The United Methodist Church is moving toward a future of regionalization, where Africa will keep its values and a clear position on homosexuality as spelled out in the current *Book of Discipline*. The regionalization proposed in the Christmas Covenant, a piece of legislation written and presented from the Central Conferences—by a majority of Africans from across the three African central conference—defines the future of The United Methodist Church globally.

Africans have had nothing to do with these two initiatives: The Protocol for Reconciliation and Grace through Separation and the Global Methodist Church, whose development was a clear demonstration of neocolonialism in The United Methodist Church. Both processes and outcomes approached Africa in a disrespectful and neocolonial manner, yet there were efforts to try to legitimize them, to offer a decent face in order to force Africans to accept it. It is important to note that anything about the church of our Lord Jesus Christ that is planned and negotiated in dark corners and back rooms, where only a few people have authority, power, and control to think for other groups of people, lacks any decency. This only perpetuates the history of the United States whereby people of African descent have been regarded as not human, subjected to slavery, torture, murders, and police brutality in recent years.

The culmination of The Protocol and the formation of the Global Methodist Church as instruments to facilitate the formation of splinter groups, with the claim that they have been representing and speaking for and on behalf of Africans, should be viewed as sacrilege. The GMC does not deserve the attention of African people. Attempts by anyone of African descent to legitimize such a venture would be a slap on the faces of our ancestors and forefathers who have struggled for Africa's sons and daughters to have justice, freedom, liberty, human dignity, and respect as equal human beings created in the image of God.

Conclusion

As I come to the end of this writing, it is important to clarify that the reasons that have been given as justification for forming a splinter group denomination named the Global Methodist Church are not disagreements we have in Africa. While the GMC was formed because of supposed disagreements on theological issues in the UMC in the United States, for many African United Methodists, the disagreements are more political than theological.

The United States is different from Africa. As African United Methodists, we have no conflicts such as those always propounded by the WCA and the Reform and Renewal Coalition as the basis of their justification to form a splinter group. Their differences are based in the United States; the conflicts are in the United States; they are not global. When Americans decided to exclude Africa in the negotiations and formations of The Protocol, the Liberation Methodist Connexion (LMX), and the GMC, they were clear that it addressed American problems and created American solutions. Why do they want others to be involved unless it is as voting machines or resources to be exploited?

There has been no reason for Africans to labor in supporting The Protocol and the formation of other American denominations. The processes of The Protocol agreement cast Africans as sub-humans in the church of our forefathers. The United Methodist Church is the church of our grandparents and parents. Since the Protocol of Reconciliation and Grace through Separation, the Liberation Methodist Connexion, and the Global Methodist Church are all U.S. ventures, they should be preserved for discussion in the future U.S. regional conference, not made matters of debate to which the whole world must respond. This sense by Americans of the importance of U.S.-only issues may be coming from American exceptionalism, which leads to the imperialistic thinking that they are the world and, therefore, whatever is American is global. That is why, even when they play a game on their own, they will still come up with a *world* champion of a purely American sport. The Protocol, the LMX, and the GMC are purely American ventures that have no place in any General Conference agenda. They can wait to be discussed, debated, and voted upon in the U.S. regional conference, when that body is created by General Conference. There is no need to continue to load down and belabor all delegates from other parts of the world to spend time debating U.S. issues and conflicts.

The African people have lived under colonialism, fought and defeated colonialism, and, therefore, shall stand ready to interrupt it in whatever form or manner it shows its face, especially when it shows up in the church. Africans and others from the other Central Conferences, having seen the differences and premises for the conflicts in the United States, propose that it is time The United Methodist Church becomes a real global church with a global structure. The Christmas Covenant, written by a majority of Africans working with other central conference representatives, will help The United Methodist Church move into the future as a worldwide denomination. The Christmas Covenant will strengthen African United Methodism and maintain our unity as a worldwide denomination doing ministry and mission in a variety of contexts.

Through the Christmas Covenant, there is a greater future for the people called United Methodists from all over the world. The United Methodist Church will keep growing. The growing parts of the denomination will always be ready to support the struggling regions if they call for help in a respectful, Christian form of mission, carried out through non-colonial partnerships. God is not yet done with the people called United Methodists all over the world. The better days are ahead of us. The best is yet to come.

My final words to proponents of divisions as an African, like many of my kith and kin, sons and daughters of the soil, my many brothers and sisters in The United Methodist Church in Africa: We will continue being part of the church of our parents and grandparents. We will continue being part of the church that raised us. We will continue in the church that focuses on things that matter to us like health, education, malaria, poverty eradication, human rights advocacy, opportunities for the poor, and justice. Africans want to be part of The United Methodist Church that shapes the world. African United Methodists are not going anywhere. We don't want to join the other church; we don't want to join a church we don't know; we don't want to join a church no one has ever heard of. God bless the people called United Methodist.

8

THE CHRISTMAS COVENANT

Toward Decolonizing UMC Polity

Cristine Carnate-Atrero and Izzy Alvaran

Historical Setting

The United Methodist Church faces structural difficulties in living out its commitment to being a global denomination. Past experiences in General Conference display how issues that are pertinent to United Methodists in one region might not be as important to others in a different region of the world. Given the historical roots of the denomination, ecclesial and theological issues that are prominent in the United States tend to dominate the debate during General Conference. For delegates from central conferences, it often seems like we are treated as guests and not as full members of the connection. In our view, addressing this issue demands a long and difficult process of shifting the structures and polity of United Methodism. In this chapter, we argue for regionalization as the best way to address the systemic problems in the denomination.

Regionalization is not a new phenomenon. Trade, economics, geography, politics, and even the weather have been conceptualized regionally for centuries by a variety of peoples around the world. In fact, regionalization precedes globalization. The networks that make up globalization often emerged out of the integration of preexisting regional networks, a process carried out through economic trade, political colonization, and human travel. Colonization might be understood as a process where the world was created according to the image and the categories of the regions where the center of colonial power took residence. In the colonial era, religion also influenced communities where the movements of trade and the Western conquest of the world played out. Cultural values were part of this exportation of Western norms. European-influenced food, fashion, arts, music, and words were inculcated into local areas. Christianity was often a part of this cultural package exported from the West.

The Philippine Islands have long been linked to other lands regionally and globally. For centuries, the Philippines were in the trade routes of neighboring Chinese and Malay merchants, and eventually, the Spaniards, seeking Indonesian spices, landed inadvertently on Philippine shores. The Philippines became an important layover in Spanish trade between China and the New World, and the islands were incorporated into Spain's colonial empire. The Spanish introduced Christianity in the form of Catholicism to the Philippines. At the end of the 1898 Spanish-American war, which saw colonial control of the Philippines transferred from Spain to the United States, Americans brought Protestantism, including the Methodist church, to the Philippines. Methodism became a way for American culture and values to make their way to the Philippines. While indigenous Filipino leadership would eventually assume control of Methodism in the Philippines, there were early clashes over American control over the Filipino church, most notably in the person of Nicolas Zamora, who left the American church to found the independent Iglesia Evangélica Metodista en las Islas Filipinas. Tension between local control and global connection has recurred throughout Filipino Methodist history.[1]

Today, American-centric religious movements continue to influence the activities and conversations on the priorities of missions and ministries

---

1. For overviews of Filipino Methodist history, see Jose Gamboa, Jr., *Methodism in the Philippines: A Century of Faith and Vision* (Manila: Philippines Central Conference, The United Methodist Church, 2003); Luther Jeremiah Oconer, *Spirit-Filled Protestantism: Holiness-Pentecostal Revivals and the Making of Filipino Methodist Identity* (Eugene, OR: Pickwick, 2017).

in The United Methodist Church (UMC) despite local and regional structures through the central conferences and jurisdictional conferences. This is true in the Philippines and throughout the world. Since the 1970s, the United Methodist movement has been struggling with divergent opinions and theology on what is acceptable regarding LGBTQ+ clergy and same-sex unions, as well as the concept of tribalism and polygamy within Africa. This has been a global debate with significant variations in views between, as well as within, regions.

This struggle in the UMC has led the church to the point of formal division. As of this writing, disaffiliation conversations and votes are being held in some local churches in the United States and Eastern Europe to decide whether to leave The United Methodist Church. Congregations in the United States must do so by the December 31, 2023, deadline of *Book of Discipline* ¶2553, which allows local churches to depart with their property if certain requirements are fulfilled.

The Emergence of the Christmas Covenant

While some are eager to leave and some are eager to see them go, there are others who have been working to preserve the unity of the church amid this conflict. To keep The United Methodist Church under a broader, big-tent theology despite differing missional and cultural contexts, a coalition of grassroots lay and clergy leaders from several central conferences and the United States gathered to work on the package of legislation called "The Christmas Covenant: A Gift of Hope."[2]

The advent of the Christmas Covenant was the tumultuous, special, called General Conference in February 2019, where United Methodists narrowly approved the Traditional Plan—a set of legislative proposals that

---

2. Portions of this chapter are taken from material found on the Christmas Covenant website, https://www.christmascovenant.com/. All references and quotations are used by permission. The authors of this chapter had a role in developing the material on that website, along with other contributors. Thus, while Cristine Carnate-Atrero and Izzy Alvaran are listed as the authors of this piece, we recognize the entire team that has worked to produce the Christmas Covenant as having contributed to this chapter. We believe this collective approach to authorship better reflects the more collectivist cultures prevalent in the central conferences of The United Methodist Church, rather than the individualistic culture prevalent in the United States, which leads to an emphasis on sole authorship, even when insights have been collectively generated.

affirmed the current stance of the church on how it relates to LGBTQ+ persons and made some prohibitions against the ordination of LGBTQ+ clergy more stringent. The backlash was a tidal wave of protests from progressives. Those sitting on the fence about LGBTQ+ inclusion joined a movement to roll back the denomination's policies against LGBTQ+ persons and their allies. During the U.S. annual conference season that year, a supermajority of delegates committed to repealing the Traditional Plan were elected to the next General and Jurisdictional Conferences.

Another response to the 2019 General Conference was the preponderance of legislative proposals that sought to split up or dissolve the UMC. All these petitions emanated from the United States. These were generally not received well in the denomination's central conferences, regions of the church outside the United States. The college of bishops of the Philippines Central Conference released a statement in August 2019 saying: "We, United Methodists in the Philippines are intensely opposed to any move that dissolves The United Methodist Church. From the beginning of the Church in the New Testament, division and schism in the Church are to be avoided and unity must be achieved and maintained." They also said that "there is now a need to reimagine the future of United Methodism because the world both locally and globally has changed, and we need to take this change as the context for witnessing to our faith regionally, in doing our mission and living our life as a church."[3]

In response to this statement from the Filipino bishops, a petition was sent to General Conference by Filipino delegate Rev. Jonathan Ulanday to hold off discussing any petition related to the dissolution of the denomination. Titled, "Oppose Dissolution and Preserve the Unity of The United Methodist Church," the petition says,

> After the 2019 General Conference passed the Traditional Plan, various groups of United Methodists in the United States have put forward plans that call for disaffiliation, separation, segmentation, and worse, dissolution of The United Methodist Church. These plans are wantonly against the spirit of unity and the inclusiveness of the church enshrined in the Preamble

---

3. Philippines Central Conference College of Bishops, "United Methodists in the Philippines seek UMC unity," September 9, 2019, https://www.unitedmethodistbishops.org/newsdetail/united-methodists -in-the-philippines-seek-umc-unity-12904170.

and Articles 4, 5, and 6 of The UMC Constitution. Any plan to dismember or dissolve the church is harmful to the Body of Christ through whom people of faith seek to connect and live in gracious relationships.[4]

It asks General Conference to:

1. Suspend all actions furthering any dissolution, disaffiliation, and separation plans in favor of preserving the unity of the church in compliance with our Constitution and the biblically founded values of unity, inclusiveness, and contextualization in our Preamble.
2. Authorize the Connectional Table and the Standing Committee on Central Conference Matters to jointly study and submit a report with proposals to the next General Conference session that preserves and strengthens the unity of the church in mission through a restructured polity that affirms and values broad contextual ministry policies and practices, including parity in contextual authority among existing central and jurisdictional conferences and/or any future regional bodies established by General Conference.[5]

The following month, September 2019, the African college of bishops issued a statement saying, "We do not support any legislation that calls for the dissolution of The United Methodist Church. We uphold our values as a connectional and worldwide church committed to 'Making disciples of Jesus Christ, for the transformation of the world.'" Furthermore, they said:

We cannot allow a split in the global church to split up the African church again. We cannot allow a split in the church to further reduce us to second-class citizens in a church that only needs us when they want our votes. We have been in second class for too long. We believe that as Africans, we have the right of self-determination and we have the right to speak for ourselves and determine who we want to be.[6]

As these voices were rising to oppose calls to dissolve the UMC, a group of lay and clergy leaders from central conferences and some from

---

4. Jonathan Ulanday, "Oppose Dissolution and Preserve the Unity of The United Methodist Church," https://www.facebook.com/notes/3373605182720765/?sfns=mo.

5. Ulanday, "Oppose Dissolution"; see also Petition Number: 20641-CO-NonDis-G, *2020 Advance Daily Christian Advocate*, Vol. 2, Section 1, 372.

6. Council of Bishops, The United Methodist Church, "African Bishops issue statement on future of United Methodist Church," September 6, 2019, https://www.unitedmethodistbishops.org/newsdetail/african-bishops-issue-statement-on-future-of-united-methodist-church-12903732.

the United States came together to strategize another way forward that focused on shared values of church unity, contextuality, and mission. This group—which eventually gave birth to the Christmas Covenant—supported the petition against dissolution from the Philippines, the passage of the new revised version of the Social Principles, and the Connectional Table proposal to establish a U.S. Regional Conference.

At that time, the group learned from one of its members, who also happened to be a member of the Connectional Table, that a six-year-long study conducted by the Connectional Table resulted in the group bringing the proposal to create a U.S. Regional Conference before General Conference. It took a while for the legislation to be brought to the Connectional Table Board of Trustees, which eventually approved the language submitted to the 2020 General Conference, as reflected in a collection of petitions in the *Advance Daily Christian Advocate* (ADCA).[7] The Connectional Table legislation focuses on enabling U.S. matters like clergy pensions to be considered by only American delegates. In this way, U.S. concerns were an important part of the motivation for the U.S. Regional Conference legislation.

In late October 2019, at Lake Junaluska, North Carolina, the central conference bishops met ahead of the regular fall meeting of the Council of Bishops. Three members of the pre-Christmas Covenant team were there to ask the bishops to support calls against the dissolution of the UMC. The Connectional Table leadership was also there to present its U.S. Regional Conference proposal, which the bishops received and supported. However, one member of the pre-Christmas Covenant team raised concerns about getting central conference support to pass the U.S. Regional Conference proposal without educating all General Conference delegates on the scope and ramifications of this American-centric legislation. Another member suggested expanding regionalization to cover the whole

7. See Petition Number: 20725-CO-¶11-C-!-G, Petition Number: 20723-CO-¶500-!-G, Petition Number: 20726-CO-¶500-!-G, Petition Number: 20722-CO-NonDis-!-G, and Petition Number: 20724-CO-NonDis-!-G, *2020 Advance Daily Christian Advocate*, Vol. 2, Section 1, 312, 323, 324, 373, 374. See also "Summary Report to General Conference by the Connectional Table" and "Bringing Missional Adaptation and Focus: A Report to General Conference by the Connectional Table," *2020 Advance Daily Christian Advocate*, Vol. 2, Section 2, 629–35. See also Connectional Table, "Creation of a U.S. Regional Conference," https://www.umc.org/-/media/umc-media/2019/12/02/21/51/usrc-petition-on-linecopy.ashx?la=en&hash=EBC9DC690112F5C036A3CB3E88DA54B57D3BA2FA.

UMC connection, making central conferences into new regions like the proposed U.S. Regional Conference. It was also envisioned that this major restructuring legislation would be submitted by an annual conference from one of the central conferences.

Upon further conversations on values and mission ministries among the central conference outreach team (later also known as the Christmas Covenant team), legislation was developed on worldwide regionalization to include improved amendments to the Constitution, expanding those from the Connectional Table proposal. Conversations with The Connectional Table's US Contextual Committee members enabled the incorporation of their U.S. Regional Conference legislation with clearer deadlines and implementation guidelines in the new legislation named "The Christmas Covenant: A Gift of Hope."[8] It was born during the Christmas season of 2019 and named in honor of the Christmas Conference of 1784. In January 2020, members of the Philippines' Cavite Annual Conference held meetings to share information about this legislation and its historical implications. In February 2020, the Cavite Annual Conference of the Philippines Central Conference unanimously approved The Christmas Covenant in time for the 45-day submission deadline for General Conference 2020.[9]

What Is the Christmas Covenant?

The Christmas Covenant[10] is a set of legislation and constitutional amendments submitted to The United Methodist Church's General Conference with the goal of establishing regional equity in the structures of the church for missional effectiveness while sustaining connectional unity. In its preamble, proponents declare: "We envision a Church that connects globally, engages in mission together, respects contextual ministry

---

8.   For full text of the legislation, see Christmas Covenant, "Legislation," https://www.christmascovenant.com/pagecc.

9.   For more on this process, see Gladys P. Mangiduyos and Sam Hodges, "Conference acts on protocol, Christmas Covenant," *UM News*, February 13, 2020.

10.   Material in this section is adapted from Christmas Covenant, "FAQs," https://www.christmascovenant.com/faqs, and Christmas Covenant, "Legislation," https://www.christmascovenant.com/pagecc.

settings, celebrates the diversity of God's creation in its many beautiful expressions, and values mutually empowering relationships in order to strengthen our core mission of evangelism, discipleship, and social witness for the transformation of the world."[11]

The Christmas Covenant achieves regional equity by transforming Central Conferences into Regional Conferences. The change in name will undo the negative connotation associated with the term "Central." (The Central Jurisdiction segregated Black churches and clergy in the United States until 1968.) The proposed constitutional amendments will strengthen the ability of Regional Conferences to adapt the *Book of Discipline* to meet the unique missional needs of each region. The Christmas Covenant also creates the United States Regional Conference with regional equity and structure (as proposed by the Connectional Table) and authorizes contextual adaptations of the *Book of Discipline* for missional effectiveness.

Yet the Christmas Covenant reflects more than just legislation. It is an expression of principles and values dear to United Methodists in the central conferences and around the world. These principles and values are the heart of the Christmas Covenant. To celebrate equity and mutuality, it draws from principles cherished by United Methodists from different regions of our global connection.

Principles

We are all children of God. Our United Methodist Social Principles state, "We believe that our primary identity is as children of God. . . . The Church seeks to fully embrace and nurture cultural formation and competency as a means to be fully one body, expressed in multiple ways" (2016, ¶161.A) To consider one another siblings of equal stature and rights is a key human value upheld by our Christian faith. "There is no longer Jew or Greek , there is no longer slave or free, there is no longer male and female; for all of you are one in Christ Jesus" (Galatians 3:28 NRSV). In appreciation of our differences as equals, it is our sacred covenant—anchored

---

11. Christmas Covenant, "Our Vision," https://www.christmascovenant.com/pagecc.

in grace—to share with one another the freedom to live out the gospel in accordance with our various missional contexts.

Ubuntu. Ubuntu is an African concept that embodies a way of life where humanity is based on the understanding of interdependence and community life. It is lived recognizing that we are all created in the image of God and should do unto others as we wish it to be done unto us. Bishop Desmond Tutu of South Africa declares, "The profound truth is, you cannot be human on your own. . . . You are human because you participate in the relationship. It says a person is a person through other persons. This is what we say. This is what the Bible says. This is what our human experience teaches us."[12]

Bayanihan. Bayanihan is a cherished ancient Filipino concept of community spirit and cooperation to achieve communal goals. Rooted in the word bayan, which means nation or community, bayanihan has been traditionally expressed through concrete community support for families that need to relocate. The able-bodied persons of the barrio carry the entire wood and bamboo house and transfers it to a new location, especially in anticipation of typhoons, floods, and landslides. This might be rare in these modern times, but the spirit of bayanihan is alive in the hearts of Filipinos when they act as one community in support of one another in times of need, even when it is deemed impossible to do so.

We celebrate these principles as we commit to building and prospering a church rooted in community, one that welcomes and affirms the sacred worth of all God's children and extends extravagant hospitality in caring for their welfare, working faithfully to keep them from any harm. The guiding principles mentioned above ground this legislation in stated values.

Values

Respect for contextual ministry settings. This is a missional, structural, and connectional endeavor that expresses faithful stewardship of

---

12. Desmond Tutu, "Who we are: Human uniqueness and the African spirit of Ubuntu," Templeton Prize, April 3, 2013, https://www.youtube.com/watch?v=0wZtfqZ271w.

God's mission in a diverse and changing world. Such respect implies understanding that our church needs to find appropriate ministry expressions in different mission contexts. Doing otherwise fosters relationships that are essentially colonial.

Connectional relationships rooted in mission. Our unity is not for unity's sake but for the effective proclamation of the Gospel, to invite all into a loving relationship with God and with one's neighbor. We welcome and affirm the sacred worth of all God's children and embrace everyone's participation in building God's beloved community.

Legislative equity for regional bodies of the church. The diversity of our ministry settings is real. Fulfilling the mission of the church together can be strengthened by identifying our contextual differences and allowing for authority to be exercised equitably by regional conferences or any regional structure formed by General Conference to address our respective mission contexts.

Proponents of the Christmas Covenant believe that we are stronger as a church when we work together. Being on a mission together as a global church celebrates our unity in diversity and positively impacts the different contexts we represent. While diversity is a challenge, we do not believe dissolution is the right way to heal the wounds that cause us pain as Christ's body. A truly global church committed to being on a mission together embraces its differences and allows for self-determination. It is able to find common ground in affirming how we do effective ministry in places we serve. Acknowledging that our different contexts need different solutions is a better way forward and fosters mutuality. This path affirms a stronger common witness to the global community. God's grace is present everywhere and in everyone. We are called to humbly respond to this grace in recognizing its many expressions around the world. This call we do best together.

The various geographical regions of the UMC, sharing closely related ministry context, will benefit from an opportunity to engage in conversations related to the life and ministry of the church within their respective regions, while maintaining missional and connectional relationships with other regions. This offers United Methodists in all regions of the UMC the space to engage in context-specific conversations for each region that otherwise would have been brought to the General Conference. United Methodists at General Conference can then focus their time on meaningfully considering matters related to global Christian witness.

The Christmas Covenant and the Philippines

The Christmas Covenant is the result of the work of people from around the world, and it has the potential to benefit the ministry of United Methodists from around the world. This is true in our context of the Philippines as well as in other locations. We see two benefits in particular.

First, the Christmas Covenant empowers our voices. Everybody will be heard. All voices—lament, pains, sufferings, and longings—of our people will be given affirming value by listening to our common hopes, dreams, and aspirations in designing the future direction of the church. When we are unmuted after a long time of being in "mute" mode at the general church level, our voices are full of energy and passion. Our voices will be fully recognized at the new table that the Christmas Covenant seeks to create.

Second, it enriches our ministries. I (Carnate-Atrero) am serving in a district that includes an indigenous community, our Aeta siblings. I hear, feel, and see how they aspire for an authentic way of growth in all aspects of life. One time, we appointed an Aeta pastor to a non-indigenous church. He tried his very best, giving it all he's got, but to no avail. I strongly believe that the context of our ministry is our deepest identity, which will make us bloom when we are planted and affirmed in our context.

The Christmas Covenant also carries forward the spirit of the previously mentioned 2019 Philippines College of Bishops' statement, which recommends that "The UMC is to be restructured into regional conferences, within which will remain central conferences, annual conferences and local churches." The statement presents this recommendation as an expression of three core elements of United Methodist structural polity:

> 1. Locality or contextuality: that is why we have local churches, annual conferences, and central conferences; being responsive to our missional context is obligatory.

2. Connectionality in relationships; that is why there is a General Conference and a Council of Bishops; having a global identity and organic structure are necessary.

3. Globality in inclusiveness; that is why the UMC reaches out in mutual relations with all governments and civil communities that promote Christian values and principles.[13]

The bishops make clear in their statement that this is the dominant understanding of United Methodists in the Philippines.

This message has been reiterated by others as well. Speaking as part of the pre-General Conference Briefing in January 2020, Rev. Igmedio Domingo, district superintendent of the Southwest Metro Manila District and a signer of the Christmas Covenant, emphasized the importance of contextual adaptation in the Philippines. He said, "As a central conference, we have a distinct missional context. We have a diverse culture with many languages. We minister in a country of 1,641 islands. We have three episcopal areas: Baguio (Ilocano region), Manila (Tagalog region), and Davao (Visayan region). We have differences in culture, location, language, and theological leanings, but we are united in being United Methodists." Rev. Domingo emphasized, though, that contextualization cannot mean secondary status. He continued, "Central conference perspectives should not be an afterthought. In fact, we should be an equal partner at the table envisioning the future of the church, and not just an audience whose perspectives are being asked after others have made plans and decisions that affect our mission work. This demands equity and respect."[14] He concluded by expressing support for the Christmas Covenant as an expression of these values.

The strong resonance of the Christmas Covenant in the Philippines can also be seen in the many Filipino leaders who have contributed video testimonies in support of the Christmas Covenant.[15] In a video released

---

13.   Philippines Central Conference College of Bishops, "United Methodists in the Philippines seek UMC unity."

14.   Igmedio Domingo, "Philippine Central Conference Perspective on the Future of The United Methodist Church," *UM & Global*, February 17, 2020, http://www.umglobal.org/2020/02/igmedio-domingo-philippine-central.html.

15.   See Christmas Covenant, "Testimonies," https://www.christmascovenant.com/testimonies.

on the first anniversary of the Christmas Covenant, Bishop Rudolfo Juan connected the principles of the Christmas Covenant to his episcopal experience across the Philippines Central Conference. He noted the importance of unity in the gospel amid diversity of contexts in the Philippines:

> Here in the Philippines, we speak different dialects, and as workers, pastors, lay leaders, we have varied theological perspectives. But I want to tell you, my dear friends, that even if we have differences in opinions regarding theology and interpreting the Scripture, we share the same gospel—the gospel of Christ, gospel of love and salvation, the gospel that inspires and empowers us to love one another as we love God, with all our mind, our heart, our soul, and all our being.

He continued by linking this concept to the practice of unity in mission in The United Methodist Church in the Philippines:

> And we care, my dear friends, for the lost, the least, and the last in our society. Unity in mission is what the Christmas Covenant is all about. . . . My country, the Philippine Islands, has experienced many calamities—typhoons and earthquakes—but our church, I would like to say, rose up to meet and face all these challenges bravely and courageously because we work together in the name of Christ. And in the midst of all these natural calamities, my dear friends, in the means of the pandemic, we continue as Filipino United Methodists who work together focused on God's mission of love in the name of Christ, through the ministries of the church.

Bishop Juan concluded his remarks by expressing the view of many in the Philippines: "Friends, I believe that the Christmas Covenant is God's gift to our church."[16]

Out of Chaos, Creation

In addition to sharing the Christmas Covenant, it is also important to lift up the work of an ad hoc group of fifteen lay and clergy grassroots leaders from central conferences and the United States who worked on a parallel process. Some are also members of the Christmas Covenant team.

16. Bishop Rudolfo Juan, video testimony, The Christmas Covenant, December 24, 2020, https://www.youtube.com/watch?v=q7stkk__gsY.

They created a vision map document entitled, "Out of Chaos, Creation: Imagining a Way to Be a Better United Methodist."[17] In partnership with the Connectional Table, the group surveyed and listened to numerous United Methodist groups and individuals about the denomination. The intention was not to create new legislation but to have conversations and listening time for non-delegate United Methodists to speak their thoughts about The United Methodist Church. This group and the Connectional Table support the language and legislation of the Christmas Covenant. One of the aspirations of "Out of Chaos, Creation," cited under their "table manners" affirmation about "U.S.-Centrism, Colonialism & Neo-colonialism," states that:

> At the Lord's Table, we meet eye-to-eye. As such, we lament the harm done by racism, colonialism, and neo-colonialism, and recognize that U.S.-centrism is an outgrowth of colonialism in The United Methodist Church. Therefore,
>
> - We give full support to the passage of regionalization legislation, such as the Christmas Covenant or the Connectional Table's U.S. as a Regional Conference petitions, so that ministry can be developed contextually and so that the issues that divide within one region do not get inordinate weight in our global connection.
> - Doing so would help the church reject U.S.-centrism and U.S. normativity, as well as colonialist/neo-colonialist power dynamics, and fully commit to an identity as a global church expressing ministry regionally.
> - We also call our church to commit to decolonizing our missional relationships both locally and globally, altering power dynamics to honor the voices, aspirations, and leadership of those often seen as recipients of our mission.

---

17. Out of Chaos, Creation, "Out of Chaos, Creation: Imagining a Better Way of Being United Methodists." The English version of the statement is no longer available online, but a German translation remains available at www.emk.de/fileadmin/meldungen/2021/210224-Out_of_Chaos_Anlage_Statement _DE_vorl_Fassung.pdf. For coverage of the statement, see Heather Hahn, "Delegates map out vision for church future," *UM News*, February 23, 2021; Klaus Ulrich Ruof, "Auch an Gottes Tisch sind gesittete Manieren nötig," Evangelisch-methodistische Kirche in Deutschland (EmK), February 24, 2021, https:// www.emk.de/meldung/auch-an-gottes-tisch-sind-gesittete-manieren-noetig; Cynthia B. Astle, "'Out of Chaos' to Create 'Vision Map' for Church: Group Enters Second Round of Envisioning a New UMC," *United Methodist Insight*, December 1, 2020, https://um-insight.net/in-the-church/umc-future/group-enters-second-round-of-envisioning-a-new-umc/.

- And, we call our church to commit to resisting using power and money to dictate missional outcomes for others and to being in conversation with communities impacted by our actions. These conversations should be marked by transparency and mutuality.[18]

This powerful statement reminds us that we do not decide who sits at God's table. We need a church that welcomes all to the table, a church that rejects systems that devalue and divide people based on race, ethnicity, or national origin. At God's table is infinite love and grace.

Additional Support for the Christmas Covenant

Out of Chaos, Creation is not the only group that has affirmed the Christmas Covenant. As of this writing, fifteen annual conferences in the Philippines and the United States have affirmed the Christmas Covenant legislation. It has also been affirmed by a variety of regional and international UMC-related groups, including the Connectional Table, the North Central Jurisdictional Conference, the Inter-Ethnic Strategy and Development Group, MARCHA, United Women in Faith, the Love Your Neighbor Coalition (LYNC), and the Western Methodist Justice Movement (WMJM).[19] Moreover, laity, clergy, and bishops from around the world have raised their testimonies on behalf of the Christmas Covenant.[20] We believe this broad support for the Christmas Covenant reflects a growing sense in The United Methodist Church that it is time for a new way of being the church together, one that moves beyond old, colonial models to preserve the unity of the church, forward its mission, and acknowledge its regional differences.

During the five U.S. Jurisdictional Conferences in November 2022, each jurisdictional body approved by a clear majority a non-binding resolution signifying a clear shift toward the organization of the U.S. Regional

---

18. Out of Chaos, Creation, "Out of Chaos, Creation: Imagining a Better Way of Being United Methodists."

19. For a current list of endorsements, see Christmas Covenant, "Endorsements," https://www.christmascovenant.com/endorsements.

20. See Christmas Covenant, "Testimonies," https://www.christmascovenant.com/testimonies.

Conference along with other regions during the 2024 General Conference.[21] The resolution also covered endorsement of the Christmas Covenant written by international United Methodists, aimed toward greater contextual autonomy for non-U.S. regions, and the reduction of the U.S.-centric nature of General Conference. Regionalization is an agenda and key topic of conversations in the months leading to this global gathering.

Furthermore, during the 2022 special session of the Philippines Central Conference, a forum on the future of the UMC was hosted by Wesleyan University–Philippines, Wesley Divinity School, and the Kapatiran-Kaunlaran Foundation (a social justice agency of the Philippines Central Conference).[22] In that panel presentation, Bishop Thomas Bickerton (president of the UMC Council of Bishops) said that the UMC *Book of Discipline* is very colonial in nature and U.S.-centric, and that it is time to create equity among all United Methodists across the globe through a new regional structure as proposed by the Christmas Covenant. This was echoed by Bishop Christian Alsted, president of the Connectional Table. He said that regionalization is a pressing need, given that the face of United Methodism has changed in the last quarter of a century. From being a largely American denomination, the UMC now has more than 40 percent of its membership outside the United States, predominantly in the African continent. Comparing the UMC to McDonald's—where we have the same "menu" built legislatively into the *Book of Discipline* and offered and practiced globally without regard to missional context—Bishop Alsted emphasized that this is not sustainable. Parts of the UMC around the world are confident in doing mission work contextually, but the general church has been slow to adapt and transition structurally to this new reality. Rev. Dr. Betty Kazadi, communications director of the North Katanga Conference in the Democratic Republic of Congo, powerfully pointed to decolonizing UMC polity through regionalization as the way for central conferences to move from the margins to the center. A General Conference delegate, she also stressed the importance of respect

---

21. Heather Hahn, Sam Hodges, and the Rev. Tom Kim, "Jurisdictions see shift in bishops, more cooperation," *UM News*, November 7, 2022.

22. A recording of the conference, "Forum on the Future of The United Methodist Church," can be found in https://fb.watch/hvBKQONb7l/.

for our regions' cultural differences even as we strive to collaborate in fulfilling our missional work.

Overall, the concept of regionalization has an accepted following that includes the Council of Bishops, the Connectional Table, and a host of annual conferences in the United States, Europe, and the Philippines. Due to cultural context, it remains unclear on the African continent if regionalization is accepted, since their annual conferences do not endorse legislation. Educational workshops have happened in 2020-2022, and more presentations will take place during the 2023 annual conference season globally. It becomes more important for both General Conference and annual conference delegates to understand the concept of regionalization and its organizational impact on the future of the UMC.

Responding to the task of decolonizing church polity, proponents of regionalization face legislative challenges. First, there are attempts to paint the Christmas Covenant as a proposal opposed to efforts by some groups to disaffiliate from the UMC and/or to establish their own expression of Methodism. This is farthest from the truth. Regionalization, as envisioned in the Christmas Covenant, seeks a decolonized structure for the future of the church and those who seek to remain in connection with the UMC. It does not stop or go against any legislative effort toward disaffiliation or schism. However, it does invite and engage as many United Methodists as possible to consider being church in a new way in the twenty-first century, unencumbered by conflicts brought about by perceived differences that could be addressed better locally or regionally while remaining focused on ministries we already do so well together.

Second, there are proposals that strip the Christmas Covenant of the much-needed constitutional amendments that actually give power to proposed regional conferences to enact policies that are sensible, applicable, and effective in their respective mission contexts. Third and last, and probably the most egregious of all, are proposals that conflate U.S. regional realities and needs with regionalization on a global scale. Any proposal to create regions based on differences in theological viewpoints—including how the church should be in ministry with LGBTQ+ persons—is blatantly segregationist, and very U.S.-centric. Bishops in the Philippines and the African continent have been very clear about their regions as bastions of traditional views on human sexuality. The sharpest differences and conflicts that have now risen to the point of schism and disaffiliation, are mainly in the U.S. Therefore, as Rev. Neal Christie—a member of the Christmas Covenant team—points out, "arguing about a regional U.S. issue on a global scale is colonial."[23] He correctly identifies the problem of creating regions based on theological differences. Such proposals assume that the U.S. predicament is the same across all regions of the church. This is presumptuous and colonially arrogant. The U.S. as a regional conference needs to be the arena to have these internal U.S. polity conversations.

Conclusion

Thomas E. Frank pointed out the need for new thinking in polity, writing that, "It's time for 'new paradigms' of organization. The days of bloated bureaucracy and top-down programming are over. This is the era of local initiative and control." He continues by describing the common sentiment that "[d]enominations are so badly divided over homosexuality—along with other gender, sexuality, and family issues—that there is little choice but 'amicable separation' or some kind of 'exit fee' to enable like-minded congregations to leave the current denomination and form their own associations." For Frank, such views create a "rhetoric of crisis."[24]

Crisis, though, does not need to be overwhelming or fatal. The Christmas Covenant legislation will take every detail of the denomination's crises and resiliently turn them into steppingstones for the rise of the church. The recovery of the relevant legacies of the history of Methodism shall come from the grassroots. Some of the most powerful and daring movements in the life of the church emerged in times of decline and loss. Our Methodist historical legacy allows us to envision a future of rising while celebrating diversity, reviving while affirming differences, and resurrecting while maintaining our distinct heritage. We have done it before; we will do it again in our present age.

---

23. Neal Christie, WhatsApp group conversation, December 31, 2022.

24. Thomas E. Frank, *Polity, Practice, and the Mission of The United Methodist Church,* 2006 Edition (Nashville: Abingdon, 2006), 21-22.

9

WHITHER GLOBAL METHODISM?

Filipe Maia

The globe is on our computers. No one lives there.
The 'global' notion allows us to think that we can aim
to control globality.
—*Gayatri Chakravorty Spivak*

When one opens the website of the recently launched Global Methodist Church, one finds the image of a spinning globe.[1] "The Methodist movement has always been global," reads the website. A global disposition is indisputably present in Methodism, a movement that emerged under the expansionist drive of the British Empire and exploded onto a global stage as the United States consolidated its westward and overseas expansion in the nineteenth century. But the globe to which Methodism was sent has not always been the spinning globe viewed from the atmosphere. That globe exists only on our computers. It is, in fact, a creation of the age of computerized globalization. As postcolonial critic Gayatri Spivak suggests, there has always been a subtle link between the figure of the globe and the impetus to control.[2] Mapping the globe, scanning its surface, hovering over its atmosphere,

---

1.   Global Methodist Church, Homepage, https://globalmethodist.org/.

2.   Gayatri Chakravorty Spivak, "'Planetarity' (Box 4, WELT)," *Paragraph (Modern Critical Theory Group)* 38:2 (2015): 291, https://doi.org/10.3366/para.2015.0166.

flying across it: these are activities that disclose the globe as a manageable entity. Like the spinning globe, these are familiar images. We know what the globe is and, therefore, we assume what a global denomination ought to look like. Global has become a "fully appropriate" name.[3] This is the double-bind of a denomination with global aspirations; it presents its field of action as a fully known entity, the globe, while having to shape relations and assemblages in spheres that operate under the radar, on the ground, on the dusty paths unrecognizable to the satellites capturing the globe from above. The spinning globe is a representation of a familiar totality, fully known to us. Can it become an assembly?

The Global Methodist Church, launched in May 2022, departs from United Methodism while sharing the hopes of being a global denomination. The departure will allow traditional and conservative Methodists to be in a denomination of like-minded theological spirits and a shared sexual ethic that portrays queer love as contrary to Christian teaching. The new denomination is making headway to incorporate congregations from The United Methodist Church as well as driving its own church-planting initiative. With its official and ancillary documents, the new denomination emphasizes its global character.[4] Its website states: "We are a global church that recognizes and deploys the gifts and contributions of each part of the church, working as partners in the gospel with equal voice and leadership."[5] The statement echoes Global Methodism's *Transitional Book of Doctrines and Discipline (TBDD)*: "Ours is a global church that recognizes the gifts and contributions of each part of our communion in Christ. . . . Learning from each other and sharing best practices across cultures, we follow the admonition of St. Paul that 'to each one the manifestation of the Spirit is given for the common good,' that together we are the Body

---

3. Global Methodist Church, "Vision," https://globalmethodist.org/about/#about-vision-section, accessed September 28, 2022.

4. For a summary of the arguments made by conservative United Methodists and members of the Wesleyan Covenant Association prior to the constitution of the Global Methodist Church, see David W. Scott, "The Traditionalist Bid for Africa," *UM & Global*, August 5, 2020, http://www.umglobal.org/2020/08/the-traditionalist-bid-for-africa.html, accessed June 25, 2022.

5. Global Methodist Church, "Vision."

of Christ, sharing in 'an equal concern for one another' (1 Corinthians 12). Our vision of a global church is one marked by mutual love, concern, sharing, and accountability"[6] (TBDD ¶302).

In this chapter, I argue that the vision of the "globe" that is now stamped as the name of Global Methodism unwittingly carries with it the "spirit of empire," the thought that the globe is that which one might be able to manage and control.[7] The reference to "best practices across cultures," cited above, will have to be put in tension with documents from Global Methodist leaders and theologians who present "culture" in opposition to church traditions and gospel truths. I will be suggesting that a flat reading of culture, devoid of attention to power and the history of American imperialism, puts the vision of a global denomination in peril. It further exposes the provincialism in the writings of Global Methodists. I argue that many of the slippages in the discourse of the emerging denomination are yet another symptom of the imperial condition that befalls the project of a global denomination.

My reflection is divided in three parts. I first offer a close reading of recent statements and documents by conservative and traditionalist Methodists aligned with the Global Methodist Church to identify how they have projected the "culture wars" peculiar to the United States onto other regions of the globe. Second, I suggest that Global Methodism's controversial attitude against United Methodism harbors a more profound difficulty in recognizing and acknowledging realities that cannot be captured by doctrinal statements of claims for orthodoxy. Third, in closing, I gesture in the direction of a passage from the notion of a "global" denomination to the image of a "planetary" assembly as a vision and a tactic for resisting the spirit of empire latent in global Methodism.

---

6. Global Methodist Church, *The Transitional Book of Doctrines and Discipline, 2022,* https://globalmethodist.org/wp-content/uploads/2022/04/Transitional-Discipline.2022041257.pdf. Henceforth, references to the document will remain on the body of the document marked as TBDD with paragraph numbers.

7. The expression comes from Néstor Míguez, Joerg Rieger, and Jung Mo Sung, *Beyond the Spirit of Empire: Theology and Politics in a New Key* (London: SCM, 2009).

Global Church, Local Fights

Global Methodists allude often to John Wesley's aphorism, "I consider the entire world as my parish."[8] The denomination's website suggests that leaders from many countries and many languages have expressed the desire for a new expression of Methodism. The aspirational goal is laudable, it must be stressed. At times, however, Global Methodism demonstrates an unwillingness to interrogate the imperial inheritance in Methodism, especially as it represents this global "partnership" between its constituents in the global North and those in the global South. More important, as I will demonstrate in the paragraphs below, the theological statements of Global Methodism are representative of social and cultural tensions that are unique to the United States. The ecclesial identity of Global Methodism is built upon disputes that can only be conceived of as provincial.

The setup for the emergence of the Global Methodist Church is thoroughly polemical. This is only natural considering that the denomination emerges as a result of a schism within United Methodism. The poles in the dispute are therefore understandably reflective of the tensions that have marred The United Methodist Church for the past five decades. But the terms of this tension are far from global. The polemic that shapes Global Methodism as a denomination is discernably American, as are the patterns emerging from its initial documents and doctrinal statements. In them, the church's adversary is presented as the "co-optation" of the church by "culture."[9] But whose culture? As I indicate below, this question remains unasked in the founding documents of the Global Methodist Church. These assume culture as a detrimental force, while letting typically Ameri-

---

8. For the historical context in which John Wesley made this affirmation and a reflection on how the usage of the expression amongst Methodists often neglect it, see David W. Scott, "The World Is Not My Parish," *UM & Global*, May 4, 2022, http://www.umglobal.org/2022/05/the-world-is-not-my-parish.html. In addition to the historical inaccuracy, I would also like to point out the fact that Wesley's statement came in the context of a polemic with leaders in the Church of England who deemed his preaching at certain churches to be irregular. In this reading, "the world is my parish" is Wesley's justification for breaking with church polity, which is ironic given the accusations that conservative United Methodists and members of the Global Methodist Church make against those who, today, also break with church polity and discipline in the matter of the recognition of the ministry of queer clergy.

9. See, for one notable example, Mike Lowry, "Crossing the Rubicon: A Bishop Says Goodbye to the United Methodist Church," *Firebrand Magazine*, May 1, 2022, https://firebrandmag.com/articles/crossing-the-rubicon-a-bishop-says-goodbye-to-the-united-methodist-church.

can cultural dispositions and assumptions govern the central tenets of the denomination.

The recent volume *The Next Methodism* serves as a good point of departure to track this polemic against culture. The volume promises to deliver the "foundations" for global Methodism, grounding a new denomination in right doctrine, proper ecclesial governance, and evangelical piety. The volume stresses the global nature of the denomination, even though perspectives from outside the United States are presented only much later in the volume.

The image that orients the opening pages of *The Next Methodism* is that of a funeral march: the Holy Roman Empire exemplifies the "death knell for so many heretofore thriving movements that now line the ash heap of history," writes Kenneth Collins, one of the volume's editors and author of its introduction.[10] The terms of the polemic pit the church against empire while closing off the possibility that one's view of the church is not far removed from the influence of empire. In this register, empire and culture can only "co-opt" the church. They are never acknowledged as forces that shape our very understanding of what the church is, and no attention is given to how one discerns between spirits of imperial and hegemonic cultures and the spirit of a life-giving gospel. Collins is nevertheless certain: the church must preserve its identity against the threats imposed by culture. The enemies of the church are the "co-opting forces of culture [that] over time can transform a theological tradition and thereby undermine its earlier, commonly celebrated identity."[11] As we will continue to observe through the pages of *The Next Methodism*, the narrative of a loss of identity is important for Global Methodism. For Collins, Methodism has been raised by God in continuation of this "commonly celebrated identity" as a representative of "real, true, proper scriptural Christianity."[12]

This identity is under attack by contemporary cultural forces. At points in the volume, authors will respond by engaging in an all-out culture war.

---

10. Kenneth J. Collins, "Introduction," in *The Next Methodism: Theological, Social, and Missional Foundations for Global Methodism*, eds. Kenneth J. Collins and Ryan N. Danker, Kindle (Franklin, TN: Seedbed Publishing, 2022), 12.

11. Collins, 13.

12. Collins, 14.

The enemy is now The United Methodist Church. The "UMC will increasingly accommodate the broader culture," James R. Thobaben writes. "They will agree with social media giants, academic elites, and members of the federal bureaucracy, the denominational bureaucrats in Nashville and Washington, and in the various episcopal offices while asserting that they speak the truth to power."[13] The text moves at blazing speed, comparing and somewhat equating the power of social media corporations to that of bishops in The United Methodist Church or the power of intellectuals—another familiar enemy of traditionalists—and members of the federal bureaucracy, supposedly in the United States government. A vague analysis of culture can only lead to a misplaced power analysis. That prepares the way for the fundamental attack that *The Next Methodism* will direct at United Methodists. Thobaben accuses those who "disregard . . . sexual purity, denying it is an important component of holy living." He concludes with the announcement of impending doom: "They will function as court prophets of a dying religious organization, proudly virtue signaling to a society that could not care less."[14] As one notices, the stakes could not be higher in the polemic against United Methodism. The narrative follows the pattern of a diatribe against culture, against a culture that threatens to steal the church's identity, purity, traditions, and documents.

But who has denied the importance of holy living? What social media giants? What academic elites? None of these are named, only presumed, for the force of this polemic is precisely to create its own adversary, to put them into a corner and frame them in the way that will sustain the polemic. While the force of the polemic assures Global Methodism of its identity along the "Great Tradition" of Christian orthodoxy, it also discloses its provincial origins in cultural and social tensions unique to the United States context in the early twenty-first century.

Mark Tooley, president of the Institute on Religion and Democracy, offers a chapter on political theology in *The Next Methodism*. He accuses twentieth-century Methodists of being "utterly leftists" in the 1930s under the influence of the social gospel and of abandoning "Christian moral

---

13. James R. Thobaben, "The Sexual Ethics of the Body of Christ and the Way Forward," in *The Next Methodism*, 369.

14. Thobaben, 369.

orthodoxy" in 1970 when General Conference endorsed "unrestricted abortion."[15] That tradition, according to Tooley, paved the way for the debate over homosexuality after 1972. In this context, the public witness of the church "became indistinguishable from secular left-wing activism."[16] The essay goes on to say that Methodism embraced a "mostly materialistic political theology invested in centralized government's expansive social welfare and regulatory state, rejecting or minimizing the state's vocation for police and military powers, and ratifying the sexual revolution by accepting its anthropology of atomized, self-empowered individuals liberated from nature, natural law, and traditional Christian teaching."[17] The political landscape described by Tooley discloses its American provenance.

But the real issue here emerges because this effort at producing a political theology for "next" Methodism offers more than a diagnosis of the past. Its rendition of the Methodist history in the twentieth century entails a blueprint for a desired expression of global Methodism for the twenty-first. In the adversarial tone common to *The Next Methodism*, Tooley lays out his political vision for small government combined with a recognition of the police and the military as foundational to a government's legitimate use of power, another veiled response to the context of controversies around police violence in the United States. The question must be raised: how will this political theology meet a global ecclesial body? Consider the case of nations whose recent memories include military-backed genocidal governments or cases of rampant corruption driven by the opening of its markets to international corporations under the banner of "small government." Tooley's political theology, presented as doctrinally Wesleyan, is likely to encounter a global audience that will take it for what it is: yet another instance of the conflation of American civil religion disguised under the cloak of evangelical zeal.

The belligerence against culture and the American bias of *The Next Methodism* remain flagrant in the section devoted to "global Methodism," the closing section of the volume. Peter J. Bellini celebrates a new global

---

15. Mark Tooley, "Political Theology for Global Methodism," in *The Next Methodism*, 242.

16. Tooley, 243.

17. Tooley, 243.

denomination as being able to be an "instrument of God" to renew Methodism and "spread scriptural holiness."[18] This new Methodism will correct the mistakes committed by a United Methodist Church that remained caught up in "culture" and allowed it to drive the mission of the church.[19] Bellini points out that the "global United Methodist Church was structured for U.S. dominance with minimal measures of cultural autonomy given to central conferences compared to the weight of cultural hegemony assumed by Americans."[20] The point is well taken and historically salient. It is followed by yet another important remark, this time indicating that a global denomination can only function when "it allows for people of every culture to fulfill the call of God through its own governance, propagation, support, and theology."[21] The polemical tone commonly adopted in *The Next Methodism* takes a quick rest as the need for cultural humility seems to take a more prominent role in the analysis. But this is a short-lived moment as Bellini's essay quickly resorts back to tropes common to the culture wars: "If there is to be a next Methodism, we need to treat the institutional ADHD (Attention Deficit Hyperactivity Disorder) that has plagued our sense of missional direction. For decades, we have aimlessly chased every politically and culturally correct pet interest down every rabbit hole."[22] The hostility toward culture nevertheless hides the cultural provincialism of the analysis as we are taken to the middle of the culture wars of the American context: "The difference is that now we can offer the Scripture way of salvation, which flows from the doctrine of the church, rather than offering an uncritical social wokeness peddled by the culture."[23] While filled with moral outrage, statements like this are barely legible to a cultural context beyond the United States. Its provincialism cannot be remedied by its claim to doctrinal purity nor its moral outrage.

---

18.   Peter J. Bellini, "A Global Movement," in *The Next Methodism*, 415.

19.   Bellini, 417.

20.   Bellini, 420.

21.   Bellini, 420–21.

22.   Bellini, 422. With the risk of being "politically correct," in Bellini's use of the term, I must resist the use of a mental health diagnosis as analogy for what the author understands to be doctrinal negligence.

23.   Bellini, 417–18.

After this sequence of argument, the essay goes through a quick global awakening. "Rather than responding to the impulses of the culture, the church discerns where the Spirit preveniently is already at work and submits to his purposes."[24] This has been amply established in the essay and in the volume until this point. But Bellini offers this in the next sentence: "In practical global terms, it may mean the West needs to accept the dynamic instrumentality of the church in the majority world in terms of its sheer numbers, vitality, and spiritual impact and allow the Lord to do likewise in its own churches."[25] This expression is worthy of a highlight: the West may need to resign itself to the "dynamic instrumentality of the church" in the "majority world." Bellini seems to suggest that the task of churches in the West is to follow the leadership of churches in the global South. This is most certainly a noble sentiment, and Bellini later acknowledges the "gift of the Spirit's renewal" that comes from the southern hemisphere.[26] The concerning part comes next as Bellini announces what he perceives to be the contribution of the northern hemisphere to a global Methodist connection. From the North, he states, there will be "widespread resources for development."[27]

The dynamic remains transactional: the global South has spiritual vitality; the North has the money. This is not a new claim, much less an innocent one. What appears as a strong commitment to a global expression of Methodism harbors the projection of unacknowledged imperial aspirations. On the one hand, Bellini's explicit reference to the resources coming from the northern hemisphere runs the risk of glossing over the fact that access to resources shapes power differentials. He states: "An emerging global Methodist church may recharge and resuscitate the 'valley of dry bones' (Ezek. 37:1–14) in the West that, in turn, can undergird and support mission and development throughout the world."[28] David R. Thomas's chapter in *The Next Methodism* offers a similar prognosis as he

---

24. Bellini, 418.

25. Bellini, 418.

26. Bellini, 424.

27. Bellini, 424.

28. Bellini, 424.

connects the survival of American Christianity and the values embraced by next Methodism.[29] Part of the transactional nature of the enterprise described by Bellini is the underlying assumption that the West can buy its way into a spiritual revival. On the other hand, one sees in statements such as this the typical Western anxiety about declining church membership. From a Christian ecclesiological perspective, the association between numerical growth and church vitality is anything but certain.[30] It nevertheless remains central to the analysis that authors in *The Next Methodism* offer about the reasons for their departure from United Methodism. David Scott has suggested that fear of membership decline bespeaks "theological anxieties" that are "heightened for Methodists from the United States, where there is a high cultural emphasis on numerical growth as a demonstration of success and a high cultural stigma on numerical decline as a demonstration of failure."[31] Hence, the desire to obtain the same level of "explosive growth in the global South" is not simply a matter of retrieving church vitality.[32] This might be yet another symptom of the unacknowledged sense of loss of imperial Christianity with its hegemonic power over a society.

The global aspirations of the Global Methodist Church are informed by the problematic perception that the global South is somehow a depository of primitive truths the West has neglected, a space where natives preserve what the West has lost, a location that holds the key to an imperial past that the West has disavowed. Even the somewhat benevolent recognition of the vitality of the church in the global South is problematic if perceived as an instrumental means to obtain a similar vitality in the North. These perceptions of the globe—the North and its resources, the South and its spiritual explosiveness—will undoubtedly shape the inter-

---

29. The text reads, "Clearly, it is no exaggeration to recognize how these next two or three decades are make-or-break for American Christianity. Similarly, it is no mere coincidence to see these same years as the open door for the next Methodism." David R. Thomas, "Opportunity for Awakening," in *The Next Methodism*, 322.

30. See, for example, Bryan P. Stone, *Evangelism after Christendom: The Theology and Practice of Christian Witness* (Grand Rapids, MI: Brazos, 2007).

31. David W. Scott, "US Membership Decline and the Rhetoric of the Global Church," *UM & Global*, April 21, 2021, http://www.umglobal.org/2021/04/us-membership-decline-and-rhetoric-of.html.

32. Bellini, 424.

nal dynamics of Global Methodism. The denomination and its founding documents cast a vision of a global denomination where members have equal voice and ecclesial power. These documents nevertheless continue to bespeak the cultural provincialism of their authors while attempting to shape the denominational ethos of Global Methodism. As evidenced by the transactional representation between southern and northern hemispheres in Bellini's analysis, an unacknowledged American bias is all the more concerning, for it may disguise old colonial tropes and aspirations.

The lack of *critical* cultural analysis is the danger incurred by those who blame culture for the ills of the church. This is a thought of culture that disregards how cultures get produced, negotiated, and also suppressed. As Joerg Rieger has remarked, the trope of "Christ against culture" is not new, having been famously considered by H. Richard Niebuhr's *Christ and Culture*. Rieger's own contribution in *Christ and Empire* challenges us to be wary of treating culture "apart from issues of power."[33] What gets dismissed as "culture" is often what informs the type of argument that places the "theological truths" as standing above and beyond culture. The danger is that uninterrogated and yet powerful cultural forces operate under the surface. Rieger is correct in suggesting the narrow-mindedness of this approach: "In the thick of the culture wars, it may seem that there is no way out but to pick one of these camps—determined by the current American imagination—or to stay somewhere near the center as it is gradually pulled to the right in the current climate."[34]

Culture, which is singularly understood as a corrosive force working against the gospel by the authors of *The Next Methodism*, will soon become a necessary site of negotiation for Global Methodists. Scott rightly suggests that such an approach will likely become unsustainable for a global denomination.[35] At present, homosexuality provides the battleground for the culture wars and therefore grants a temporary common ground for

---

33.   Joerg Rieger, *Christ and Empire: From Paul to Postcolonial Times* (Minneapolis: Fortress, 2007), vii.

34.   Joerg Rieger, "The Ill-Fated Impasse of United Methodist Theology: A Constructive Proposal beyond the Middle Road," *United Methodist Insight*, March 21, 2021, https://um-insight.net/in-the-church/umc-future/the-ill-fated-impasse-of-united-methodist-theology/.

35.   David W. Scott, "The Problems of a Global Traditionalist Church," *UM & Global*, August 12, 2020, http://www.umglobal.org/2020/08/the-problems-of-global-traditionalist.html.

traditionalists in the United States and their counterparts in Africa, the Philippines, Europe, and Eurasia. The formation of the Global Methodist Church will provide the end of this shared identity. U.S. Traditionalists will then likely find themselves in a denomination where their assumptions about a "global" church will be challenged by voices who do not share the same perspectives on what the global nature of the church means. When the possibility of blaming the co-opting forces of culture is gone, U.S. traditionalists in the Global Methodist Church are likely to perceive their social and economic force will stand in the way of a truly global denomination where all members share "equal voice and leadership." The tension never quite explicitly acknowledged by Global Methodism is the processes whereby doctrinal purity will be obtained in the context of power-laden cultural diversity.

Throughout the pages of *The Next Methodism*, one is drawn to the epicenter of the "culture wars" waged in the United States. Attacks directed at The United Methodist Church are abundant and reflect distinctly American social and political concerns. Quite often, the conservative and traditionalist authors of the volume perform a call to arms against culture while remaining inattentive to the cultural grounds in which they stand. In this context, what may come "next" for Methodism will run the risk of reproducing not so much the "Great Tradition" that the authors in the volume seek to preserve, but the unacknowledged continuation of the hegemonic cultural heritage of the United States.[36]

Extravagant Loves, Diverging Paths

The mission of the Global Methodist Church declares its intent to "make disciples of Jesus Christ who worship passionately, love extravagantly, and witness boldly."[37] The statement echoes the call for discipleship present in the United Methodist mission statement ("to make disciples of Jesus Christ for the transformation of the world"), but drops the call for world transformation. There might be a polemical undertone to the change that associates worldly transformation with the impositions of culture or as

36. For the reference to the "Great Tradition," see Collins, "Introduction."

37. See "Preface" in Global Methodist Church, *Transitional Book of Doctrines and Discipline.*

a secondary matter.[38] Instead, Global Methodists offer the triad of worship, love, and witness followed by their appropriate qualifiers. The dissonance in the statement is perhaps found in its call to an "extravagant" love. In some of its historical meanings, *extravagant* signifies that which "wanders out of bounds," something that is "straying" or "roaming" and "[varies] widely from what is usual or proper." It refers to something "strange" or "unbecoming." The etymology of *extravagant*, in short, refers to what is "widely divergent."[39] But a love that diverges from the norm is definitely outside the goals of the new denomination.

In January 2022, a gathering of traditionalist and conservative Wesleyan scholars in the context of the United States produced a document entitled "The Faith Once Delivered." The scope of the document is bold: "to offer 'a constructive voice' that clearly articulates the Wesleyan understanding of Christian orthodoxy'" and to "guide the theological trajectory of Methodism for the next century or more."[40] Mark Tooley joked that it could become for Methodists what the Synod of Dort was for the Reformed tradition.[41] Like documents produced in the context of the Protestant Reformation, "The Faith Once Delivered" embraces the genre of a confession of faith. Unlike other documents, however, it remains elusive regarding the source of its authority to receive, interpret, and proclaim Methodist doctrine. Historically, Methodists understood that doctrine was discerned through holy conferencing and that the creedal tradition embraced by the Christian faith is conciliar. This collective form of discernment is not ex-

---

38. Kevin Watson writes: "[The] dominant strain of Methodism actually *conformed* to the dominant culture. It did not, as the UMC presumptuously ascribes to itself today, lead the way in progress or 'the transformation of the world.' On the contrary, United Methodism in the United States was more often transformed by the world." Kevin Watson, "Methodism Dividing," *First Things*, May 2020, https://www.firstthings.com/article/2020/05/methodism-dividing; see also Mike Lowry, "The Birth Pangs of the Next Methodism," in *The Next Methodism*, 349, n. 2.

39. "Extravagant," in *Oxford English Dictionary* (Oxford University Press, 2022), https://www.oed.com/viewdictionaryentry/Entry/67142.

40. The first sentence is taken from Ryan Danker, director of the John Wesley Institute that convened the summit and helped in editing the document. Daniel Silliman, "Theologians Craft Wesleyan Agreement for a Divided Methodist Era," *Christianity Today*, May 24, 2022, https://www.christianity-today.com/news/2022/may/next-methodism-methodist-wesleyan-theology-document.html. The second sentence comes from the document itself: Ryan N. Danker, Jonathan Powers, and Kevin Watson, eds., "The Faith Once Delivered: A Wesleyan Witness," 2022, para. 1, https://nextmethodism.org/wp-content/uploads/The-Faith-Once-Delivered-FINAL-1.pdf. Henceforth, references to the document will remain on the body of the document marked as FoD with paragraph numbers.

41. Silliman, "Theologians Craft Wesleyan Agreement for a Divided Methodist Era."

plicitly named by the authors of the document. It is also concerning that a document that aims at shaping global Methodism in the twenty-first century only included authors from the United States. The document affirms that efforts were made to include voices from all areas of the globe, but these efforts were hindered by the coronavirus pandemic (FoD ¶2). I should not linger too much on the lack of global representation so as to focus more closely on how the document—and others—construct the identity of Global Methodism.

The driving image of "The Faith Once Delivered" is the concept of humanity as created in the image of God. The document presents an elegant account of Christian teaching, from the apostolic age to the present times with special emphasis on the patristic period and the Wesleyan revival. The confession does, however, reverberate the familiar vocabulary of the co-optation of the church by culture and other unnamed forces, despite the assurance given by one of its editors that the document did not aim at being polemical.[42] With some poetic license, the document analogizes between the "faith once delivered" and a river; it acknowledges that the Christian message has flowed steadily and incorporated "minerals and particles" along the way comparable to "tastes and expressions to the great old flow [that] enhance our appreciation of it." The statement adds: "Sadly, some admixtures prove to be unnecessary or even pollutants that, though they may abide in the waters for a time (even a long time), must be and will be ultimately cleansed from its course by the same faithful Holy Spirit" (FoD ¶104). The language of impurity is subtle, but its unnamed target is obvious.

The emerging Global Methodist Church seems disposed to offer silent attacks at communities of diverging gender expressions. Collins's chapter in *The Next Methodism* takes issue with the language of "love," though the reader will have to fill in the many ellipses in his text. The Methodist movement, he surmises, was indeed concerned about love. But not any love. It was "*holy* love—humble, sacrificial love—not a self-indulgent or self-referential love."[43] Queer love is not mentioned, only implied by the qualifier "holy" which signals that the appeal to love in queer experiences

---

42. Ryan Danker, director of the John Wesley Institute, told *Christianity Today* that "the document is not intended to be polemical, or even really original." Silliman.

43. Kenneth J. Collins, "Holy Love as a Key to What Sanctification Is All About," in *The Next Methodism*, 26. Emphasis in the original.

is not holy. "Therefore, the proper summation of John Wesley's practical theology . . . is both holiness (holy love) and grace (both free and cooperant)—never one without the other."[44] Collins is concerned about a view of love that, in his words, "[celebrates] the degrading and enslaving aspects of particular human *lusts*."[45] It is once again the task of the reader to fill in the blank and guess that what Collins portrays as lust is queer love. Collins goes as far as to suggest that this unnamed rival of holy love is selfish and "ethnocentric."[46] The pattern reappears as cultural elites are named as responsible for this unnamed enemy: "[The] gospel story of holy love rooted in the atoning work of Jesus Christ has effectively been switched out in which another story, an alien narrative, often championed by cultural elites, has now been declared to be the real meaning of the good news for all people."[47] Not many pages before this, readers had been introduced to the idea that love is indeed a matter of loving the "other," an outward movement. Now, it is alien forces coming from outside that are threatening holy love. Collins's text slips through this attempt at defining holy love as pure love of the other, while maintaining the need to police this alien, unnamed other that claims the name of love for itself. Collins is certain: this unnamed adversary cannot be love, cannot be holy, cannot be pure. It must be an alien imposition. Might "holy love" survive in the midst of so many other aliens in the context of a global denomination? Might this love be truly extravagant and embrace that which is divergent?

Some sections in *The Next Methodism* offer a more direct attack on queer love, though the rhetoric of policing divergence is no less stringent. Maxie Dunnam, for example, is clear about his embrace of the Houston Declaration and its opposition to the "practice of homosexuality."[48] Parenthetically—and it appears to be symptomatic that this happens within a

---

44. Collins, 45. Emphasis in the original.

45. Collins, 49. Emphasis in the original.

46. One important and intriguing observation is that the word "ethnocentrism" was originally coined by French philosopher Jacques Derrida, often accused by conservative philosophers and theologians alike of being a "relativist" and a destroyer of the great canon of Western thought. The irony in Collins's use of the term is compiled by the fact that in its first usage by Derrida, "ethnocentrism" refers to the association between written language and that which is perceived as immutable. See Jacques Derrida, *Of Grammatology*, trans. Gayatri Chakravorty Spivak, Fortieth-Anniversary Edition (Baltimore: Johns Hopkins University Press, 2016), 3.

47. Collins, "Holy Love as a Key to What Sanctification Is All About," 49. Emphasis in the original.

48. Maxie Dunnam, "Theological Accountability," in *The Next Methodism*, 73.

parenthesis—the *Transitional Book of Doctrines and Discipline* of the Global Methodist Church defines gender as "a person's immutable biological traits identified by or before birth" (TBDD ¶306). It also requires its ministers to embrace "fidelity in a Christian marriage between one man and one woman, [and] chastity in singleness" (TBDD ¶405.2). "The Faith Once Delivered" is even more economical in its reference to sexuality: "The Scripture provides God's vision for life and happiness, true wholeness, including but not limited to human flourishing, the good of singleness, the marriage of one man and one woman, true friendship, fulfillment in vocation, and holy community" (FoD ¶101). Later in *The Next Methodism* we encounter a chapter on marriage that is explicit about its normative claims about holy love and what constitutes marriage. Warren Smith is clear that marriage is divinely instituted as a "spiritual friendship" between a man and a woman for the purpose of bearing children.[49] He argues that this is a countercultural position.[50] On a similar vein, Thobaben argues that "late modern Western sexual morality" is the new embodiment of colonialism.[51]

Colonialism and imperialism make no appearance in the *Transitional Book of Doctrines and Discipline* of the Global Methodist Church nor in "The Faith Once Delivered."[52] At times, however, the terms surface in conservative Methodist circles in the polemic against the recognition of the ministry of queer clergy and same-sex unions. It is not uncommon that conservative Methodist leaders turn to the language of colonial imposition

---

49. Warren Smith, "The Significance of Marriage," in *The Next Methodism*, 358. The stress on bearing children suggests that, for Smith, a heterosexual couple with no children is outside the zone of marital purity.

50. Smith, 359.

51. Thobaben, 370.

52. In its section on "Our Witness to the World" (¶202), the *Transitional Book of Doctrines and Discipline* expressed concerns for "disparities in wealth and resources, both among individuals and nations" and suggests that this is the cause of poverty. Still, no direct mention is made to how these disparities have been historically constructed in the context of colonialism. It is also worthy of mention that none of the authors in *Next Methodism* offer any extensive account of imperialism or colonialism. The only passing reference to the topic appears in Eduard Khegay's essay:

"Today, when I ask many Methodists in Eurasia what are some of the most important factors that inspired them to become Methodists, their answers always include welcoming people and being an inclusive church. I am confident that this should be a strong characteristic of the next Methodism. The world tends to divide and exclude people. Racism and colonialism persist. The walls go higher and the labeling spreads like a virus. Does the church have a different message?" Eduard Khegay, "Eurasia: Lessons from the Past, Hopes for the Future," in *The Next Methodism*, 453.

On the matter of conservative movements in the United States suggesting that there is a colonial imposition of a "gay agenda," it must be remembered that the vast majority of conservative Christians in the United States have historically opposed twentieth-century anti-colonial struggles in Asia and Africa.

of a "gay agenda" by liberal Methodists in Western societies. This claim goes beyond the context of Methodism and is in fact a live debate in the social sciences, in gender theory, and postcolonial studies. The case of Africa is the most visible site where these disputes take place. Adriaan van Klinken has suggested that the "idea of homosexuality as 'un-African,' 'unnatural,' and 'un-Christian' was prevalent throughout the twentieth century, reinforced by European colonial administrators and Christian missionaries, and in recent decades by HIV-prevention strategies."[53] Neville Hoad illustrates how the formation of a postcolonial African identity established against the category of homosexuality is indissociable from the sexual discipline imposed by the British.[54] Furthermore, the anti-gay agenda in African countries has become a truly transnational endeavor with robust funding of anti-LGBTQ initiatives by U.S. conservative Christian groups. Between 2008 and 2018, the Fellowship Foundation, for example, sent more than $20 million dollars to fund anti-gay movements and policies in Uganda alone.[55] As amply reported by Kapya Kaoma, the turning of homosexuality as a contentious point in sub-Saharan Africa is a direct reflection of the cultural context of the United States with profound consequences for gender

---

53. Adriaan Van Klinken, *Kenyan, Christian, Queer: Religion, LGBT Activism, and Arts of Resistance in Africa* (University Park, PA: The Pennsylvania State University Press, 2019), 4. In a study conducted with Masiiwa Ragies Gunda, Klinken has analyzed "the ways in which homosexuality is addressed in contemporary African theological writing." The study concluded that "homosexuality has been actively opposed, especially by theologians working in the paradigm of inculturation theology, who tend uncritically to join the choir of those who argue that homosexuality is incompatible with 'African values,' and who adopt a rather static concept of 'African culture,' selectively ignoring the historical and anthropological evidence of same-sex sexualities in African cultures and societies." Van Klinken, 21. For a history of the formation of the idea of a "heterosexual Africa," see Marc Epprecht, *Heterosexual Africa? The History of an Idea from the Age of Exploration to the Age of AIDS* (Athens, OH: Ohio University Press, 2008).

54. Neville Wallace Hoad, *African Intimacies: Race, Homosexuality, and Globalization* (Minneapolis: University of Minnesota Press, 2007).

55. Lydia Namubiru and Khatondi Soita Wepukhulu, "Exclusive: US Christian Right Pours More than $50m into Africa," *Open Democracy*, October 29, 2020, https://www.opendemocracy.net/en/5050/africa-us-christian-right-50m/. The Fellowship Foundation defines itself thusly: "Incorporated in 1949, The Fellowship Foundation, Inc., is a faith-based, non-profit organization established for the purpose of providing fiduciary oversight and accountability to a wide range of ministries. These ministries are conducted primarily by an ecumenical, bi-partisan fellowship of laypeople of all ages, ethnicities and socio-economic backgrounds. As followers of Jesus, we seek relationally to introduce the all-consuming, transforming and reconciling person and teachings of Jesus of Nazareth to people from all walks of life and every nation of the world." See https://fellowshipfoundation.org/who-we-are.

The Ugandan case is exemplary against the claim that a queer agenda is an imposition because the so-called "Kill the Gays" policy approved by Parliament in 2009 builds upon colonial-era legislation that regulates "carnal knowledge against the order of nature." See Amar Wahab, "'Homosexuality/Homophobia Is Un-African'?: Un-Mapping Transnational Discourses in the Context of Uganda's Anti-Homosexuality Bill/Act," *Journal of Homosexuality* 63:5 (2016): 685–718, https://pubmed.ncbi.nlm.nih.gov/26503528/.

dynamics in the continent.[56] The implications for religious communities are equally vast. Elizabeth Khaxas and Saskia Wieringa have traced how homophobia was directly fomented in areas of Namibia in the context of ethnic tensions where the more urban and Christian Ovambo tended to adopt homophobic traditions compared to the more rural and less Christianized Damara.[57]

Starting with the schism between the Episcopal Church USA and the Anglican communion, sexuality has turned into a battleground that pits Western churches against African churches. As I have been stressing, the terms of the debate are often framed as a matter of allegiance or departure from Christian teaching, but the tensions are overdetermined by the afterlives of colonialism and imperialism. Amar Wahab has suggested that both the anti-gay coalition as well as the pro-gay transnational movements have to be conceived of along the lines of global structures in their current neoliberal format.[58] With the crumbling of national sovereignty at the expanse of multinational private corporations, the discourse of homosexuality as "un-African" ought to be perceived as a transnational discourse that seeks to "[invent] tradition . . . and then establish 'solidarity as a proxy' across different nations and cultures."[59] This invention of tradition functions to situate African communities as stable and as representatives of a past that the West has dangerously abandoned. What goes unnamed or unnoticed is that this "identity" has been built under the aegis of colonial power.

---

56. Kapya Kaoma, "The U.S. Christian Right and the Attack on Gays in Africa," *Political Research Associates*, December 1, 2009, https://politicalresearch.org/2009/12/01/us-christian-right-and-attack-gays-africa; Kapya Kaoma, "Exporting the Anti-Gay Movement," *The American Prospect*, April 24, 2012, https://prospect.org/world/exporting-anti-gay-movement/; Kapya John Kaoma, "How the U.S. Christian Right Is Transforming Sexual Politics in Africa" (Somerville, MA: Political Research Associates, 2012), https://www.sxpolitics.org/wp-content/uploads/2012/08/colonizingafricanvaluespra.pdf. For a summary of the literature and history on the influence of the Christian Right movement in Africa and a case study of the schism between the Episcopal Church and the Anglican Communion due to the question of homosexuality, see Marcia Oliver, "Transnational Sex Politics, Conservative Christianity, and Antigay Activism in Uganda," *Studies in Social Justice* 7:1 (2013): 90–93, https://doi.org/10.26522/ssj.v7i1.1056

57. Ruth Morgan and Saskia Wieringa, *Tommy Boys, Lesbian Men and Ancestral Wives: Female Same-Sex Practices in Africa* (Johannesburg: Jacana Media, 2005), 121–27. See also Epprecht, *Heterosexual Africa?*, 18.

58. Wahab, "'Homosexuality/Homophobia Is Un-African'?"

59. Wahab, "'Homosexuality/Homophobia Is Un-African'?", 706–7.

An interview conducted by Mark Tooley with Liberian United Methodist theologian Jerry Kulah offers an example of this.[60] Tooley is interested in how African United Methodists "prevented UMC from following other USA based Mainline Protestant denominations from abandoning biblical sexual ethics."[61] The question that follows can only be rhetorical: "Why is UMC in Africa so committed to traditional biblical beliefs?" This is less of a question and more of an invitation to confirm the premise of the question. Kulah only partially embraces those expectations, for he corrects Tooley in suggesting that the vote during the United Methodist General Conference in 2019 was itself a global vote, not an African vote. Kulah nevertheless will go on to partially confirm the expected answer from Tooley with a claim about doctrinal purity. African United Methodists, Kulah suggests, "are committed to traditional biblical beliefs because that is what we know as the unchanging, infallible Word of God since the birth of the Christian Church in Africa."[62] In this theological account of the birth of the church in Africa, we are taken to a specific time in history: "The early missionaries and episcopal leaders from America to Africa were all committed to traditional biblical beliefs. Traditional biblical beliefs form part of our spiritual DNA." Kulah has therefore confirmed the bias in Tooley's question with an inaccurate history of African Christianity.[63] The historical inaccuracy is nevertheless beside the point. The issue at stake is the charged terrain in which the dialogue between Tooley and Kulah takes place. In the dialogue, Tooley and Kulah share a common sexual ethic, but they diverge deeply on how they come to this narrative; Tooley is engaged in a polemic against pro-gay movements in his native United States, Kulah defending a certain view of African theological autonomy. Because of the charged terrain in which the conversation takes place, Kulah's claim to doctrinal orthodoxy must refer to the arrival of American bishops and missionaries in the nineteenth century. The dialogue between Tooley and Kulah is overdetermined by this colonial heritage.

---

60. For a further reflection on the interaction between Tooley and Kulah, see Scott, "The Problems of a Global Traditionalist Church."

61. Mark Tooley, "Jerry Kulah on Africa's Methodist Future," *Juicy Ecumenism: The Institute on Religion and Democracy's Blog*, May 26, 2020, https://juicyecumenism.com/2020/05/26/jerry-kulah-africa-initiative/.

62. Tooley.

63. The Christian presence in sub-Saharan Africa predates the nineteenth century.

What may appear as a reversal of roles between Americans and Africans in the interaction between Tooley and Kulah in fact confirms the authority of American missionaries and the perceived orthodoxy they represented, including their nineteenth-century sexual ethic. I insist: what is at stake here is not the history of missionary activity, which is simultaneously far more complex than a process of theological colonization and yet inseparable from it. What is really at stake is the reconstruction of a narrative that associates doctrinal authority with an imagined, homogenous Methodist identity brought by American missionaries to Africa in the nineteenth century. That Methodist orthodox identity has merged with the African postcolonial identity endorsed by Kulah. In this instance, he must speak for Africa in such a way to confirm the destiny made manifest to American missionaries in the nineteenth century. But when Kulah's narrative is appropriated by his current allies in conservative Methodist circles, the story changes completely from a story about theological and ecclesial autonomy to a story about the loss of theological truth on the part of Methodists in the United States. By narrating the crisis of United Methodism as a case study of a denomination doomed by its co-optation by culture, conservative Methodists in the United States demand their partners in the global South embrace that heritage.

The schism in United Methodism and the formation of the Global Methodist Church is therefore another chapter in a dispute that has become transnational over the past decades. The transnational character of United Methodism situates the tensions within the denomination in the difficult global crossroads. Admittedly, the denomination has not found ecclesial structures where these negotiations can be engaged in a more generative way, and some chapters in the present volume provide historical and theological perspectives about this.

As the Global Methodist Church is launched, the fundamental global structures remain intact, and the historical tensions between U.S. Christianity and Christian communities in Africa remain unaltered. As I have been trying to stress, the ecclesial identity of Global Methodism relies on theological and social animosities brewing in the United States. These tensions do not easily cross international borders without having a ripple effect in different contexts. The theological identity of the Global Methodist Church is gaining shape in a polemical context that stresses allegiance to the Christian doctrinal tradition against the impositions of culture and of that which is perceived as divergences in gender and sexuality.

Global Methodism faces challenges in meeting its noble call to "love extravagantly." Traditionally, this type of love entails something "flagrantly excessive," "widely divergent," and "discrepant."[64] One need not remain within the confines of this etymology, naturally, but such have been the traditional meanings of the term in English. Global Methodism will likely need to diverge from them.

Global Churches, Planetary Assembling

Mark Twain receives credit for having said that "history does not repeat itself; it rhymes." The historical development of The United Methodist Church in the twentieth century has its share of rhymes with the history of American empire. Global Methodism, as much as it represents its identity in a polemic against United Methodism, is starting to produce its own imperial rhymes. As familiar as the image is, the spinning globe carries with it assumptions of a notion of the globe that has been formed and developed under the spirit of empire. As a totalizing view, the globe is never just a vision of all peoples and nations of the world coming together. With that image ingrained in its name, Global Methodism is carrying uninterrogated assumptions and replicating known imperial patterns.

Throughout the second half of the twentieth century, United Methodism struggled with its global reach. Its ecclesial structures and methods of deliberation—especially its General Conference—proved inadequate. "Holy conferencing," a mark of Wesleyan ecclesiology, was rarely a means of grace for the denomination. Alongside the tensions around human sexuality, church governance, and doctrinal matters, the schism of The United Methodist Church is to be understood as yet another fracture in the history of empire and its global pretenses. As many chapters in this volume have indicated, attention to the flow of power in history and the cultural negotiations that happen in that context is central to an analysis of the schism in the denomination. The poles of conflict are themselves overdetermined by the imperial inheritance latent in Methodism.

---

64. "Extravagant."

The spirit of empire hovers above the formation of the globe, of the perception of homogeneity in that which is plural and mysteriously uncanny. Jacques Derrida has called attention to this through his concept of "globalatinization," an expression that refers to the fact that "globalization" has been the global extension of an imperial memory that extends all the way back to Rome. It is a thoroughly Christian and imperial vision of the globe, Derrida affirms.[65] When unquestioned, claims for a global denomination run the risk of carrying over norms, political suppositions, and cultural patterns that are far from global. At worst, these projects replicate global designs that have been shaped by empire. The vision of a global denomination in the twentieth and twenty-first centuries is unthinkable outside the imperial aspirations of the United States.

Yet resistance to the spirit of empire does not entail letting go of commitments that are planetary in scope and solidarities that transgress national boundaries. Pointing out the entanglement between global Methodism and this imperial inheritance does not diminish the movement but can contribute to the tracking of the counter-imperial gestures in the tradition. The hope and the bias of the analysis is that both exist and continue to rise up. In an epoch of rising nationalisms, a global ecclesial body can testify to a more excellent way. For a global denomination, that would entail turning the globe into an unfamiliar body, an assembly of living beings that escapes totalizations. That requires departing from the spinning globe as the operative metaphor and entering the unfamiliar zone of a *planetary assembling*.

Spivak has drawn the distinction between the "globe" and the "planet" to address, with regards to the former, a form of imagining the world as a homogenous entity engendered under the confines of imperialistic projects. For Spivak, we recall, the globe can exist only on the computer. As I suggested, the spinning globe is its most recent and common figuration that makes its way onto the imaginary of Global Methodism. The planet is distinct from the globe, but in a distinction that cannot be an opposition. "The planet is in the species of alterity, belonging to another

65. See Jacques Derrida, "Faith and Knowledge: The Two Sources of 'Religion' at the Limits of Reason Alone," in *Acts of Religion*, ed. Gil Anidjar (New York: Routledge, 2002), 40–100.

system," writes Spivak. "It is not really amenable to a neat contrast with the globe."[66] When she "invokes" the planet as a category, Spivak seeks to name—indeed to "nickname"—our human intendedness toward the other. We are creatures inclined in the direction of otherness. The planet is one such name for the "animating gift" of our other-bound intendedness. A planetary assembly would then be the gathering of a people committed to the unbounded mystery of the other, a community that takes upon itself the vocation to love that which is strange and "wandering." The spinning globe presents a familiar and manageable entity. The planet, living and uncanny, is of a different nature.

The turning to the other, one might say, is one way to name our desire for God. Global denominations are temporary and incomplete attempts at gathering together our shared inclinations to God in an assembly that cannot be confined to any one nation-state or vision of a unified globe. The theological project of a global denomination cannot be subsumed by any singular vision of what the "globe" is. I'm suggesting that "global" ought never to be a "fully appropriate" name for a mode of assembling that honors our shared intention for the other.[67] A planetary assembling constitutes a different public, a different social body. A planetary assembling disidentifies us from a globe that has been constituted by the spirit of empire. The planet renders unfamiliar that which empire has made familiar. The church as a planetary assembling is only legible as an act of queering, a rendering strange of what has been made familiar, too familiar.

In the age of imperial globalization, nationalist boundary-setting, and ecological calamity, a planetary assembling might be the most appropriate name for a world parish. The spirit of the old Wesleyan proverb is claimed by competing inheritors of the Methodist revival, but its planetary disposition remains elusive. The fact that we cannot pin down what a "world parish" ought to be is the hopeful sign that it does not belong to any one globe. Truly, the world that becomes a parish harbors the peculiar queerness of a warmed heart. One is entitled to hope that the strangeness of that experience will not let Methodism be consumed by the spirit of empire.

---

66. Spivak, "Planetarity," 291.

67. Global Methodist Church, "Vision."